Civil Liberties and the
Bill of Rights
Part II

Professor John E. Finn

THE TEACHING COMPANY ®

PUBLISHED BY:

THE TEACHING COMPANY
4151 Lafayette Center Drive, Suite 100
Chantilly, Virginia 20151-1232
1-800-TEACH-12
Fax—703-378-3819
www.teach12.com

ISBN 1-59803-198-8

John E. Finn, J.D., Ph.D.

Professor of Government, Wesleyan University

John E. Finn is Professor of Government at Wesleyan University. He received his B.A. in political science from Nasson College, a J.D. from Georgetown University, a Ph.D. in political science from Princeton University, and a degree in culinary arts from the French Culinary Institute. He has taught at Wesleyan since 1986, where his research focuses on constitutional theory, comparative constitutional law, the First Amendment, the legal regulation of terrorism and political violence, and cuisine and popular culture. He is the recipient of four distinguished teaching awards at Wesleyan: the Carol A. Baker `81 Memorial Prize for Excellence in Teaching & Scholarship, awarded in 1989; the Binswanger Prize for Excellence in Teaching in 1994; and on two occasions the Caleb T. Winchester Award for Teaching Excellence, first in 1997, and again in 2004. He was also the recipient of the Association of Princeton Graduate Alumni Teaching Award for distinguished teaching while a graduate student at Princeton. The American Political Science Association described his syllabus for American Constitutional Interpretation as "an ideal model."

Professor Finn is an internationally recognized expert on constitutional law and political violence. His public lectures include testimony in front of the U.S. House Judiciary Committee, as well as lectures in Chile, Bolivia, Spain, Italy, Canada, England, and France.

Professor Finn has published widely in the fields of constitutional theory and interpretation. Among his publications are *American Constitutional Law: Essays, Cases, and Comparative Notes*, 2nd edition (Rowman & Littlefield, 2004), with Donald P. Kommers of Notre Dame University and Gary Jacobsohn of Williams College, once described as "the Cadillac of constitutional law casebooks," and the highly regarded *Constitutions in Crisis: Political Violence and the Rule of Law* (Oxford University Press, 1991).

Professor Finn lives in Hartford, Connecticut, with his wife, Linda, and their two children.

Table of Contents
Civil Liberties and the Bill of Rights
Part II

Civil Liberties and the Bill of Rights

Scope:

This course is designed to introduce students to a uniquely American invention and, to some ways of thinking, a wonderfully naïve contribution to politics: The written specification of individual liberties and rights that citizens possess and can, through courts, enforce against the state. *Civil Liberties* is not, however, a course on law. It is, instead, a course that has as its subject the relationship of law to the most fundamental sorts of questions about politics, morality, and human nature.

In this course of 36 lectures, we shall see that most of the serious difficulties (and there are many) in the politics of civil liberties arise from conflicts between our commitments to two or more positive values. There are, for example, inevitable and recurrent conflicts (despite our attempts to ignore them) between the values of liberty and equality. As Felix Frankfurter once wrote, these and other such conflicts are "what the Greeks thousands of years ago recognized as a tragic issue, namely the clash of rights, not the clash of wrongs." We examine these clashes in light of the broader philosophical and institutional problems of the constitutional order. I hope to show that constitutional "answers" to problems like those of abortion, freedom of speech, and affirmative action require a coherent understanding of the U.S. Constitution and of the assumptions it makes about human nature and the proper ends of government and civil society.

We will, therefore, examine the doctrinal development of specific liberties and rights, such as due process and privacy, the ultimate denial of liberty entailed by the death penalty, freedom of speech and religion, and equal protection, but we shall consider them in a broader theoretical context. We shall want to know what overall conception of liberties, rights, and governmental powers most nearly reflects and promotes our best understanding of the Constitution and the polity it both constitutes and envisions.

The course is divided into three sections. We begin with the institutional and interpretive foundations of the American constitutional order. Our purpose here is to provide students with background on the U.S. Supreme Court and its role in the constitutional order, as well as an overview of the process of constitutional interpretation. In our first lecture, for example, we focus on the organization, composition, and decision-making authority of the Court. In our second lecture, we take up the "why" and the "what" of constitutional interpretation. We shall see that interpretation is both a choice and a necessity: a choice because we must choose among many diverse methods and strategies, and a burden because such choices are often difficult to justify or even to explain. In Lectures Three and Four, we take up the intersection of Lectures One and Two by considering how and why the power of constitutional interpretation—and, hence, the power to decide the most pressing issues of civil liberties—came to rest with the Supreme Court through the mechanism of judicial review.

In the second section of the course, we begin our inquiry into the Bill of Rights. In every case that arises under the Bill of Rights, we must reconcile our desire for individual liberty with the need for public order, personal autonomy with the needs of the community. Considered in its totality, and not simply provision by provision, a bill of rights sketches the broad outlines of the relationship between individual liberty and the needs of the community. In this larger sense, a bill of rights indicates how conflicts between liberty and community should be conceived and, to some extent, resolved. In our fifth lecture, we consider the history and theory of the Bill of Rights. Was a bill of rights really necessary? And why, initially, did its protections run only against the federal government, not the states? In the sixth lecture, we take up the fascinating doctrine of *incorporation*, or the torturous and winding road the Court followed to make the Bill of Rights applicable to state and local governments—arguably a constitutional revolution no less significant than the Founding in Philadelphia.

In the third and, by far, the largest section of the course, comprising 30 lectures, we consider the individual provisions of the Bill of Rights and the development of several other specific liberties. In deference to the Founders, we begin with the constitutional right to property. The protection of private property, broadly defined, was a central purpose of the constitutional order, and the rise, fall, and possible resurgence of property as a constitutional right of magnitude has had important implications for civil liberties more generally. After property, we take up the fundamental rights of privacy and personhood, rights that cover a broad spectrum of liberty issues, including procreation and abortion, the definition of family, sexual orientation and preference, capital punishment, and the right to die.

We then devote a series of lectures to the speech and religion clauses of the First Amendment. We start with speech. Among the issues we will consider will be the definition of speech, hate speech and fighting words, indecency and pornography, and freedom of association. Our examination of the religion clauses likewise includes questions concerning the definition of religion, as well as consideration of the meaning of the establishment and free exercise clauses and how they interact.

In the final part of the course, we explore the many intricacies of the equal protection clause of the Fourteenth Amendment. When, if ever, does the equal protection clause allow the state to discriminate on the basis of race? Is there a constitutional difference between malignant discrimination, such as Jim Crow laws, and affirmative action, or so-called "reverse discrimination"? Should the Constitution be colorblind? The equal protection clause also applies to other forms of discrimination; thus, we will want to consider how the Supreme Court has addressed discrimination based on gender, sexual orientation, and national origin.

In addressing these issues, whether under the equal protection clause, the First Amendment, or the Eighth Amendment, we will confront a welter of difficult and controversial questions. It is unlikely that we will succeed in our attempts to answer them fully or finally. What we can hope to achieve, however, is an improved and more sophisticated appreciation of the importance of our commitment to civil liberties and of the sacrifices we must make if we choose to honor that commitment.

Lecture Thirteen
Other Privacy Interests—Family

Scope:

As we saw in Lecture Eleven, the right to liberty is less a single right than a collection of diverse interests. The same is true of the right to privacy: Privacy is an umbrella that covers a wide collection of more specific interests, including, among other things, procreation, abortion, marriage, and sexuality. In *Moore v. City of East Cleveland* (1977), for example, the Court struck down an ordinance that prohibited, under its definition of "immediate family," a grandmother from living in the same house with her son and two grandchildren (who were first cousins). The Court wrote, "when the government intrudes on choices concerning family living arrangements, [we] must examine carefully the importance of the governmental interests advanced...." The Court has since considered a fair number of other family cases. Hence, in *Michael H. v. Gerald D.* (1989), the Court refused to find a fundamental right on the part of a biological father (not married to the mother) to be guaranteed visits with his child. And in *Troxel v. Granville* (2000), although the Court noted its recognition of "the changing realities of the American family," it nonetheless struck down a statute that gave grandparents increased visitation rights with their deceased son's children as an unconstitutional infringement of the parents' fundamental right to rear their children.

Outline

I. The Court has long recognized that the right to privacy encompasses more than reproductive freedom and sexuality.

   A. The right to privacy, like the rights to liberty and property, is an umbrella term for a wide range of more specific liberty interests, such as rights concerning the family unit.

   B. As with the other rights we have seen, judicial determination of what those other protected interests include, and what is not included, raises important issues about the nature of constitutional interpretation and the proper limits of judicial power.

II. In *Moore v. City of East Cleveland* (1977), for example, the Court struck down an ordinance that prohibited, under its definition of "immediate family," a grandmother from living in the same house with her son and two grandchildren who were first cousins.

   A. In its plurality decision, the Court wrote that a government action that "intrudes on choices concerning family living arrangements" must be subject to careful scrutiny.

   B. The plurality decision suggests that these kinds of choices are protected as fundamental rights, because "unless we close our eyes to the basic reasons why certain rights associated with the family have been" protected, "we cannot avoid applying the force and rationale" of prior cases to this case.

   C. The Court also directly addressed the difficult issues of judicial power and legitimacy raised by privacy cases, noting: "Substantive due process has at times been a treacherous field for this Court."

   D. In dissent, Justice Stewart noted that "although the appellant's desire to share a single-dwelling unit also involves 'private family life,' that desire can hardly be equated with any of the interests protected" in previous privacy cases.

III. In *Michael H. v. Gerald D.* (1989), the Court considered a somewhat different set of family-related issues.

   A. In this case, the Court refused to find a fundamental right on the part of a biological father (not married to the mother) to be guaranteed visits with his child.

   B. Noting the importance to the state of promoting and protecting the nuclear family, the Court upheld a California statute that created a legal presumption that a child born to a married woman is a product of the marriage.

   C. In refusing to find a fundamental right on the part of the biological father, Justice Scalia wrote that to be so protected, the interest must "be so rooted in the traditions and conscience of our people as to be ranked as fundamental."

D. In dissent, Justice Brennan argued: "The plurality's interpretive method is more than novel; it is misguided.... In a community such as ours, 'liberty' must include the freedom not to conform."

IV. Family and parental rights were also the issue in the case of *Troxel v. Granville* (2000). Noting its recognition of "the changing realities of the American family," the Court nonetheless struck down a statute that gave grandparents increased visitation rights with their deceased son's children as an unconstitutional infringement of the parents' fundamental right to rear their children.

    A. Justice O'Connor's plurality decision relied on a series of precedents to sketch a parental due process right to "make decisions concerning the care, custody, and control" of children.

    B. In individual dissents, Justices Stevens, Scalia, and Kennedy each expressed discomfort with the Court's apparent willingness to displace the judgments of popularly elected state legislatures.

Essential Reading:

Moore v. City of East Cleveland (1977).

Michael H. v. Gerald D. (1989).

Troxel v. Granville (2000).

Kommers, Finn, and Jacobsohn, *American Constitutional Law*, chapter 6, pp. 252–253.

Robert A. Burt, "The Constitution of the Family," 1979 *Supreme Court Review* 329.

Supplementary Reading:

James S. Fishkin, *Justice, Equal Opportunity, and the Family*.

Susan Moller Okin, *Justice, Gender, and the Family*.

Questions to Consider:

1. Unlike some other late-20th-century constitutions, the American constitutional text has little if anything to say about the family proper. How has this relative silence influenced the Court? Does it make judicial decisions about family or parental rights more troublesome as exercises of judicial authority in a democracy?

2. According to Justice Powell in *Moore*, why does the Constitution protect "the sanctity of the family"? Does he respond persuasively to Justice White's complaints about the Court's use of substantive due process?

3. According to Justice Scalia, "a right of parents to direct the upbringing of their children is among the 'unalienable Rights' mentioned in the Declaration of Independence." However, he went on to say that the Declaration "is not a legal prescription conferring powers upon the Courts." Why not?

Lecture Thirteen—Transcript
Other Privacy Interests—Family

Until now, our discussion of the privacy right has tended to center on issues of reproductive freedom and reproductive autonomy. That's true even of our discussion of *Griswold,* which, you'll recall, involved birth control, or at least access to information about birth control and to specific contraceptives.

In this lecture, and in the subsequent lectures concerning privacy, we'll begin to broaden our focus a bit, and we'll begin to consider, especially in this lecture, how the privacy right really refers to a diverse set of particular interests, none of which, necessarily, has a direct, immediate connection to the other sets of interests that we'll concern ourselves with. In particular, here, in this lecture, we're going to concern ourselves with liberties that surround the family unit. I'm going to call them "family rights," or "family privacy rights;" but that too is an umbrella term for a very wide-ranging set of interests, as we'll begin to see.

I also may have left you with the impression, because we started with *Griswold,* that the right to privacy is really a child of the 1960s, until now. That's not entirely true. Some of the Court's earliest privacy cases actually occurred at around the same time that *Lochner* was decided in the early 1900s.

So, for example, in the case of *Meyer v. Nebraska*, decided in 1923, the Court concluded that there is a right to receive instruction in foreign languages in public schools. The right described in *Meyer* might be a right that attaches to a child—the right to receive a particular kind of education. Alternatively, you might think the right in *Meyer,* or the liberty interest in *Meyer*, is a liberty interest that attaches to the teachers their right to instruct students in a particular subject. But I think most of us would also agree that *Meyer* is fundamentally about the rights of parents to direct the upbringing and the education of their children.

In a similar case, decided two years later, in 1925, in *Pierce v. Society of Sisters,* the Court struck down a rule that required a public school education for all children in the state between ages eight and sixteen. And again, this case is probably best described as yet another case concerning the rights of parents to direct their family, or to direct the upbringing of their children. Those cases are, more or less, contemporaneous with *Lochner*.

Now, just by way of review, you'll recall that, when the Court used substantive due process to strike down economic-related laws in *Lochner*, that ultimately that became the gravest of constitutional errors; and that the *Lochner* line of cases has long since been repudiated. On the other hand, the due process cases decided in *Meyer* and *Pierce*; those two privacy cases remain good law. And one of the great questions of constitutional theory is, how could it possibly be that the use of substantive due process in economic cases is now ridiculed as completely illegitimate; and yet, the use of substantive due process to construct the early privacy cases in *Meyer* and *Pierce* is still considered good law? This is an open question, and one that the Court itself continues to struggle with, as we'll see in today's cases.

We will begin, however, with a case that is far more recent. In *Moore v. City of East Cleveland*, decided in 1977, the Court struck down an ordinance—a city, a municipal ordinance—that prohibited, under its definition of "immediate family," a grandmother from living in the same house with her son and two grandchildren. The two grandchildren however, were first cousins, not brothers.

The first thing we need to ask, as we should in any privacy case, is, what privacy interest is actually implicated on this set of facts? And here, the privacy interest seems to concern what the definition of a family will be; or alternatively, who gets to make choices about what constitutes a family? Here, the city had defined "immediate family" in a particular kind of way, a way that made it very close to the traditional nuclear family. This seemed to be in direct conflict with the grandmother's definition of family, which did not fit this traditional definition.

The second thing we need to do in any such case is to ask ourselves, what state interests are meant to be advanced by the legislation or the action in question? And it is worth taking a little bit of time here to think about what the city hoped to accomplish in *Moore v. City of East Cleveland*.

The part of East Cleveland that we are talking about was in the midst of gentrification. By gentrification, I mean that traditionally impoverished parts of the city, traditionally impoverished neighborhoods, were undergoing a kind of urban renewal; and the city was very anxious to make sure that this process continued. Part of what the city was trying to accomplish was to define a family in a particular way, to eliminate the existence of extended families, which would impose costs—or so the city imagined—upon city resources. In particular, the city was concerned about the number of parking spaces and cars that might be available on the streets, or that might be seen on the streets. The idea here (whether it was a sound one or not is beside the question) is simply that, if we define family in a particular way, we might be able to eliminate some urban overcrowding, and contribute to this process of gentrification.

You'll recall that, under the current set of doctrinal frameworks, we are now left with a case that looks dramatically like every other case we've seen, at least at the level of constitutional theory. We have, presumably, a fundamental right, although the Court has actually yet to say that it is a fundamental right; but assuming it's a fundamental right, we must weigh that fundamental right, that fundamental privacy or liberty interest, against the state's interest. And if the right is in fact fundamental, then we must ask ourselves, are the city's interests compelling? That is the kind of analysis the Court took upon itself.

I want to stress first that, like so many of the privacy cases, *Moore* gives us a Court that is deeply fractured. Once again, as we have seen so many times with the abortion cases in our last two lectures, the Court was unable to construct a majority opinion. Instead, in its plurality decision, the Court wrote that a government action that "intrudes on choices concerning family living arrangements" must be subject to careful scrutiny. This is a very interesting way to describe the case. Does careful scrutiny equate to strict scrutiny or to the compelling state interest test?

The plurality decision continued by suggesting that the reasons these kinds of family choices must be protected as fundamental rights is because, "unless we close our eyes to the basic reasons why certain rights associated with the family have been protected in the past, we cannot avoid applying the force and rationale…" of prior cases to this case.

Here I want to step back a minute and ask you to take a look at the methodology, the interpretive methodology, that the Court has chosen to utilize. The Court appears to be relying largely on precedent. It is saying, in effect, if we look at the other cases where we have decided that some set of privacy interests should, indeed, be ranked as fundamental, we will see that, in terms of this case, there are no real differences. The same kinds of interests that are articulated in precedent cases are present in this case, and the force of precedent, the logic of precedent, requires us to conclude that this set of interests—how one defines a family—must, in fact, be ranked as fundamental.

The Court was very careful here. The plurality opinion acknowledged that this kind of analysis, this use of substantive due process, is always a touchy matter. So, the Court wrote, "Substantive due process has, at times, been a treacherous field for this Court."

Now, what the Court is suggesting here, of course, is that it is attuned to the problem of *Lochner*. It is worried, in other words, that the constant creation of new fundamental rights might be seen as an exercise in simple, judicial creativity. And as much as we might admire creativity in our children, in our students, in our colleagues, creativity is not something you want the Court to be engaged in. "Creativity" is a set of buzzwords, a particular way of describing illegitimate judicial action. Creativity, in other words, is a way of talking about a Court that is no longer tethered to the constitutional text. That, of course, was the fundamental problem in *Lochner,* and the fundamental problem the Court was concerned with avoiding in *Moore v. City of East Cleveland.*

There are some other interesting opinions in *Moore v. City of East Cleveland,* as well. In his strongly worded dissent, Justice Stewart noted that, "although the appellant's desire to share a single-dwelling unit also involves 'private family life,' that desire can hardly be equated with any of the interests protected" in earlier privacy cases. What we have here is a simple dispute between the majority, and Justice Stewart writing in dissent about what the precedent cases actually mean. It is worth, again, stepping back from the particulars of the case to understand what the larger issues are in this case.

Reaching all the way back to our first set of lectures, you will recall that we discussed a number of different methods of constitutional interpretation. We spoke, for example, about appeals to originalism, or to Founders' intent; to structuralism; to balancing; and especially, the use of precedent. Why does any judge ever take the time to think about which interpretive methodology to adopt? We might ask ourselves, in the abstract, who cares what method of interpretation they use?

Judges worry about methods of interpretation because they want to avoid the charge of Lochnerizing. A method of interpretation is a way of constraining "judicial creativity," or, perhaps it would be better to say, a way of constraining judicial decision making. A method of interpretation is a coat you can wear to guard against the "ill chill wind" of *Lochner*. Of course, this coat only protects you if, in fact, the method of interpretation you choose to adopt does constrain judicial decision making.

On the other hand, if the method of interpretation you choose to adopt doesn't actually constrain, if it doesn't limit your choices about how to rule, when to rule, and in favor of whom to rule; then the method of interpretation is, at best, useless, and, at worst, a charade.

I mention that because, here, both the plurality opinion and Justice Stewart in dissent seem to agree that—in this case at least—the critical method of constitutional interpretation is the appeal to precedent. But note what happens: the plurality thinks if one reads the precedents in one particular way, it yields a fundamental liberty interest that should be protected in this case. Justice Stewart looks at the same line of cases and concludes that those cases do not protect the family interest involved here. What we have is, I think, an honest, authentic dispute about how to utilize precedent; which suggests, as we probably have seen before, that no method of interpretation is so convenient, is so perfect, that it absolutely constrains judicial decision making. Every method of interpretation might reduce the arena of discretion; might reduce the arena, the occasion, for interpretation; but interpretation is still necessary, nonetheless.

Consider another case, a fantastically complicated case, and a wonderfully complex case. In 1989, the Supreme Court considered the case of *Michael H. v. Gerald D.,* a case that arose out of California. I would like to read for you the opening paragraphs of Justice Scalia's opinion for the Court:

> Under California law, a child born to a married woman is presumed to be a child of the marriage. This case presents

the claim that this presumption infringes upon the due process rights of a man who wishes to establish his paternity of a child born to the wife of another man. And the claim that it infringes upon the constitutional right of the child to retain a relationship with her natural father.

What a fascinating set of issues! And, as Justice Scalia describes them, there is not one, but, in fact, two privacy interests that are implicated by this set of facts. The first privacy interest is the interest of the so-called natural father to establish a relationship with his daughter; and the second claim, almost a mirror image, is the constitutional privacy right of the child to maintain a relationship with the biological father.

Before we inquire into what state interests might be behind such a statute, we should again ask, as we should in every privacy case, how do we know—how can we know—if these sets of interests, these two interests in particular, are, in fact, fundamental rights? And again, by way of review, how do you know if any claim of interest is a fundamental right, or, alternatively, a non-fundamental right?

You'll recall, when we discussed the incorporation doctrine, that *Palko v. Connecticut* distinguished between two classes of rights— explicit or implicit—in the Bill of Rights. The first are those rights that are fundamental; the second are those that are non-fundamental. What did *Palko* tell us about which rights are fundamental? Quoting *Palko* again, "Those rights are fundamental that are implicit in the scheme of ordered liberty."

You'll recall, we had a certain amount of fun trying to parse what that actually means in any particular case; but there is the test. So the first task that we are charged with in *Michael H.* is asking ourselves the following question: Does the biological father's putative right to establish a relationship with his child, or does the child's putative right to have a relationship with her biological father—are either of those implicit in the concept of ordered liberty?

To be frank, I don't know how to answer that question. On good days, I think I know what the question means; but I still can't answer it. On bad days, I'm not confident that I understand the question at all. I'm not confident Justice Scalia and a majority of the Court understood how to answer the question, as well. And, in fact, Justice Scalia proposed another test for determining which rights are fundamental and which ones are not. This test has become profoundly persuasive and important over time, and we need to spend a little bit of time with it.

Here is Justice Scalia's reformulation—or new answer, if you prefer—to the question, how do we know when a right is fundamental? He said, "The claimed liberty need not only be fundamental, but also it must be an interest traditionally protected by our society." I want to say that again: a right will only be fundamental, for purposes of due process, if it is an "interest traditionally protected by our society."

There are, potentially, serious, perhaps fatal, flaws with this test; but before we examine them, it is worth trying to answer Scalia's question. Is either of the two interests that Scalia described in the opening paragraphs interests that are "traditionally protected by our society"? According to Justice Scalia, neither could be. Justice Scalia goes so far as to say that the whole point of the California law is to suggest that these are not interests that are "traditionally protected by society."

Here's what he means by that: the California law establishes a presumption of paternity. Why does it do it? Remember, we want, also, in every privacy case, to ask ourselves, why does the state adopt the law in particular? What state interest does it mean to advance? And here, according to the majority, the state interest is trying to establish a clear sense of parenthood, or of family identity, so that the child grows up in a secure, stable environment; and so that society understands what the definition of a family will be. Hence, the presumption that a child born to a married woman is the product of the marriage. As you can imagine, there are difficult and vexing issues of paternity and, perhaps, of legitimacy; and ultimately, particular legal issues concerning inheritance and other kinds of rights that will attach to the family relationship, which the California law seeks to settle by engaging in this presumption.

So, according to the Court, these two kinds of claimed interests—the interests of the biological father, the interests of the child—are not, in fact, interests that society has traditionally sought to protect. Because they are not traditional interests that society has sought to protect, neither one rises to the level of a fundamental right.

This doesn't conclude the analysis. The next step in the analysis must still be, if it's not a fundamental right, may the state act whenever it wants to? Of course not; the state is still obligated to advance a set of rational interests. And, of course, the interests, which we have spoken about, will clearly satisfy the rationality test, at least as it has been used by the Court in the past.

So, the majority opinion—whether you agree with it or not—is, in some ways, very traditional, and covers no new ground. I say that because it adopts the language of fundamental rights and compelling state interests, and applies the doctrine in a way that is fundamentally consistent with what we have seen before.

On the other hand, there is one novel dimension to the majority opinion, and that is this new test—we will call it the "*Michael H.* test"—for determining which interests will, in fact, be protected under the rubric of privacy and which ones will not. That interpretive method is, for us, what is genuinely significant about *Michael H.*

I want to be very careful here. You'll recall that, when we spoke about *DeShaney*, that I wanted to remind you in *DeShaney* that behind all of these doctrinal tests are real people; that it's easy to deal with these at the level of abstraction; but we shouldn't do so at the cost of understanding that, in nearly every case, somebody live wins, and somebody live looses. The consequences in any case can be profound to the individuals involved. And I don't think we should underestimate the degree of distress that must have attached to all the participants in this case.

That said, for us, the importance of *Michael H.* must be in the test; and in his dissent, Justice Brennan went directly to that issue. I want to quote Justice Brennan, in dissent here, responding to the new test for determining which rights are fundamental. Justice Brennan argues, "The plurality's interpretive method is more than novel; it is misguided…. In a community such as ours, 'liberty' must include the freedom not to conform."

Now I hope it's clear what Justice Brennan is making a reference to here. His argument is this: if the test for determining a fundamental right is whether or not, historically, as a matter of tradition, American society has tended to embrace that interest; then, presumably, the only things that will count as fundamental rights are those that are explicitly delineated by the Bill of Rights, and those embraced in the past by the American people. Hence, the use of the word, "conformity."

Presumably, fundamental interests that involve some notion of diversity—an exception to the norm, an exception from historical practice—will not rise to the status of a fundamental liberty under Justice Scalia's formulation. Justice Brennan finds that to be a grave difficulty, noting, instead, that part of what liberty must mean, in the abstract, is precisely the liberty to diverge from communitarian norms. I will leave it to you to determine which of these two opinions you find more persuasive; but we will rarely, if ever, encounter such a clear, such a stark and important distinction.

We saw that *Moore v. City of East Cleveland* was a plurality decision, and I suggested that that plurality opinion was indicative of underlying conflict within the Court. *Michael H.* was also a plurality opinion. Our next case, and our last case for this lecture, involves, yet again, a plurality opinion.

Before we go into the specifics of this case, I think it is worth noting that the plurality opinions in these cases are, in fact, a sign of continuing disagreement within the Court; but disagreement over what? I think *Michael H.* and the *Moore* case and, perhaps, also our next case, *Troxel*, ought to suggest that that division, that disagreement within the Court, isn't simply about how to read the facts of any particular case; that disagreement isn't simply about whether or not certain kinds of activity ought to be protected under the constitutional right to privacy. Instead, the discussion seems to embrace—or perhaps to be caused by—different understandings about what is the correct way to interpret the Constitution.

As *Michael H.* makes especially clear, much of the disagreement in these cases is fundamentally about methodology, and not so much about substance. By methodology, I mean these are judges who now appear to be engaged in fundamental disputes, not about what the Constitution protects, what it fails to protect, so much as a fundamental dispute about how to make sense of the Constitution; about what sorts of interpretive strategies one ought to bear in trying to make sense of these complicated factual patterns.

Why do judges argue about how to interpret the Constitution? Let me play the role of cynic for just a minute. Perhaps what we should take from today's cases, and from the cases of earlier lectures, is a simple, straightforward lesson. Perhaps that lesson is, people can reasonably disagree about what the Constitution means in any particular case; and because they can reasonably disagree about it, there is, in fact, no way to explain these cases on the basis of a neutral objective, impartial, constitutional principle. Instead, each case simply reflects the changing politics of the Court and, perhaps, the changing politics of society.

To put this as bluntly as possible, perhaps there is no substance, no irreducible core to constitutional theory. Perhaps, in every case, what we have are judges who just make it up; and, if that is true, then why do judges bother to argue about what method of interpretation is superior to another method of interpretation? And the cynic responds, I suppose, by saying, judges are engaged in a game of post-hoc explanation. No judge, especially following *Lochner,* could write an opinion that says, "Here is what I think, but I cannot tell you why I think it. It is simply my preference." So judges manipulate verbal formulas, methods of interpretation, or doctrines, to justify, after the fact, a result they have reached on some other set of grounds.

And I cannot tell you with any confidence that that position is wrong; but I am skeptical. I am skeptical because I believe that judges believe, for themselves, at least, that it does matter what method of interpretation you use; and that some methods of interpretation will foreclose certain kinds of results, or, at least, preference other kinds of results.

Perhaps that's what's involved in the case of *Troxel v. Granville,* decided in 2000. *Troxel* involved a so-called third-party visitation statute. Many states have these statutes—statutes that give third parties rights to visitation of children, grandchildren, cousins, or nieces or nephews. In this case, the Washington state third-party visitation statute gave grandparents increased visitation rights with their deceased sons' children. The parents argued that this increased set of visitation rights was a violation of the parents' fundamental right to rear their children as they wish; a right that, as we saw at the beginning of this lecture, reaches back at least as far as the 1920s, through cases such as *Meyer v. Nebraska* and *Pierce v. Society of Sisters.*

What a fascinating set of conflicts we have in this case! Grandparents who argue that they have both a statutory and, perhaps, a constitutional right to maintain some kind of a visitation relationship with their grandchildren; and parents saying, choices about who my children will visit, about who my children will have contact with, are fundamentally not choices that ought to be legislated by the state; but are, instead, a part of our parental right to liberty to raise our children as we see fit.

Once again, a plurality decision; this plurality decision was written by Justice O'Connor. Her interpretive method was to rely on precedent. She relied on a series of cases, a series of precedents, to sketch out what she called a "parental due process right," "to make decisions concerning the care, custody, and control" of the children. This probably does not cover a lot of new ground. The existence of such a right is, in fact, probably well established by precedent. But remember, the key issue isn't whether there is a precedent; the key issue is how far, how expansive, how narrow, how constricted, we're going to read these precedents. If we read them broadly, then we can, in fact, cover the kinds of issues that are claimed in *Troxel*. On the other hand, it's just as possible to read those precedents in a way that is more constricted, that is narrower; and in individual dissents, justices Stevens, Scalia, and Kennedy all thought that the precedents did not reach as far as Justice O'Connor wrote for the plurality.

Perhaps more importantly, justices Scalia, Stevens, and Kennedy reminded the Court—and hence, reminded us—that in all of these cases—that in every case where the Court finds a fundamental constitutional right to privacy, in this case of parental control over children—the Court is engaged in a relationship with the majoritarian political process more generally.

Now think about what that means in this case—the popularity of third-party visitation statutes may partly be traced to growing concern, to growing awareness in American society, about the changing nature of the American family itself. Indeed, the Court acknowledged the so-called changing realities of the American family, but nevertheless went on to conclude that those changing realities were not sufficient to overcome a parent's right to control the rearing of their children. In other words, what's involved in these cases, at least according to the dissents, is the familiar problem of under what conditions, if any, the Court should set aside majoritarian judgments about what constitutes sound public policy.

Lecture Fourteen
Other Privacy Interests—Sexuality

Scope:

Does the Constitution protect the choices we make about sexuality? Few areas of life, it might seem, are as "private," but most societies also recognize that society sometimes does have a collective interest in regulating certain kinds of sexual conduct. Incest, for example, is clearly an area in which the state has an interest in protecting the individual members of society, as well as a larger collective interest. In this lecture, we consider the Court's work in this controversial area. We begin with a review of *Griswold v. Connecticut* (1963) and *Eisenstadt v. Baird* (1972), in which the Court found a privacy right that did extend to certain kinds of sexual behavior but not to all. The Court's sense that privacy does not extend to every kind of sexual practice was underscored in the important case of *Bowers v. Hardwick* (1986), in which the Court refused to find in privacy what it called a "right to homosexual sodomy." The Court reversed its position in *Texas v. Lawrence* (2003), this time holding that "Liberty presumes an autonomy of self that includes … certain intimate conduct." The Court's decision in *Lawrence*, like its earlier decision in *Bowers*, provoked controversy both on and off the Court, controversy that once again revolves around great questions of morality and judicial power.

Outline

I. In this lecture, we continue our examination of the constitutional right to privacy. Our cases involve an area of profound importance and complexity: human sexuality.

   A. Does the Constitution, perhaps through a right of privacy, protect certain kinds of sexual behavior? If so, which ones and why?

   B. It is important to remember here, as with the other kinds of privacy cases we have considered, that there is always some tension between the individual right and the community's interests in regulating those rights.

II. It is important to remember, too, that the issues in these cases are

©2006 The Teaching Company Limited Partnership

made even more complicated because they also involve important issues about the limits of judicial power.

A. Such concerns arise in part because, again, the constitutional text has little if anything to say directly about such matters. Consequently, constitutional interpretation has to struggle with familiar questions—about how broadly or narrowly to read the text and about when, if ever, it is appropriate for judges to go beyond the text itself.

B. As we shall see, the Court's work in this area has been especially sensitive to issues about judicial power and the use of substantive due process.

III. All these issues came into play in the important case of *Bowers v. Hardwick* (1986), in which the Court first addressed so-called "unconventional sexual practices." In *Bowers*, the Court ruled that the right to privacy does not prohibit states from making consensual sodomy between same-sex partners a criminal offense.

A. Writing for the Court, Justice White concluded, "There is no fundamental right [of] homosexuals to engage in sodomy."

   1. Justice White reasoned that the Court's earlier privacy cases did not reach so far and that protection for homosexual activity is "not deeply rooted in this nation's history and traditions."

   2. In addition, Justice White voiced concerns about the limited role of courts in a democracy. The Court should be reluctant "to expand the substantive reach of the Due Process Clause," he wrote, because in doing so, "the Judiciary necessarily takes to itself further authority to govern the country."

B. In an impassioned dissent, Justice Blackmun described the privacy interest in very different terms, arguing that this case was less about sodomy than the right to be let alone and self-determination.

C. *Bowers* is important in part because it demonstrated again that the Court has been unable to develop a method or procedure for determining what "privacy" includes or excludes.

D. *Bowers* is important, too, because it demonstrated that cases involving privacy rights are profoundly influenced by how one characterizes the interests involved in any specific case. These, in turn, may be influenced by the Court's understanding about the nature and limits of its own power, as well as by larger visions about the relationship of the individual to society.

IV. The same issues were still very much alive 17 years later, in *Lawrence v. Texas* (2003).

    A. In this case, the Court struck down a Texas law that prohibited sodomy between same-sex partners. Unlike the Georgia law, however, the Texas statute did not criminalize the same acts when performed by heterosexuals.

    B. Writing for a 6–3 majority, Justice Kennedy said, "Liberty presumes an autonomy of self that includes freedom of thought, belief, expression, and certain intimate conduct."

        1. The majority thus concluded that the description in *Bowers* of the right of privacy as a right to sodomy had profoundly mischaracterized the liberty interest in this case and that *Bowers* must, therefore, be overruled.

        2. The majority opinion discussed at some length when precedent should control a decision and when it may be overruled.

    C. In a strongly worded dissent, Justice Scalia accused the majority of taking sides in a "culture war" that was better left to the democratic process and that threatened a "massive disruption of the current social order."

        1. As he had in *Casey*, Justice Scalia again reminded the Court that it had little constitutional warrant for displacing the choices of democratic majorities absent a clear constitutional basis for doing so.

        2. Responding to the majority's discussion of precedent, Justice Scalia wrote: "I do not myself believe in rigid adherence [to precedent], but I do believe that we should be consistent rather than manipulative in invoking [precedent]."

V. Like so many of the Court's privacy cases, the decisions in

Bowers and *Lawrence* provoked a storm of both support and criticism in society at large. In that sense, Justice Scalia may well have been correct when he predicted "massive social disruption." Following *Lawrence*, for example, some members of Congress have spoken openly about ways to discipline the Court. Other critics have explored the possibility of amendments to the Constitution, one of which, for example, would define marriage as between a man and a woman.

Essential Reading:

Griswold v. Connecticut (1963).

Eisenstadt v. Baird (1972).

Bowers v. Hardwick (1986).

Texas v. Lawrence (2003).

Kommers, Finn, and Jacobsohn, *American Constitutional Law*, chapter 6, pp. 249–253.

Supplementary Reading:

Richard Posner, *Sex and Reason*.

Cass Sunstein, *One Case at a Time: Judicial Minimalism on the Supreme Court*.

Questions to Consider:

1. *Lawrence* invites comparisons to *Planned Parenthood v. Casey* (1992), in part because in both cases the Court seemed to adopt fairly expansive definitions of *liberty*. Are there implications in these cases for "morals" legislation more generally? Does either case give conscientious legislators any clear guidance about to what extent or when the community may regulate sexual practices?

2. Do you agree with Justice Scalia's claim that in *Lawrence*, the majority of the Court chose to take sides in a larger "culture war" concerning the criminalization of homosexual conduct?

Lecture Fourteen—Transcript
Other Privacy Interests—Sexuality

Does the Constitution protect the choices we make about sexuality? Few areas of life, it might seem, are as private, but most societies also recognize that the community sometimes does have a collective interest in regulating certain kinds of sexual conduct. In this lecture, we take up issues involving sexual conduct, including sodomy and related forms of behavior. I'd like to begin by reminding you that this isn't the first time we've considered the Constitution's relationship to sexuality. In some ways, that was the issue that was underlying all of the other issues involved in *Griswold v. Connecticut*. In this lecture, however, I'm going to concentrate largely on two cases. The first, *Bowers v. Hardwick*, decided in 1986; and the second, *Lawrence v. Texas*, decided in 2003.

Let's begin with *Bowers v. Hardwick*. Before we get into the specifics of the case, though, I think it is worth reminding ourselves what kind of analysis, what kind of doctrinal issues, we need to address. So, the first thing we will need to do in both of these cases is to identify precisely what the claimed liberty interest will be. Second, we need to assess whether or not that interest rises to the status of a fundamental constitutional right. And then, thirdly, we'll need to examine the various state interests advanced to regulate the right, and we'll need to assess whether or not those rights pass the compelling state interests test if that is what is required; or alternatively, whether they pass the rationality test.

All of the kinds of issues involving an individual's status in society, individual rights to self-determination, and individual rights to autonomy were involved in the case of *Bowers v. Hardwick*. This might have been the first case in which the Court first addressed so-called unconventional sexual practices. And before we get into the specifics of the case, let me just give you the holding: in *Bowers*, the Court finally ruled that the right to privacy does not prohibit states from making consensual sodomy between same-sex partners a criminal offense. I want to say that again. Under *Bowers,* a state is perfectly within its constitutional authority to prohibit same-sex sodomy and, presumably, related sexual activities.

Now, before we actually go into the nature of the liberty interest, I would like to spend a little bit of time articulating what state interests might support a criminal prohibition on same-sex sodomy. In Georgia, the defendant in this case articulated at least three possible such interests. First, one might imagine that the state engages in sexual regulation, or in the regulation of sexual practices, because it sometimes wants to protect vulnerable members of society. One can easily see how incest laws, for example, or bestiality laws, advance, or might advance, that state interest. In addition, we could imagine the state might advance certain kinds of sexual regulations to promote the public health in all sorts of different ways. Consider, for example, the transmission of STDs and related things. And then, finally, we might imagine that the state might sometimes engage in the regulation of sexual practices because such regulations advance or protect the moral preferences of the community at large. And before we immediately dismiss that as inappropriate, I again need to remind you that under the states' police power, the states have always had the authority to protect the health, safety, welfare, and morals of the community.

Let's begin with the case itself. Writing for the majority, Justice White first asked whether or not the privacy cases the Court had already decided protected homosexual activity. He concluded that the Court's earlier cases did not reach to this particular form of behavior. That would be essentially an appeal to precedent. Justice White began his opinion by asking, does the Constitution protect a right of homosexuals to engage in sodomy? His way of addressing that question was to appeal first, or to inquire first, into precedent; and he concluded from the *Griswold/Roe* line of cases that no such right existed.

Please recall, however, that after *Michael H.,* there is another way to determine whether or not a set of protected interests rises to the status of a fundamental constitutional right. Following Justice Scalia's formulation in *Michael H.*, the next question would be the following—and was for Justice White, for the majority—is this kind of behavior—and let's be precise about it—is homosexual sodomy, "deeply rooted in this nation's history and traditions"? And, to be completely precise—I misspoke—the issue isn't whether or not the behavior is rooted in history and tradition; the question is, rather, does history and tradition counsel us that such behavior ought to be beyond the reach of law? Justice White and the majority had no difficulty at all in concluding that such behavior was not traditionally protected by the nation's legal system, or by American traditions, more broadly.

In an additional opinion, in a concurring opinion, Chief Justice Burger elaborated on Justice White's comments by noting that nearly every state, at some point in the nation's history, had had criminal proscriptions against such behavior, and that many states still had such proscriptions. "Such proscriptions against homosexual sodomy," Chief Justice Burger wrote, "have a long-standing history in the American legal system."

In addition, Justice White spent a fair amount of time worrying about the limited role of courts in a democracy. In other words, he was worried that every time the Court is faced with a constitutional liberty that might be subsumed under privacy, the Court runs the risk of increasing the category of fundamental rights; and that, perhaps, is not so much the difficulty as the difficulties instead of, is it legitimate for the Court to do so?

Here is precisely what he was worried about: he wrote, again, "Does the Constitution confer on homosexuals a fundamental right to engage in acts of sodomy?" You can see, when you formulate the question in that way, what he is concerned about. Where could one possibly derive such a right from the constitutional text? If we are to find such a right—Justice White would have concluded—that would simply be another instance of the Court, or a majority of the Court, simply making up, simply creating, a new constitutional right out of whole cloth. That, of course, is fundamentally illegitimate in our constitutional democracy.

I want to quote Justice White on this point. He said that the Court should be reluctant, "to expand the substantive reach of the Due Process Clause," because in doing so "the judiciary necessarily takes to itself further authority to govern the country." And that is perhaps as direct and as obvious a way of stating the problem as one could imagine. I want to read it again. "The Judiciary necessarily takes to itself further authority to govern the country"—not to interpret the Constitution; not to apply the Constitution to specific sets of facts; not to apply the Constitution or the Bill of Rights to a specific set of issues; but rather to usurp to itself the authority to govern the nation, and in so doing, to subvert the democratic process itself.

Justice Blackmun wrote an impassioned dissent. He described the privacy interest involved in *Bowers* in very different terms, arguing that the case was less about sodomy, or a constitutional right to engage in sodomy, than it was to be about the right to be let alone, and about self-determination. I want to read you part of his opinion: "We protect such rights, not because they contribute in some direct and material way to the general public welfare, but because they form so central a part of an individual's life."

I'd like to step back for a moment and counsel you again about how important it is to be precise about identifying what constitutional liberty is actually implicated in any particular case. How one frames, or how one poses a constitutional issue; how one characterizes the liberty interest involved in that case may be substantially related to the question of whether or not that liberty is actually protected by the text.

I don't want to suggest that the question always begets the answer; but it is worth asking ourselves what answer we thought would follow when Justice White wrote, "Does the Constitution confer upon homosexuals a fundamental right to engage in sodomy?" Is anybody terribly surprised that the immediate answer the majority followed with was, "Of course not;" and indeed, one can't actually find anything that remotely looks like that in the text.

On the other hand, if one formulates the question as, does the Constitution protect the kinds of fundamental choices we make about our intimate lives? Does the Constitution, perhaps through liberty or privacy, protect the kind of autonomy that most of us feel we are entitled to with at least certain kinds of choices? Are we surprised when Justice Blackmun, in the minority, concluded that, "Of course the Constitution protects that;" what other meaning could be possibly attached to the notion of liberty? How one describes the issue doesn't necessarily dictate the answer. I don't mean to go that far; but it does go a long way toward influencing how we think about the answer and how we think about the analysis that's necessary to achieve a particular result. Again, how one frames the issue in *Bowers* is, ultimately, if not of final significance, at least of large significance in concerning or in determining what's actually protected and what is not.

Bowers is important, not so much because it tells us anything new about how to do the constitutional analysis—unlike *Michael H.,* where the plurality, writing through Justice Scalia, contributed a new method for thinking about how to find constitutional rights—nothing like that happens in *Bowers. Bowers,* in some ways, covers no new ground at all, by which I mean only, nothing changes in the methods of analysis; nothing changes in the doctrinal tools that are at our disposal.

What *Bowers* does show is that, within those tools, within the analytical framework we have, there is great room, a wide expanse, for disagreement. I can't say—I would not say—whether the majority's interpretation of the precedents is superior to the dissents' interpretation of the precedents; that I will leave to you as you read the case for yourself. But try not to read *Bowers* in exclusion. You can't really determine whether the majority's understanding of precedent is superior to the dissents' understanding of precedent without reading *Bowers* in conjunction with all of the cases that preceded it. Nor can I say whether or not history and tradition counsel toward an expansive concept, an expanding concept, of individual liberty, or whether or not we should read it in the more narrow fashion that the majority adopted.

Both of those readings are likely to be influenced, in turn, by the Court's understanding about the nature and limits of its own power, as well as by larger visions of the relationship to the individual in society at large. Again, without assuming that the position Justice Blackmun adopted as correct, it is worth noting what I quoted earlier: "We protect such rights, not because they contribute in some direct and material way to the general public welfare, but because they form so central a part of an individual's life." They do indeed form so central a part of an individual's life. With that, there is little room to argue.

The difficulty comes in whether or not the Constitution advises us, or commands us, to protect all such decisions. One might argue that there is inescapably an individualistic cast to Justice Blackmun's dissent, in the same way that one might argue that Justice White's opinion for the majority tends to privilege community sentiments more than it privileges individual liberty. Those are difficult balances to strike, and it's not clear that the Constitution absolutely commands one reading in preference to another reading.

Bowers touched off a firestorm of controversy in American society at large. A few years after he retired, Justice Powell, one of the key votes in *Bowers*, was at the New York University Law School in a seminar on constitutional law. One of the students in that classroom asked Justice Powell if he had regretted any decision he had ever made, or if he had simply thought that perhaps he had reached the wrong decision. And the case that came to mind for Justice Powell was *Bowers v. Hardwick*. He admitted that he might have made a mistake; and on second thought, might have voted with the minority. Recall *Bowers v. Hardwick* was a 5–4 vote.

What are we to make of such a judicial admission? I'm not inclined to read too much into it. The Constitution isn't a self-executing document. What it means is not self-evident in any case. Please recall our discussion much earlier in the course about the differences between hard cases and easy cases. Clearly, *Bowers* is a hard case; and clearly, it is a mark of maturity, of intellectual discipline, to rethink the choices we have made in our lives. If there is a difficulty with Justice Powell's remark, it might be a second point he made in the same seminar, where he admitted that he didn't think the case was all that important, and he was annoyed that the case had been brought to the Court's attention in the first instance.

I don't mean to criticize Justice Powell by name. It might have been any other justice; but this is an appropriate point, I think, to remember a recurrent theme of this course. It's too easy to get caught up in the doctrine. It's very easy to play a game in which we shift different doctrinal formulas like we shift mathematic equations—plug in different numbers, plug in different values, and come up with different results. When we do that—when we treat *Bowers* simply as a case of fundamental rights and ask, are there compelling state interests?—we run the risk again of dehumanizing constitutional law, of dehumanizing the Bill of Rights, and forgetting that there was a young man in this case who was convicted of a crime.

The controversy ignited in *Bowers* was readdressed by the Court in the important case of *Lawrence v. Texas*, decided in 2003. Again, I want to foreshadow what the case held and then go into the details. In this case, *Lawrence*, the Court struck down a Texas law that prohibited sodomy between same-sex partners. That is nearly the opposite result from Bowers. And indeed, later, as we'll see the opinion, the majority, speaking through Justice Kennedy in *Texas v.*

Lawrence, explicitly overruled *Bowers v. Hardwick.* Nevertheless, there was an important factual difference between the two cases. In Georgia, the law that prohibited sodomy applied to everyone. It made no distinction between heterosexual forms of sodomy or heterosexual couples, and homosexual forms of sodomy or homosexual couples. That was not true in the *Texas* statute. The *Texas* statute said nothing at all about heterosexual sodomy, and instead, prohibited only homosexual sodomy.

Why do we need to concern ourselves with this distinction? To be honest, we might overlook it. But I ask you to think about it now, because it suggests an issue that will occupy at least five lectures of our time later on. One might argue that there is a particular kind of constitutional issue suggested by the distinction in these factual patterns. That issue, as we shall see later on, would be called an "equal protection" issue. Here, the equal protection issue simply refers to this distinction: is a law that is directed only against homosexual couples different in kind than a law that is directed to all couples engaged in sexual behavior? If so, does that law implicate the Constitution's protections for equal protection?

As it turns out, this seems like the most obvious difference between the two cases; but only one justice, Sandra Day O'Connor, chose to address the equal protection issue. Notwithstanding the obvious distinction, in other words, *Lawrence v. Texas* is squarely a privacy case and not an equal protection case.

I will begin with Justice Kennedy's majority opinion. He notes that *Bowers* must be specifically overruled. But before he gets there, he writes, in language that is very reminiscent of the Court's decision, of the plurality decision, in *Casey,* "Liberty presumes an autonomy of self that includes the freedom of thought, belief, expression, and certain intimate conduct."

Please recall the opening paragraphs of the plurality opinion in *Casey,* where Justice O'Connor wrote, in that plurality opinion, "Liberty finds no refuge in a jurisprudence of doubt." And then she continues to expand in truly descriptive terms how profound, how expansive, the liberty interest is. The same language appears in Justice Kennedy's opinion.

Justice Kennedy and the majority then go on to conclude that, in light of this description of the interest involved, *Bowers'* description, or at least the majority's description, of the right involved in *Bowers* was profoundly wrong. He wrote:

> To say that the issue in *Bowers* was simply the right to engage in certain sexual conduct demeans the claims that the individuals put forward in that case. Just as it would demean a married couple were it to be said that marriage is simply about the right to have sexual intercourse.

Now let me elaborate for a moment on Justice Kennedy's point. One might reach all the way back to *Griswold*—where the right was described as a right to privacy, or sometimes, alternatively, as a right to marital privacy—and instead say, "No, what's involved in *Griswold* is the right to have sexual intercourse by virtue of having access to contraceptive devices." But nobody in *Griswold* described the right in that way. You'll recall that it was described, in overarching terms, about the sacredness of the marriage relationship, "We deal with a right of privacy that is older than the Bill of Rights;" that is essentially the point Kennedy wants to make here.

Here is another way to put this. Of the two descriptions we encountered of the right in *Bowers,* the majority's description in the dissents, the majority of the Court in *Lawrence* firmly embraces the description that was advanced by Justice Blackmun in dissent. The right is no longer about engaging in sexual sodomy, much less in homosexual sodomy; the right is about self-determination, about the right to make certain kinds of intimate choices without the intervening prospect of the state.

The opinion continued at some length on a secondary issue, an issue of constitutional interpretation; and that issue was simply this: under what conditions, if any, should the Court overrule itself? Again, the same kinds of issues that we addressed in *Casey.* What kinds of issues are involved whenever a Court makes a decision to overrule an earlier case? For the majority, at least in this case, it was more important to get the Constitution correct than it was to worry about the kinds of inconsistency or threats to the Court's legitimacy that might occur if the Court changes its mind too frequently.

Now, just as *Bowers* produced strongly worded dissents, so did the *Lawrence v. Texas* case. Justice Scalia, in particular, wrote at some length and with great passion. Justice Scalia first accused the majority of taking sides in a culture war. He wrote:

I now turn to the ground on which the Court squarely rests its holding, the contention that there is no rational basis for the law here. This proposition is so out of accord with our jurisprudence, indeed with a jurisprudence of any society we know, that it requires little discussion.

And something very interesting has happened in this little part of the dissent. I want to return to it in a few minutes, but note that he says the Court's discussion—the majority's discussion—concludes that the law was irrational. That is an issue to which we will have to return.

He also wrote, angrily, about some other issues: "Today's opinion is the product of a Court which is the product of a law profession culture that has largely signed on to the so-called 'homosexual agenda.'"

Now, it's difficult to imagine a more frank, direct exchange of views. We can only understand Justice Scalia's anger in the context of the larger set of constitutional issues that are implicated here. I want to go through just a couple of those things.

First, as he had done in *Casey*, Justice Scalia again reminded the Court that it had little constitutional warrant for displacing the choices of democratic majorities, and that the Court may never do that unless it has a clear, constitutional basis for doing so. Did the Court have a clear, constitutional basis for doing so? Not according to Justice Scalia. Remember, Justice Scalia is the person, the justice, who wrote in *Michael H.* that:

> Something achieves the status of a fundamental liberty interest, a fundamental privacy interest, only if it is explicitly protected by the text [clearly it is not here] and secondarily, only if we can find some support for the liberty interest in American history and American traditions.

Justice Scalia had no difficulty concluding that no such support could be found. Indeed, his primary piece of evidence, that no such tradition existed, was the Court's opinion in *Bowers* itself, decided only 17 years earlier.

Let me put this in a slightly different formulation. According to Justice Scalia, it was inconceivable that there would actually be a fundamental liberty interest advanced on this set of facts—because precedent could not clearly support it; the constitutional text had no relationship to it; and, perhaps more importantly, two centuries of an unbroken legal tradition had made it clear that states had traditionally proscribed such conduct. There was no basis in the majority opinion, according to Justice Scalia, for suddenly deciding (and I use the words "suddenly deciding" deliberately) that there was now some fundamental constitutional right that covered same-sex sodomy.

One wonders—we cannot know—how Justice Scalia would have voted in the *Bowers* case. I know that must sound strange. Surely, if he dissented in the *Lawrence* case, he would have dissented in *Bowers;* but I'd like to come full circle on that. Remember, in *Bowers*, the legislative proscription applied to both heterosexual and to homosexual couples; not so in the *Lawrence* case. Is there a difference—not in fact, but in importance—in constitutional relevance between homosexual sodomy?—and, let's not call it "heterosexual sodomy;" let's say, "sodomy between a married couple."

Imagine the issue now as simply this: does a state statute that prohibits heterosexual sodomy for everybody, including heterosexual married couples, violate the privacy line of cases, or those parts of the Constitution that contribute to a right to privacy?

I don't know how to answer that. One might look at the *Griswold* line of cases and suggest that the Constitution, or, at least, precedent, suggests a greater degree of autonomy for a married couple engaged in sexual activity within the marriage; not a complete degree of autonomy—not even *Griswold* goes that far. *Griswold*, for example, doesn't necessarily mean that state adultery statutes would be unconstitutional. But *Griswold* might be read as saying certain kinds of choices made about sexuality in the context of a heterosexual marriage are entitled to some degree of constitutional protection. So, perhaps we can read precedent in a way that yields a different result in my hypothetical case than yielded in *Bowers* or *Lawrence v. Texas*.

Alternatively, we might use the analytical framework proposed by Justice Scalia, and ask ourselves, what about American history and tradition? Do they counsel the state to withdraw from the sanctity of the marital relationship? I don't know the answer to that question either. I assume—but it is only an assumption—that Justice Scalia will be able to point to a long-standing tradition of laws, such as the Georgian one that prohibits sodomy for all individuals; but on the other hand, such statutes are not as common as those that seem to isolate or to choose out homosexual sodomy. Perhaps that's a constitutionally relevant distinction.

Let's try to conclude our discussion of the sexuality cases in the following way. Like so many of the Court's privacy cases, the decisions in *Bowers* and *Lawrence* provoked a storm of both criticism and support in society at large. It is worth again consulting Justice Scalia's dissenting opinion, where he predicted, following *Lawrence v. Texas*, "massive social disruption."

What happened following *Lawrence v. Texas*? Some members have spoken openly about ways to discipline the Court. How might we discipline the Court? I'm not sure "discipline" is the correct word here; but there have been different movements in state governance, and certainly in Congress, to propose constitutional amendments that would allow the prohibition of sodomy, especially same-sex sodomy. Is that a form of discipline? Perhaps. It might also be a form of democratic accountability.

Lecture Fifteen
Same-Sex Marriages and the Constitution

Scope:

Does the Constitution protect same-sex marriages? No decision by the Supreme Court has addressed this question directly, but there are several cases that might be relevant to the issue, including *Loving v. Virginia* (1967), *Romer v. Evans* (1996), and *Lawrence v. Texas* (2003). The issue has received a bit more attention in the state courts. In *Baehr v. Lewin* (1993), for example, the Supreme Court of Hawaii held that a law limiting marriage to opposite-sex couples violated the state constitution. An amendment to the Hawaiian Constitution overturned the decision. Similarly, in *Baker v. Vermont* (1999), the Supreme Court of Vermont held that a state law denying the statutory benefits of marriage to same-sex couples violates that state's constitution. And in *Goodridge v. Mass. Department of Public Health* (2003), the Massachusetts Supreme Court ruled that the Massachusetts Constitution prohibits the state from discriminating against same-sex marriages. On the other hand, at least 39 states have laws similar to the federal Defense of Marriage Act (1996), which prohibits same-sex marriages. And President George W. Bush has called for a constitutional amendment barring same-sex marriages. The controversy surrounding same-sex marriages should remind us that civil liberties are matters of importance, not just for lawyers and judges, but also for every citizen.

Outline

I.   As you know by now, there is a great deal of material we must cover in this course, and in every lecture are several cases and issues that demand our attention. Every once in awhile, however, I think we would do well to narrow our focus by examining just one issue and just a few cases in greater detail.

    A. In this lecture, then, I would like to take up a particular privacy issue and consider it at length: Does the right to privacy offer some degree of constitutional protection for same-sex marriages?

B. We shall see that the U.S. Supreme Court has yet to address this question directly, but there are several opinions, both federal and state, that are relevant to the question.

II. Again, no decision by the U.S. Supreme Court directly addresses this question, but there are a few cases that might bear on it.

    A. For example, in *Loving v. Virginia* (1967), the Court ruled that a Virginia statute that prohibited interracial marriages was a violation of the fundamental right to marriage and of the equal protection clause of the Fourteenth Amendment.

        1. It is interesting that the Court identified two distinct constitutional grounds upon which the law could be invalidated—the fundamental right to marry and equal protection.

        2. As we shall see in Lectures Thirty-Two through Thirty-Five, the equal protection argument can be made entirely independently of the fundamental rights argument.

    B. In *Romer v. Evans* (1996), the Court invalidated an amendment to the Colorado Constitution that barred local governments from adopting ordinances that prohibited discrimination against homosexuals.

        1. The majority concluded that the amendment could not survive the rationality test that we explored in earlier lectures.

        2. Although *Romer* was decided on equal protection grounds, there are aspects of the Court's majority opinion that might be of relevance to the fundamental rights question as well.

    C. As we saw in Lecture Fourteen, in *Lawrence v. Texas* (2003), the Court struck down a Texas law that prohibited sodomy between same-sex partners. Unlike the Georgia law, however, the Texas statute did not criminalize the same acts when performed by heterosexuals.

        1. Writing for a 6–3 majority, Justice Kennedy said, "Liberty presumes an autonomy of self that includes freedom of thought, belief, expression, and certain intimate conduct."

        2. One must wonder if that same liberty includes the right to marry the partner of one's choice.

3. *Lawrence* is also relevant because, at least in the opinion of many observers, the Court seemed to use a heightened form of rationality, a somewhat more aggressive version of the rationality test.

4. There was also an important dissent in *Romer* from Justice Scalia. He wrote:

> The Court has mistaken a *Kulturkampf* for a fit of spite. The constitutional amendment before us here [he means the Colorado amendment] is not the manifestation of a "bare ... desire to harm" homosexuals, but is rather a modest attempt by seemingly tolerant Coloradoans to preserve traditional sexual mores against the efforts of a politically powerful minority to revise those mores through the use of the laws.

D. In addition to the foregoing cases, several states have adopted statutes, sometimes called Defense of Marriage Acts, that typically define marriage as an institution reserved to heterosexual couples. There is also a federal version, the Defense of Marriage Act, or DOMA.

III. Although the Court has yet to say, this issue has been a matter of exceptional controversy since at least the early 1990s, when the Supreme Court of Hawaii ruled that the state's ban on such marriages violated the Hawaiian state constitution.

A. In the controversial case of *Baehr v. Lewin* (1993), the state Supreme Court ruled that such prohibitions were a violation of the equal protection clause. The court in part relied on a U.S. Supreme Court decision, *Loving v. Virginia* (1967), which had ruled that state prohibitions of interracial marriages violated the equal protection clause and the fundamental right to marriage, protected under the due process clause. In 1997, however, voters in Hawaii passed an amendment to the state constitution giving the legislature the right to limit marriage to male-female partners.

B. Six years later, in *Baker v. Vermont* (1999), the Vermont Supreme Court ruled that the Vermont Constitution requires equality of treatment between heterosexual and same-sex marriages. The Vermont legislature responded by passing a law offering such couples "civil unions" with all the benefits that attach to marriage, including the right to adopt children, to own real estate, and to dispose of one's estate.

C. In 2003, the Massachusetts Supreme Court, in the controversial case of *Goodridge v. Mass. Department of Public Health* (2003), ruled that a prohibition against same-sex marriages violated both the fundamental right to marriage and the right to equal protection under the state constitution.

IV. The federal government has also taken up the issue of same-sex marriages, notably with the passage of the Defense of Marriage Act (1996), which prohibits federal recognition of same-sex marriages and allows states to refuse to recognize such marriages performed in other states.

A. Thirty-nine states have enacted similar laws, but many have been challenged on constitutional grounds. In particular, litigants have claimed that such laws violate the "full faith and credit" provision of Article IV, Section 1, which generally requires state courts to honor judicial rulings and decisions in other states.

B. Doubts about the constitutionality of DOMA and its counterparts in the states have led some, including President George W. Bush, to call for a constitutional amendment barring same-sex marriages.

V. Now, having reviewed the relevant case law, let's turn to a constitutional analysis of same-sex marriage.

A. Imagine that the Supreme Court takes up such a case, and for purposes of analysis, imagine that the Court restricts its analysis to the privacy and substantive due process issues.

    1. Our first inquiry, probably, should concern whether such a right exists and whether it is fundamental.

    2. We might use the *Palko* test to address this question: Is the right to same-sex marriage "implicit in the concept of ordered liberty"?

3. Or we might use the test advanced by Justice Scalia: Is such a right one that is traditionally protected as a part of American history, or is it rooted in the nation's history and tradition?

4. The answer, under either test, is not as obvious at it might first seem.

5. What is obvious, though, is that many if not all of the justices will introduce another factor into the analysis—that issue, of course, is whether, in the absence of any clear constitutional guidance, the Court should even undertake to resolve the issue or, instead, should leave it to the democratic process to resolve.

B. Assume, for purposes of analysis, that a majority of the Court overcame the previous difficulties and held that there is a fundamental right to same-sex marriage. There is more that we must do to complete the analysis.

1. We must next address: What state interests are advanced to regulate the right, and are those interests compelling?

2. We have yet, in this course, to come up with a clear or concise definition of *compelling*.

C. Alternatively, suppose the Court finds that such a right does not exist, or at least, it is not a fundamental right.

1. The Court must still assess whether the state's interests would pass the rationality test.

2. As we have seen, historically, this has not proved to be much of a hurdle. But *Romer*'s use of the rationality test to strike the Colorado amendment might suggest a more subtle analysis.

VI. Finally, let's consider another hypothetical situation. Imagine this time that the requisite number of states passes a constitutional amendment that carefully defines marriage as a heterosexual institution.

A. Could the Supreme Court declare an amendment—passed in cheerful and complete compliance with every other constitutional requirement—"unconstitutional"?

B. Suppose the amendment—this one or some other—seems to be at odds with some other basic constitutional commitment?

1. What if we passed an amendment, for example, that repealed the First Amendment?
2. Or if we passed an amendment repealing the antislavery provisions of the Thirteenth Amendment?
C. Behind these questions is another, perhaps more basic question: Does our commitment to democratic self-governance trump every other constitutional value?

Essential Reading:

Loving v. Virginia (1967).

Romer v. Evans (1996).

Baker v. Vermont (1999).

Lawrence v. Texas (2003).

Goodridge v. Mass. Department of Public Health (2003).

Supplementary Reading:

Anita Bernstein, "For and Against Marriage: A Revision," 102 *Michigan Law Review* 129 (2003).

Evan Gerstmann, *Same-Sex Marriage and the Constitution.*

Mark Strasser, *On Same-Sex Marriage, Civil Unions, and the Rule of Law: Constitutional Interpretation at the Crossroads.*

Cass Sunstein, "The Right to Marry," 26 *Cardozo Law Review* 2081 (2005).

Questions to Consider:

1. Does it matter, either politically or constitutionally, if we consider the same-sex marriage issue a fundamental rights/due process issue or an issue of equal protection?

2. At bottom, same-sex marriages raise an old and familiar problem about the relationship between our commitment to democratic self-governance and the protection of civil liberties: When, if ever, should the interests of the community trump individual liberty? Or is this a false conflict?

Lecture Fifteen—Transcript
Same-Sex Marriages and the Constitution

At certain points in this course, I think it makes a certain amount of sense to take one particular issue and to perhaps examine it in more detail than would otherwise be possible. So for much of the privacy cases, for example, we've had to consider a wide array of cases, a long line of precedents. I'd like to just change course a little bit in this lecture and focus on one single issue in some detail. Does the Constitution protect same-sex marriages?

No decision by the Supreme Court has addressed this question directly, but there are several cases that might be relevant to the issue, including one called *Loving v. Virginia,* decided in 1967; a second called *Romer v. Evans,* decided in 1996; and then *Lawrence v. Texas,* which we addressed in the last lecture. Although the federal courts haven't spent an inordinate amount of time—and certainly the Supreme Court has not spent any time—considering the constitutionality of same-sex marriages, the issue has received a certain amount of attention in some of the state courts. Before we go to those state court decisions, let's at least review the few federal decisions that might be appropriate or might be relevant.

In *Loving v. Virginia*, decided in 1967, the Supreme Court ruled that a Virginia statute that prohibited interracial marriages was a violation of the fundamental right to marriage and of the equal protection clause of the Fourteenth Amendment. We'll take up the equal protection issue in a later lecture. For now, it's important to understand, I think, that *Loving v. Virginia* does assume, does hold, that certain kinds of decisions one makes about who to marry will, in fact, be protected under the privacy provisions of the Court's jurisprudence. So we have some sense, anyway—although not a very articulate or detailed one—that some marriage choices probably will be protected by the Fourteenth Amendment.

Loving v. Virginia establishes the baseline that the right to marry is fundamental. That doesn't actually answer the question about whether your fundamental right to marry includes the right to marry anyone. It doesn't address under what conditions the state might have a compelling state interest in prohibiting certain choices about whom to marry, but it does at least establish that fundamental baseline.

Alternatively, in the important case of *Romer v. Evans*, decided in 1996, the Court invalidated an amendment to the Colorado Constitution that prohibited local governments, including Denver, Aspen, and Boulder, from adopting ordinances that prohibited discrimination against homosexuals. The majority in this case decided that the Colorado constitutional amendment involved could not survive the rationality test that we have seen in previous cases. I want to be careful—*Romer* was actually decided upon equal protection grounds—but there are aspects of the opinion that might be relevant to our privacy inquiry, as well; in particular, that use of the rationality test, which drives us back to *Lawrence v. Texas*.

You'll recall that I mentioned, just in passing, that there was something unique about *Lawrence*'s use of the rationality test in our last lecture. Here's what I mean. Let's go back to *Lawrence* for just a second. *Lawrence,* you'll recall, involved a Court that struck down a Texas law prohibiting sodomy between same-sex partners.

Interestingly, however, the Court does not clearly indicate that homosexual sodomy is a fundamental right protected by the Fourteenth Amendment. At no point in the opinion does the Court unequivocally say, "Yes, the right to engage in these kinds of activities is fundamental." Instead, it appears as though the Court sidesteps that question, and, instead, spends most of its time, most of its attention, addressing whether or not the particular statute in *Texas* is, in fact, rational.

Now you'll recall that, historically, when the Court uses the rationality test, the result is almost always a foregone conclusion; but that was not true in the Texas sodomy case. Instead, the Court concluded that the distinction made between heterosexual sodomy and homosexual sodomy, although not directly relevant to the holding, at least opened up the question about whether or not the Texas statute was, in fact, rational, and the Court concluded that it wasn't.

I can't be terribly precise about this other than to say the following: it appears to many observers as though what the Court did in the *Lawrence v. Texas* case was to adopt a heightened form of rationality. I mentioned that because in *Romer,* too, it appears as though the Court utilized a heightened form of rationality, a more aggressive form of judicial scrutiny, to strike down that amendment to the Colorado Constitution; and that suggests that, perhaps, there is a class—or will soon be a class—of constitutional liberties that might not be described as fundamental, but which might, nonetheless, receive more protection than they would have, historically; because the Court will—or might—invoke this heightened sense of rationality in its evaluation of the law. *Romer v. Evans* and *Lawrence v. Texas* together, then, might make some suggestion that the Court's analysis in this area isn't as predictable as one might have thought it would be.

There's also an important dissent in *Romer*, which, again, I think will be relevant to the issues in same-sex marriage cases. Justice Scalia, dissenting in *Romer*, wrote the following. Please forgive me; this is rather a long quote, but it is important to our understanding. He wrote:

> The Court has mistaken a *Kulturkampf* for a fit of spite. The constitutional amendment before us here [he means the Colorado amendment] is not the manifestation of a "bare…desire to harm" homosexuals, but is rather a modest attempt by seemingly tolerant Coloradoans to preserve traditional sexual mores against the efforts of a politically powerful minority to revise those mores through the use of the laws.

Now, you can imagine, of course, continuing with this opinion, that Justice Scalia thinks it is inappropriate for the Court to engage itself in this kind of culture clash; that this is precisely the sort of arena that ought to be left to the purity and to the integrity of the democratic process, more generally.

Of course, what I didn't quote for you is the obvious corollary to his opinion. In Justice Scalia's view, there would be nothing in the Constitution that would speak directly to the efforts of Colorado citizens to impose—or to enact, I should say—these kinds of state amendments. I also want to stress, again, that it was an amendment to a state constitution; because, when we conclude this lecture, I want to return to the possibility of constitutional amendment.

Now, let's continue with federal efforts to concern themselves or to address themselves to same-sex marriage. Although the Court has yet to issue a definitive opinion, the federal government has been apt. In particular, several states have adopted statutes, sometimes called Defense of Marriage Acts, which go out of their way to specifically identify that marriage as an institution reserved to heterosexual couples. And, indeed, there is a federal version of this statute—the Defense of Marriage Act—which defines marriage, for purposes of federal law, as between a man and a woman.

As I said, the Court has yet to weigh in on the constitutionality of that statute. The Court has yet to indicate its opinion about these state efforts; and there have been several state efforts.

Perhaps the first of these state efforts came about in 1993 in the Hawaiian case of *Baehr v. Lewin*. In that case, the Hawaii Supreme Court ruled that prohibitions against same-sex marriages were a violation of the equal protection clause. Again, that's not our issue here—we're interested in the due process issues—but it is interesting that the Hawaii court cited the case of *Loving v. Virginia*, which was decided partially on due process grounds. You'll recall *Loving v. Virginia* was that decision by the Supreme Court that struck down the interracial marriage laws in Virginia.

In 1993, however—the same year—voters in Hawaii passed an amendment to the state constitution, which gave to the legislature the right to limit marriage to male-female partners. And, again, you see the connection with the *Romer* case. Both the *Romer* case and the Hawaiian case ultimately, or finally, evolved the passage of state constitutional amendments, an issue to which we'll return.

Two other cases are directly relevant to our inquiry: in 1999, in a case perhaps better known than the Hawaiian case, the Vermont Supreme Court ruled in *Baker v. Vermont* that the Vermont State Constitution requires equality of treatment between heterosexual and homosexual, or same-sex, marriages. The Vermont legislature responded to the state Supreme Court's decision by passing a law offering such couples so-called civil unions, or unions that have all of the benefits that attach to marriage, or that are traditionally attached to the marriage relationship; including the right to adopt children, to own real estate, and to dispose of one's estate—and those, indeed, are typically privileges that attach to the marital relationship.

Four years later, in 2003, the Massachusetts Supreme Court, in the wildly controversial case of *Goodridge v. Massachusetts Department of Health*, ruled that a prohibition against same-sex marriages violated both the fundamental right to marriage and the right to equal protection under the state constitution. That case, perhaps more than the other two, provoked widespread social controversy.

In 1996, I mentioned that the federal government had taken up the Defense of Marriage Act. That Defense of Marriage Act is a statutory provision. The Court's ruling in Massachusetts suggested to some in the federal government, including President Bush, that the Defense of Marriage Act would not be enough as a statutory measure to protect or to limit the institution of marriage to heterosexual couples; and as a consequence, many states and the federal government are considering constitutional amendments to limit marriage to heterosexual couples. *Goodridge* didn't cause that controversy; but *Goodridge* did accelerate that controversy in profound ways.

Now let me just step back for a moment here. Does the Constitution protect same-sex marriages? We don't have a Supreme Court decision that answers that question unequivocally. We don't have a Supreme Court decision that even gives us much guidance about how to answer such a question. If the court were to take the issue up, it certainly would consult the decisions of various state courts; but, as a matter of law, it is important to understand that none of those decisions would bind the United States Supreme Court. None of them are precedent in the strict legal sense. None of them are binding authorities, as an attorney would say; although they might have— again, as an attorney would say—some kind of persuasive merit, or some kind of persuasive value.

What will the Court do in such a case? It is at this point, I think, that we have an opportunity to do the kinds of analysis that we have seen the Court use in earlier cases. Part of the reason I wanted to stop the course at this point and to consider the issue in detail is to give us an opportunity to see what we've learned; to give us an opportunity to utilize the kind of tools that we have been exposed to.

So, let's work our way through a hypothetical. Imagine the Court does take up the issue of same-sex marriage; and just for purposes of convenience, imagine that it limits its analysis to the privacy issues or to the substantive due process issues (we'll leave the equal protection issues to a later time). So think about, now, how we, the Court, will react to such an issue. We do have certain kinds of analytical devices that are at our disposal, and now is the time to think about how to use them. Where should we begin?

The first question that we should ask is whether or not there is a fundamental right to a same-sex marriage. How do we know what the answer to that question will be? We do have, at our disposal, certain kinds of tools that we should think about using to try to answer that question.

Let's begin with the first test we encountered. How do we know whether a right is fundamental, or a claimed set of interests should be fundamental? The first place we should consult, presumably, would be the Supreme Court's decision in *Palko v. Connecticut*. You'll recall that discussion from our incorporation lecture. The test in *Palko* is straightforward. It is simply this: is this claimed liberty interest—the right to a same-sex marriage, "Implicit in the concept of ordered liberty?" In other words, could we imagine a system, devoted to the protection of individual liberty, that did not privilege or immunize the decision to engage in a same-sex marriage from state regulation? That is our first question.

I hope you can see that the answer to that question is not immediately obvious; or, I should say, there is certainly room to argue it on either side. Let's try a different test. Let's use the test proposed by Justice Scalia in the *Michael H.* case; in which case, we would ask ourselves, does the behavior involved, does the interest involved in this case—again, the right to pursue a same-sex marriage—one that is traditionally protected by American history, or by American traditions more generally? Is that behavior deeply rooted in the nation's history and traditions?

Here, I think we have a fairly straightforward answer, at least if we ask the question in the way I've described it. I think we would have to conclude, that, in point of fact, it's not deeply protected, or not historically protected, in American tradition. To the best of my knowledge, no state historically has protected same-sex marriages. I think we would have to conclude that the overwhelming weight of history counsels against that conclusion.

On the other hand, it is worth remembering, too, Justice Brennan's objection to this interpretive method when we considered *Michael H.* Remember, he argued, that the problem with the Scalia test is that it allows no room for diversity. Remember, he argued, that a constitutional right to liberty at its core must include the right not to conform.

There is another objection that we didn't consider when we addressed *Michael H.,* but now would be a good time to bring it up. Whether we find some particular set of human behaviors protected in American history and tradition might well depend on what level of abstraction we use to consider that behavior. So, in some ways, I have prejudiced the question by asking, is there a history and tradition in American law and society of protecting, or allowing, or recognizing homosexual marriage or same-sex marriage? But surely that is only one way to ask the question.

We might ask, instead, does American history, do American traditions, counsel that individuals ought to be allowed to marry whomever they like? Do you see the difference in the level of abstractions? If we describe it as, is this particular form of marriage historically protected?—then, of course, the answer is, no. But if we ask, do we protect, or want to protect, the autonomy that is involved in allowing individuals to make decisions about whom to marry?— we might come up with a different answer.

I want to be careful here too. I'm not suggesting that, if we categorize the question in this way, that the answer is obviously, yes; because surely, throughout American history, there have always been limits on whom you can marry. *Virginia v. Loving* indicates that, historically, such decisions were limited on the basis of race. They have been limited on several other bases, as well, and continue to be so. So, a liberty to marry whomever you please certainly doesn't exist with regard to adults marrying children, for example. The question would be, under this new kind of analysis, which forms of state regulation are legitimate, and which forms threaten the underlying liberty that we have always sought to protect?

Just like the *Palko* test, the answer that we should reach under the *Michael H.* analysis is, perhaps, not as obvious as it might first seem. Alternatively, we might use the language that Justice O'Connor used in the plurality opinion in *Casey,* and that Justice Kennedy used in *Lawrence v. Texas.* In both cases, you'll recall, these justices wrote of a broad expanse of liberty that protects certain kinds of intimate decisions one should be able to make for themselves without the interfering force of the state. It is a nice prospect. Certainly, as handled, or as written, or as developed by justices O'Connor and Kennedy, it is remarkably eloquent as a test; but whether it addresses us or drives us to any particular conclusion in this case seems far less obvious.

To be blunt, I'm not confident that I know what the correct answer is to the question of same-sex marriage under *Casey,* or under the *Casey* test; I'm not confident I know what it is under the *Michael H.* test; and I'm not confident I know what it is under the *Palko* test. I do know this, however: if a Court were to take up the question of same-sex marriage, and to engage the analysis of, is there a fundamental right here? Several members—perhaps every member of the Court—will want to introduce an additional complicating factor; and that factor will be, should the Court be involved in these cases at all? Surely, you can hear Justice Thomas or Justice Scalia, and perhaps even Ginsburg or Breyer, saying that we need to be especially attentive, as a Court, to the use of judicial power. "Perhaps, same sex marriage," these justices would write, "is precisely the set of issues or the kind of issues that ought to be left to the democratic process in general."

Why would that be? Well, at least one reason would be this: these kinds of issues ought to be left to the democratic process just because the Constitution doesn't seem to speak clearly to the issue at all. In the absence of any kind of clear constitutional guidance, then, presumably, the issue ought to be left to the people themselves to decide. Perhaps one of the ways that the people might choose to involve themselves in this process——as we saw in the *Romer* case and as we saw in the Hawaii same-sex case—is by passing different kinds of constitutional amendments. But before we get there, we need to continue with the analysis.

Let's assume for a minute that you, as Chief Justice, manage to persuade a majority of your brethren that there is, in fact, a fundamental right under the due process clause to marry a partner of the same sex. That hardly concludes our analysis. At best, we've established only that there's a fundamental right.

You'll recall that the second part of the analysis is an inquiry into the state's interests. A complete analysis then requires us to ask the following question: What state interests are advanced by prohibitions on same-sex marriages? I sometimes worry that when we take up this question, we find the state interest, and we tend to concentrate on it so exclusively that we don't imagine the full array of different kinds of state interests that are involved. So, if we can think of one, we ought not to end our inquiry there; we ought to ask, are there others?

What might those interests be? Is there a public health interest in limiting marriage to different-sex couples? Alternatively, is there a social moray kind of interest? What might that interest be? We have seen before that there are times when it is permissible for the state, acting through its police power, to pass laws that do little more than reinforce prevailing modes of morality, prevailing modes of social expectations surrounding sexual behavior.

In other words, would it not be a legitimate state interest for the state to say that we act to preserve a historical institution, an institution that has always been defined in this way? And you can imagine how the argument will play itself out. This is an institution (presumably the heterosexual, nuclear family) upon which much of civil society historically rests. I don't ask you to agree with that proposition or to disagree with that proposition. I ask you to imagine, is it not inevitable that that kind of discussion will be presented as one of the state's interests?

I deliberately use the phrase, "legitimate state interest," because I have not yet opened up the question about whether or not that state interest is compelling or merely rational. If we have concluded that there is a fundamental right to a same-sex marriage, then it is not enough for the state interests—let's call it in preserving traditional notions of a marriage relationship— to be legitimate. That interest must be compelling. And we have to ask ourselves here, are we not simply playing with words?

We have yet to identify at any part in this course, we have yet to develop at any part in this course, a clear, concise definition of the word "compelling." We have been playing with it. We have been ignoring it. What does it mean to say that an interest is compelling, as opposed to merely rational? I hope you can see that there is an element of judgment involved here; and ultimately, again, constitutional interpretation always involves elements of judgment. This provides one path through the doctrine, one way of understanding how the Court might take up the issue of same-sex marriage. But we've been dealing in the conditional; I have used, "if this happens, then this follows."

Let's continue with this analysis. Let's assume, instead, that a majority of the Court concludes that the right to a same-sex marriage is not a protected fundamental constitutional liberty; that it can't be found in history and tradition; that it's not implicit in the concept of ordered liberty; that it's not a part of the liberty interest described in *Casey* and in the *Lawrence v. Texas* case. Presumably, if we follow the analysis, if the right to a same-sex marriage is not fundamental, then the state may regulate that right, this putative right, whenever it is rational to do so.

Continuing with our analysis, the state interests here are no different from the state interests we identified earlier in the analysis. The only thing that changes is our assessment of them. Instead of asking, are they compelling? We need only ask, are they rational? Historically, at least, there would be little room for doubt. Historically, these interests, whatever we might think of them individually, would clearly pass the rationality test.

On the other hand, it is worth again reminding ourselves about what happened (or what might have happened) in the *Romer* case, and what appeared to happen in *Texas v. Lawrence*. The reason I treated these two cases together, at such length earlier in this lecture and in the past lecture, is because in both cases, the Court appeared to use a rationality analysis, and yet, nevertheless, concluded the state statutes involved were irrational.

Historically, at least, the Court's use of the rationality test has always meant, or nearly always meant, that the underlying state action will pass constitutional muster. But *Romer* and the *Lawrence* cases suggest that we may be entering new territory. It might be possible, in other words, that some justices will attempt to carve out what looks to be a middle course in a same-sex case by arguing that, no, there is no fundamental right to same-sex marriage; but nonetheless, the state cannot articulate a reason for prohibiting same-sex marriages that would pass the rationality test. I think there may be room in the middle of the Court for such an analysis.

Let me step back for a second. Are same-sex marriages protected by the Constitution? I hope you can see, through our quick use with the analytical tools that we have, that nobody can say with confidence what the answer to that question is. It is possible to make very persuasive arguments on both sides. That uncertainty is part of what drives the political process to take up questions of same-sex marriage; and imagine that that political process continues to do so.

You'll recall that I asked you to remember, in a way, that the Hawaii case and the *Romer* case both involved state constitutional amendments. And you'll recall, also, that I indicated that, following the *Goodridge* case, the federal government—certain members of Congress and President Bush—decided to at least consider the possibility of a federal constitutional amendment that would limit marriages to heterosexual couples.

While we're playing hypotheticals, let's finish with this one. Imagine that the requisite number of states pass a constitutional amendment, and that constitutional amendment, with as much care is as humanly possible, defines marriage as between a man and a woman. I don't want there to be any doubt about the propriety, from a legal perspective, of this amendment. Assume every "i" has been dotted, and every "t" has been crossed; that are no procedural objections to this amendment. Might a Supreme Court nevertheless rule that an amendment to the Constitution is itself unconstitutional? Can we imagine, at least as a matter of constitutional theory, as opposed to reality, that a constitutional amendment might so fundamentally violate some other core provision of the Constitution that it can't be reconciled with that test?

If autonomy, if privacy, is so central a constitutional value, could we imagine an amendment that is fundamentally incompatible with that constitutional value? I'm not saying this amendment would be; but consider, just by way of example, an amendment that purported to repeal the First Amendment's provisions on speech or religion? Or imagine a constitutional amendment that purported to repeal the Thirteenth Amendment's prohibition on slavery? The same kind of fundamental issue is involved in the proposal that I have put before you.

Can we imagine, in other words, that there are times when the democratic political process ultimately trumps, or has the authority to trump, every other constitutional value and every other constitutional imperative? I don't believe—and I am not suggesting—that same-sex marriages will take us to that place. I mean nothing of the sort. I mean only that the issue hides behind it all.

Lecture Sixteen
The Right to Die and the Constitution

Scope:

Does the Constitution include a right to die? Few issues in civil liberties are as controversial as this question. In 1994, for example, Oregon voters adopted the Death with Dignity Act, which legalized physician-assisted suicide in certain instances. The federal government has since sought to have the statute declared unconstitutional. On the other hand, dozens of states have passed laws making physician-assisted suicide illegal. The Court has yet to issue a definitive ruling concerning the right to die in general, but there are several cases in which the Court has addressed the issue, and they have all sparked controversy, both inside the Court and in society more generally. Following the Court's decision in *Cruzan v. Director, Missouri Dept. of Health* (1990), for example, protesters occupied Cruzan's hospital room to prevent her removal from life-support systems. The Court had ruled that there is a limited "fundamental liberty interest" in terminating life-support systems. Even so, the Court upheld a Missouri statute that required "clear and convincing" evidence of a person's desire to refuse life-prolonging treatment. Seven years later, in *Washington v. Glucksberg* (1997) and *Vacco v. Quill* (1997), the Court refused to extend that liberty interest to include a right on the part of terminally patients to "physician-assisted suicide." Together, these cases nicely illustrate how the most fundamental questions in civil liberties are not so much legal as they are moral.

Outline

I. Does the Constitution include a right to die? Privacy issues often include questions that concern the quality of life, and cases involving an individual's right to refuse certain types of medical treatment have appeared with increasing frequency in the past two decades.

    A. Perhaps the first case to command public attention was that of Karen Ann Quinlan. In 1976, the New Jersey Supreme Court decided that the right to privacy included a right to be removed from a respirator and for her family to decline other life-maintaining procedures.

B. This is an issue, like so many others in civil liberties, that is not confined to the courts. In 1994, for example, Oregon voters adopted the Death with Dignity Act, which legalized physician-assisted suicide in certain instances. The federal government has since sought to have the statute declared unconstitutional. On the other hand, dozens of states have passed laws making physician-assisted suicide illegal.

C. The Supreme Court was scheduled to take up the Oregon case in the fall of 2005. [**Update**: In Gonzales v. Oregon (decided 2006), the Court ruled, in a 6–3 to decision, that the federal government had exceeded its authority by threatening to prosecute doctors who prescribed lethal drugs. Writing for the Court, Justice Kennedy noted that the government had failed to recognize "the background principles of our federal system."]

II. The issue has come to the Court before, and each time, the Court has avoided coming to a definitive decision about whether there is a constitutionally protected right to die or how far it might extend.

A. In *Cruzan v. Director, Missouri Dept. of Health* (1990), the Court considered the case of Nancy Cruzan.

1. In this case, Nancy Cruzan suffered a severe brain injury in a car crash in January 1983. Although she survived the crash, her brain was deprived of oxygen for at least 12 minutes, and the doctors advised Cruzan's parents that she would never regain consciousness. Her parents approved the insertion of a feeding tube to keep her alive.

2. In 1988, a state court granted Cruzan's parents permission to remove the feeding tube. The state appealed to the Missouri Supreme Court, which reversed the lower court. The Cruzans appealed to the U.S. Supreme Court.

B. In his opinion for the majority, Chief Justice Rehnquist assumed but did not decide "that the United States Constitution would grant a competent person a constitutionally protected right to refuse lifesaving hydration and nutrition."

1. Please note that the Chief had not decided anything about the particulars of this case just yet.

2. Instead, he had postulated, for purposes of argument, that a competent individual might have a constitutionally protected right to refuse certain kinds of lifesaving treatments.

C. In this case, however, Nancy Cruzan was in a vegetative state and, therefore, not competent. Hence, the question was whether the state of Missouri may require "clear and convincing evidence" of Nancy's wishes before permitting her surrogates—her parents—to make a decision for her.

D. The majority upheld the evidentiary requirement, noting that Missouri had two distinct interests it sought to protect.

1. First, Missouri had an interest in "the protection and preservation of human life, and there can be no gainsaying this interest."

2. Second, Missouri had a "more particular interest" in protecting "the personal element" of the profound choice between life and death, and "Not all incompetent patients will have loved ones available to serve as surrogate decisionmakers."

E. In a sharply worded concurrence, Justice Scalia sounded a familiar theme about the role of courts in such matters: "While I agree with the Court's analysis today … I would have preferred that we announce, clearly and promptly, that the federal courts have no business in this field…."

F. In dissent, Justices Brennan, Marshall, and Blackmun argued: "Nancy Cruzan has a fundamental right to be free of unwanted artificial nutrition and hydration," and the state's interests were not sufficiently strong to overcome that right.

G. As you read the various opinions in the *Cruzan* case, I'd like you to consider the following question: What, precisely, is the point of disagreement between the majority and dissenting opinions?

1. Both sets of opinions, I might suggest, are willing to at least consider the possibility of a fundamental right.

2. And, to a certain extent, there is agreement about the sorts of interests the state seeks to address.

3. The disagreement, then, might be in how the various opinions try to "balance" these diverse sets of interests.

III. In 1996, just six years after *Cruzan*, two lower federal courts extended the logic of the case to prohibit states from enacting laws that prohibited doctors from prescribing lethal doses of medication to terminally ill patients who had requested the prescription.

A. In one case, arising from Washington State, the court struck down the law on the ground that it violated a fundamental right of privacy protected by the due process clause. In the other, a federal court struck down a New York State law on equal protection grounds, finding that the state could not distinguish between a terminally ill patient's right to refuse treatment and a right to physician-assisted suicide.

B. In *Vacco v. Quill* (1997), the U.S. Supreme Court overruled the equal protection case, finding instead: "On their faces, neither New York's ban on assisting suicide nor its statutes permitting patients to refuse medical treatment treat anyone differently than anyone else or draw distinctions between persons."

C. In *Washington v. Glucksberg* (1997), the Court weighed a liberty of "personal choice by a mentally competent, terminally ill adult to commit physician-assisted suicide" against "our Nation's history, legal traditions, and practices."

1. The Court concluded that bans against suicide and assisted suicide are "longstanding expressions of the States' commitment to the protection and preservation of human life." Unwilling to find a fundamental right, the Court then weighed the liberty against the state's interest using the rationality test. The Court had little difficult in identifying a number of rational state interests that would support the ban.

2. On the other hand, the majority opinion by Chief Justice Rehnquist did suggest that the strength of the liberty interest might be different in other cases. As a consequence, the issue is not finally settled.

3. It is important, too, to consider some aspects of Justice O'Connor's concurring opinion, in part because she raises a familiar concern about the role of courts in addressing these kinds of issues. She wrote: "There is no reason to think that the democratic process will not strike the proper balance between the interests of terminally-ill, competent individuals and the state's interest in protecting those who might seek to end life mistakenly or under pressure."

4. Surely, that is about as blunt a way of putting the issue as one can imagine. She says that there is, indeed, a potential conflict between these two interests, but "there is no reason to think," she writes, "that the state or the political process, more generally, cannot fairly, justly, sensibly resolve the tensions between those two interests."

5. It is worth giving some thought to Justice O'Connor's claims. What if we suspect, or know, that the political process is "defective" or compromised?

IV. As a final issue, consider this: Up to this point, we have spoken often about the nature and importance of constitutional rights. Are there are also constitutional duties?

A. Hence, in the *Cruzan* case, should we ask if the state of Missouri has a constitutional duty to protect life or "to safeguard the element of personal choice"?

B. Or should the Court generally defer to other decision makers, recognizing, as did Justice Scalia in a famous dissent, that the materials necessary to decide such cases "are neither set forth in the Constitution nor known to the nine justices of this Court any better than they are known to nine people picked at random from the Kansas City telephone directory"?

Essential Reading:

Cruzan v. Director, Missouri Dept. of Health (1990).

Washington v. Glucksberg (1997).

Vacco v. Quill (1997).

Kommers, Finn, and Jacobsohn, *American Constitutional Law*, chapter 6, pp. 253–254.

Supplementary Reading:

Ronald Dworkin, *Life's Dominion*, chapter 7.

Alan Meisel, *The Right to Die*, 2nd ed. (1995).

Michael W. McConnell, "The Right to Die and the Jurisprudence of Tradition," *Utah Law Review* 665 (1997).

Questions to Consider:

1. If there is a constitutional right to die, what is its source in the Constitution? Is it a necessary part of a constitutional right to liberty? Is it grounded in a right to privacy?

2. The majority opinion in *Glucksberg* suggested that the state's interest in protecting the disabled includes protecting against more than coercion: "It extends to protecting disabled and terminally ill people from prejudice, negative and inaccurate stereotypes, and 'societal indifference.'" How does a law prohibiting physician-assisted suicide advance that broader interest?

Lecture Sixteen—Transcript
The Right to Die and the Constitution

This might be an overly dramatic way to put it, but let me ask: does the Constitution include a right to die? Few issues in civil liberties are as controversial as this question. In 1994, for example, Oregon voters adopted the Death with Dignity Act, which legalized physician-assisted suicide in certain instances. On the other hand, dozens of states have passed laws making physician-assisted suicide illegal.

There is no particular case, or at least no single case, in which the United States Supreme Court has issued a definitive ruling on this issue, although there are several cases that at least touch upon the issue. Although the Court has yet to finally resolve it, every time the Court has touched it—indeed, any time any state court has touched it—the decisions seemed to spark profound controversy, both inside those courts and in society, more generally. Following the Court's decision in *Cruzan v. Missouri Department of Health* in 1990, for example (a case we will describe in some detail later), some protesters physically occupied Cruzan's hospital room to prevent her removal from life support systems. That was just one case. Almost all of the Court's cases seemed to provoke certain kinds of similar reactions. The *Cruzan* case was decided in 1990.

Seven years later, in *Washington v. Glucksberg* and in *Vacco v. Quill*, the Court refused to extend that liberty interest to include a right, on the part of terminally-ill patients, to assisted suicide. We'll deal with that case in some detail, but together, the two cases suggest that these most fundamental of questions—questions about the right to die—are not so much questions of constitutional interpretation—or, I should say, are not only questions of constitutional interpretation—but are, instead, questions that go to the very way we look at the world. They implicate questions of morality, ethics, and, perhaps, faith.

Perhaps the first case to command public attention was that of Karen Ann Quinlan. In 1976, the New Jersey Supreme Court decided that the right of privacy did include a right to be removed from a respirator, as well as a right on the part of her family to decline other life-maintaining procedures. The *Quinlan* case generated enormous controversy in society at large, even resulting, at one point, for at least one made-for-T.V. movie. *Quinlan,* however, did not go to the United States Supreme Court. In reaction to *Quinlan,* several states passed laws designed to regulate physician-assisted suicide, as well as the conditions under which a mentally competent individual might choose to refuse life-saving treatment, more generally.

As I mentioned, the Court has yet to finally resolve this issue in single case, but there are several cases in which the Court has begun to take it up, and perhaps the best-known of these cases is *Cruzan v. Director,* which I referred to earlier, decided in 1990.

The facts of the case—the facts of almost all of these cases—are very tragic. In January of 1983, Nancy Cruzan was in a terrible car crash. She survived that crash, but the doctors estimated that her brain was deprived of oxygen for at least 12 minutes. They advised Nancy Cruzan's parents that Nancy would never regain consciousness. Her parents, at that time, did approve of the insertion of a feeding tube and a hydration tube to keep her alive. In 1988, however, five years later, a state court, in response to a petition from Nancy Cruzan's parents, gave her parents permission to remove the feeding tube. The state appealed to the Missouri Supreme Court, which reversed the lower court. I want to make sure we understand the procedural posture here: the lowest Missouri state court agreed that her parents had the right to remove the feeding tube. The Missouri Supreme Court reversed that decision, which meant, at least for the time being, that the feeding and hydration of Nancy Cruzan would continue.

The Cruzans appealed to the United States Supreme Court. In his opinion for the majority, Chief Justice Rehnquist assumed, but did not decide, "that the United States Constitution would grant a competent person a constitutionally protected right to refuse lifesaving hydration and nutrition."

Now I want to be careful here; I want to stop here and make sure we understand what kind of a move, intellectually, Chief Justice Rehnquist has made. He has not decided anything at all about the particulars of Nancy Cruzan's case. Instead, he has postulated, only as a matter of theory, only for the purposes of argument, only in the abstract, that a "competent" individual, a sentient, competent individual, capable of making decisions for him or herself, might sometimes have a constitutionally protected right to refuse lifesaving treatments. That, however, does not describe the factual situation we have in Nancy Cruzan's case. I am sorry to be so blunt about it, and I wish I could think of a more delicate way to put it, but Nancy Cruzan was not mentally competent. She was not possessed of the legal authority to make decisions for herself, because the doctors had diagnosed her as being in a persistent, vegetative state, and advised that it was not likely that she would ever regain consciousness.

In such circumstances, the state of Missouri had provided the following: Missouri had passed a law saying that, "the state may require clear and convincing evidence of Nancy's wishes before permitting her surrogates [in this case, her parents] to make a decision for her."

The key difference between where Chief Justice Rehnquist has started and where he needs to be in Cruzan's case is, in other words, this problem of surrogacy. Nancy Cruzan cannot make the decision for herself. The law provides that somebody else will be permitted to make the decision for her. In this case, it is the parents.

Missouri has attached a condition to that parental authority. The condition is that a Court must have, "Clear and convincing evidence of what Nancy would want." At the level of a trial court, then, what happens, or what might happen, would be the following. The state would ask a trial judge to conduct an inquiry as to whether or not there is in fact "clear and convincing evidence;" and Cruzan's parents and her attorneys would presumably produce whatever kind of evidence they have that would indicate that Nancy, in this state, would not wish to be kept alive through extraordinary or artificial life-preserving measures.

What kind of evidence might that look like? I am sure that many of you will have heard of a concept of a "living will." A living will is a process, a procedure, and a device that you may use to instruct others about what your issues would be. Nancy Cruzan did not have a living will. Alternatively, her parents might produce a diary; a letter to a friend; or, in this case, conversations with friends in which Nancy, presumably, indicated that she would never want to be kept alive under such conditions.

The precise, narrow issue in *Cruzan,* in other words, is not, is there a constitutional right to die? Instead, the issue is, is this evidentiary requirement, the requirement of "clear and convincing evidence" a constitutional violation of Nancy's surrogates' rights to make decisions on her behalf?

The majority, speaking through Chief Justice Rehnquist, upheld that requirement. As you know, in assessing any state action under the privacy provisions of the Bill of Rights, we ask first, what state interests are advanced by the regulation in question? The majority upheld the evidentiary requirement, noting that Missouri had two such interests. First, Missouri had an interest in the protection and preservation of human life; and the Court said, "There can be no gainsaying this interest." Let's be clear about this. According to the Court, a state has a legitimate interest in the preservation and the protection of human life, generally. That is a perfectly legitimate state interest.

Second, Missouri had a "more particular interest" in protecting what the Court called "the personal element" of the profound choice between life and death. I want to make sure we understand that. In this case, according to a majority of the Court, Missouri has a particular interest, a legitimate interest, in protecting the personal element of the choice; in other words, in making sure that this is actually the choice, or at least potentially the choice—probably—the choice that Nancy would have made. The idea here is to make certain that whoever actually makes the decision makes it in a way that would be consistent with Nancy's pre-existing wishes; not to impose their own set of wishes, not to impose the state's set of wishes, but to act in accordance with Nancy's wishes. The Court continued by noting in a sentence, profoundly moving, "Not all incompetent patients will have loved ones available to serve as surrogate decision makers."

Now, I hope you can see the kind of difficulty the Court is referencing here. No one in this case seriously advanced the argument that Nancy's parents were not acting on her behalf. But it doesn't take a great deal of imagination to conjure up situations in which mentally ill or mentally incompetent patients will not have individuals who are primarily determined to advance their wishes. Without going into this troublesome area in any great detail, it's not difficult to imagine "surrogate decision makers" who are, perhaps, more concerned about the cost of healthcare. Or, alternatively, without imputing ill will to anybody, can we not imagine decision makers who simply cannot bear to see their loved one in this condition, and act on the base of what they cannot handle emotionally, or what they would prefer emotionally, as opposed to what the individual in question might actually want? We don't have to attribute ill will to understand that there may, indeed, be times when a surrogate decision maker's analysis of the situation and determination of a decision may not be completely consistent with the individual's. That precisely is the kind of interest that *Missouri* is attempting to advance through this evidentiary rule.

There is an important concurrence in the case, written again by Justice Scalia, who sounds what should be, by now, a familiar theme about the role of Courts in such matters: "While I agree with the Court's analysis today...I would have preferred that we announce, clearly and promptly, that the federal courts have no business in this field...."

There is an important difference between Justice Scalia's concurrence and the majority opinion. The majority opinion is open to addressing the issue, and, indeed, goes ahead and resolves it on its merits. Its resolution of the particular factual and legal problem does not trouble Justice Scalia. He agrees that the Court reached the correct decision—the decision to uphold the Missouri law; but he would have preferred the Court not open the issue at all, and simply announce instead there are some kinds of issues—this is one of them—where judges have no special competence, can find no special instruction in the Constitution, and as a consequence, ought simply to leave to the people and to the states to resolve for themselves.

In dissent, Justices Brennan, Marshall, and Blackmun argued that, "Nancy Cruzan has a fundamental right to be free of unwanted artificial nutrition and hydration," and that the state's interests simply are not sufficiently strong to overcome that right. This is a classic dispute on the merits. The majority engages almost the exact same analysis that the minority engages. We don't have, in *Cruzan*, a majority opinion that is intent on looking at the case in one particular way, with one set of doctrinal or interpretive tools, and a dissent or several dissents that disagree with that approach.

Let me put this in more specific terms. Read these opinions for yourself, and ask yourself the following question: What, precisely, is the object of disagreement between the majority opinions and the dissenting opinions? I don't want to suggest that there is only one correct answer to that question, but I would like to propose an answer to that question—to test it against the materials.

In my view, both the majority and the dissents seemed to agree upon the existence of a fundamental right. Granted, for the majority, it's conditional. They, perhaps, didn't directly decide on the question, but they did seem to assume that there would be some kind of fundamental right; and the dissents argued explicitly that there is a fundamental right. Both the majority opinion and the dissenting opinion seemed to agree about what the various state interests are in these cases.

The area of disagreement I propose is simply in how to weigh the balance. How much weight do we attach to the fundamental liberty interests? How much weight can we attach to the state interests? What we have to do, as judges in such cases, as students in such cases, is weigh the balance and come to a conclusion. In this case, arguably, the only thing that separates the majority from the dissenting opinion is how they weigh that balance. Read the opinion carefully, please, and ask yourself the following question. Each opinion, I suspect, does an admirable job of telling you in the end where the balance lays.

Neither opinion, I propose, does a very good job of telling you how they actually reached that conclusion. This is, perhaps, one of the clearest cases involving a method of interpretation that we have not yet addressed, sometimes called "balancing." We will see many cases, especially when we take up the First Amendment, where the Court purports to balance one set of interests against another set of interests; to weigh them; and then to tell you that one interest is weightier than another, and is, hence, constitutionally superior to another. The difficulty with balancing, as a method of giving meaning to the Bill of Rights, is that it is too easy to announce the conclusion—this interest is heavier than another interest—and exceptionally difficult to know why they were assigned the weight that they possess. Anybody can say, "I have weighed the two opinions, and I find one more persuasive," but that is the announcement of a conclusion. That's not an argument.

You'll recall from our earliest lectures that one of the most basic aspects of constitutional responsibility that judges must follow is that they have an obligation, not simply to announce opinions, but to explain opinions; and one difficulty with balancing—it's a difficulty that can be overcome—but one difficulty with balancing is that, too often, it's closer to announcement than it is to explanation.

Now, to just step back for a minute, I want to make sure we understand the precise holding in *Cruzan*. *Cruzan* does not establish a constitutional right to die of any kind. It simply establishes that sometimes there might be a defensible constitutional interest in refusing life-saving treatment, and that interest must be weighed against whatever the state's interests are in that particular case.

Seven years later, in the important case of *Washington v. Glucksberg*, the Court again addressed the issue of physician-assisted suicide. Actually, there are two cases here: *Glucksberg*, the one I just referenced; and a second, called *Vacco v. Quill*, also decided in 1997. We won't take up *Vacco* here, because it's essentially an equal protection case, but the two cases did come to the Court together. The *Washington* case is exceptionally interesting. In that case, the Supreme Court struck down a Washington state law on the ground that it violated a fundamental right of privacy protected by the due process clause. This case seems more directly on point with the right-to-die issue than *Cruzan*.

However, the Court, for lack of a better word (and I hope you will forgive this piece of jargon), waffled. Constitutional law professors like to describe certain kinds of reasoning in precise terms. The precise term that most of my colleagues have used in describing the reasoning in *Washington* is that the Court's reasoning is (and again, please forgive the jargon) "fuzzy."

First step in analysis (this must seem awfully familiar by now): Is there a fundamental right—to what? Is there a fundamental right to physician-assisted suicide? How would you know if that right is fundamental? What kinds of inquiries would you have to ask? We have been through this analysis before.

The Court concluded that bans against suicide and assisted-suicide are "longstanding expressions of the state's commitment to the protection and preservation of human life." In other words, the Court concluded that there is not a fundamental right to a physician-assisted suicide; and perhaps the primary reason is because a right—such a protected liberty interest—cannot be located in the nation's history or in American traditions, more generally. You'll recognize that test as the test the Court proposed in its plurality opinion in *Michael H.*

Because we have done this in other lectures, I will not parse the Court's explanation at any great length here, other than to point out that there are objections to this interpretive method. We have seen Justice Brennan articulate them on more than one occasion; and one might ask, instead, is the tradition that we seek to find a tradition to commit physician-assisted suicide, or is it a tradition to control the circumstances of our own life and our own death? One might reach an alternative conclusion.

Now, because the Court concluded that there is not, in fact, a fundamental right to a physician-assisted suicide, the next question inevitably becomes, if we are going to follow the doctrine, is the state's interests in this case rational? And the Court, as you might imagine, had no difficulty at all in identifying a distinct number of rational state interests that would support the ban. I'm sure you can supply these interests for yourself, but obviously one of them would be the state's interest in preserving human life—the first interest articulated in the *Cruzan* case, as well as the more particular interest in the *Cruzan* case, of making certain that we protect the element of personal choice.

So far, this might seem as though it is a reasonably definitive ruling on the question of physician-assisted suicide. But, at different places in the majority opinion, Chief Justice Rehnquist did suggest that the strength of the liberty interest might be different in other cases that presented different facts. The majority, in other words, was anxious to avoid a definitive ruling on the question of physician-assisted suicide, and instead, issued an opinion that might be considered a train ticket "good for this ride only." It remains to be seen what will happen in the future.

I think it is worth again considering precisely how the Court formulated the issue in *Glucksberg*. So now I want to quote from the majority opinion. The Court weighed a claimed liberty, "of personal choice by a mentally competent, terminally ill person to commit physician-assisted suicide."

Before we pass, it's worth spending just a little bit of time with Justice O'Connor's concurring opinion in *Glucksberg*. Addressing, once again, issues that concern the proper role of the Court and its supervision of the political process, more generally, she writes:

> There is no reason to think that the democratic process will not strike the proper balance between the interests of terminally ill, competent individuals and the state's interest in protecting those who might seek to end life mistakenly or under pressure.

Surely, that is about as blunt a way of putting the issue as one can imagine. She says that there is, indeed, a potential conflict between these two interests; but "there is no reason to think," she writes, "that the state or the political process, more generally, cannot fairly, justly, sensibly resolve the tensions between those two interests." That speaks directly to the limited role of Courts in supervising the democratic process, and opens up a question that has been at least implicit every time we have asked this question, but now I want to put squarely on the table: how can we know—what sorts of evidence will be available to us—if she's correct?

It is all well and good, one might argue, to leave something to the political process, if we can be confident that the political process will strike the correct result. And one might respond to that that there is no correct result; that "correct" doesn't refer to a substantive position about which is the correct, or right, or sensible resolution of the issue; that "correct" refers, not to substance, but to the process we use to reach substantive decisions.

On this line of analysis, it will not do to complain five years in the future that the democratic process reached a result we are uncomfortable with, or that I am uncomfortable with, or that you are uncomfortable with. That is the nature of the democratic process. If there is an objection to Justice O'Connor's opinion, if there is a constitutional objection, it rests somewhere else; and presumably, the place it rests is here. Are we confident? Can we be confident that the political process will work properly to adjust these competing tensions? If we fear the political process, or if we worry that the political process might somehow be corrupted or polluted, then will there be a role for judges to step in and correct or to supervise the process? What would a defect in the political process be? What if the political process routinely silences the voices of some members of the community? That's the kind of issue we'll take up when we address the equal protection clause.

Not to put too fine a point on it, but what if the political process is racist, or biased on the basis of gender or some other characteristic? Do we then trust the political process to resolve the kinds of tensions that are in *Glucksberg* without judicial oversight or supervision? Perhaps. There are undoubtedly Supreme Court justices who would acknowledge that the political process makes mistakes. But, as Justice Rehnquist once wrote, "Having a Supreme Court position does not give you a roving license to correct every social ill you find." On the other hand, why do we have a Supreme Court?

At this point, there's not much else to be said about the right-to-die cases. They are not, in kind, dramatically different than any of the other privacy cases that we have dealt with. This would be the point, in other words, where we should think about not so much the right-to-die cases, but of all the privacy cases we have dealt with.

The right-to-die cases—indeed, most, and probably all of the privacy cases we have examined—nicely illustrate how the underlying issues here are fundamentally about different conceptions, different theories of human personality, and the relationship between individual self-determination and our status as members of larger communities.

I want to say that, implicit in these cases, are questions such as the following: What obligations do we have to ourselves? What obligations do we have to others? What obligations do we have to the state? And, just as important, when, if ever, do those obligations run in the alternative direction?

We have spoken almost entirely about constitutional rights. Are there not constitutional duties as well? Duties, for example, that might be illustrated in the *Missouri* case? Does the state have a constitutional duty to protect life, for example, or to safeguard "the element of personal choice," as Chief Justice Rehnquist suggested in that case? Or should the Court routinely defer to legislatures in addressing these kinds of issues? Recognizing, as did Justice Scalia, in perhaps his best-known dissent—also in the *Cruzan* case—that the information, that the materials necessary to resolve such issues, "are neither set forth in the Constitution, nor known to the nine justices of this Court any better than they are known to nine people, picked at random, from the Kansas City telephone directory."

Lecture Seventeen
Cruel and Unusual? The Death Penalty

Scope:

In the past few lectures, we have explored issues that go to the very heart of what it means to be a human being. In so doing, we have opened up questions that consider the relationship between self and society, between rights and responsibilities, and, indeed, about the meaning and definition of life itself. In this lecture, we take up those issues in their most profound form: the death penalty. In the case of *Furman v. Georgia* (1972), Justice Potter Stewart wrote, "The penalty of death differs from all other forms of criminal punishment." A majority of the Court has never come to the conclusion that the death penalty is by definition cruel and unusual and, hence, a violation of the Eighth Amendment. But if there is one distinguishing aspect of the Court's death penalty jurisprudence, it is the persistence and intensity of disagreement over its constitutionality. Among the issues we address in this lecture are the mechanics of the death penalty—what procedures must a judge or a jury follow in imposing the ultimate sanction?—as well as questions that consider its actual application. Consider, for example: Who gets the death penalty? In the important case of *McCleskey v. Kemp* (1987), the Court rejected a challenge premised on academic studies showing that African-Americans who murdered white victims were substantially more likely to receive the death penalty than whites who murdered blacks. We close with two important cases. In *Atkins v. Virginia* (2002), the Court concluded that states may not execute individuals found to be mentally retarded. And in *Roper v. Simmons* (2005), the Court ruled that the death penalty may not be applied to minors under the age of 18.

Outline

I. In the past few lectures, we have explored issues under the rubric of a constitutional right to privacy or substantive due process that go to the heart of what it means to be a human being and to live in community with others.

   A. In so doing, we have opened up questions about the relationship between self and society.

B. In this lecture, we consider perhaps the most profound version of those questions: the death penalty.

C. Among the issues we must consider are, first, the mechanics of the death penalty and, second, the question of who actually gets the death penalty, why, and how often.

II. Is the death penalty a violation of the Eighth Amendment's prohibition of cruel and unusual punishments? In this lecture, we will see that a majority of the Court has never ruled that it does violate the Eighth Amendment. On the other hand, most of the justices have agreed with an observation by Justice Stewart, who once wrote, "death is different."

A. We take up the death penalty here because these cases, like the privacy cases we have just explored, raise troubling and awe-inspiring questions about the meaning of life, about the relationship between the individual and society, and about the proper limits of judicial power.

B. And like the privacy cases, the only enduring and stable feature of the Court's work in this area has been the persistence and intensity of disagreement, both within the Court and in society more generally.

III. The current jurisprudence begins with the Court's decision in *Furman v. Georgia* in 1972.

A. A sharply divided Court concluded that Georgia's death penalty system did violate the Eighth Amendment but could not agree why. Every member of the Court issued an opinion.

B. Two justices—Brennan and Marshall—concluded that the death penalty is by definition unconstitutional.

C. Three other justices—Douglas, White, and Stewart—concluded that the Georgia scheme was unconstitutional because it gave the sentencing authority (in this case, the jury) too much discretion.

D. Justice Stewart wrote: "The penalty of death differs from all other forms of criminal punishment, not in degree, but in kind. It is unique in its absolute renunciation of all that is embodied in our concept of humanity."

E. In a separate opinion, Chief Justice Burger sounded a theme that should be familiar: "Since there is no majority of the Court, the future of capital punishment in this country is in limbo. If today's opinions demonstrate nothing else, they starkly show that this is an area where legislatures can act far more effectively than Courts."

F. The other four justices dissented.

G. Following *Furman*, well over 30 states adopted new death penalty laws. The inability of the Court to find a majority voice for its majority judgment in *Furman* meant that, as a practical matter, the lower federal and state courts were left without any clear guidance about when the death penalty might pass constitutional muster.

IV. In *Gregg v. Georgia* (1976), the Court again considered the death penalty, and again it could not find a majority voice. Writing for a plurality, Justice Stewart concluded that mandatory death schemes would be unconstitutional. He went on to limit a state's ability to impose death by imposing a number of conditions on the process, including a suggestion that the Court's concerns might be alleviated if states adopted "a bifurcated proceeding."

A. Justice Stewart also noted that opponents of the death penalty must bear "a heavy burden" in attacking the "judgment of the representatives of the people."

B. Nevertheless, the Court did attach a number of conditions to the death penalty. The best known of these is the requirement of *bifurcated proceedings*, which means only that there must be separate hearings to determine guilt and sentencing.

C. In an impassioned dissent, Justice Brennan challenged the majority's deference to the people, noting, "This Court inescapably has the duty, as the ultimate arbiter of the meaning of the Constitution, to say whether 'moral concepts' require us to hold that the death penalty is cruel and unusual."

D. *Gregg*, like *Furman* before it, initiated another round of state experimentation with death penalty procedures.

V. Who gets the death penalty? As far back as *Furman*, some justices had argued that the death penalty is racially biased.

   A. In 2002, there were just over 300 persons on death row in the United States. More than 98% were male, 56% were white, 35% were black, 7% were Hispanic, and 2% were of other racial backgrounds. What, if anything, do these numbers tells us about race and the death penalty?

   B. In *McCleskey v. Kemp* (1987), the Court considered an academic study that had concluded that African-Americans who murdered white victims were substantially more likely to receive the death penalty than whites who murdered blacks.

   1. The Court concluded that "at most ... the evidence presented indicates a discrepancy that appears to correlate with race. Apparent disparities in sentencing are an inevitable part of our criminal justice system."

   2. Moreover, Justice Powell sounded familiar themes about the reach of judicial power, noting that such "arguments are best presented to the legislative bodies."

VI. What is the state of death penalty jurisprudence? *McCleskey* suggests a Court that stresses deference to the democratic process.

   A. On the other hand, in two other cases, the Court appeared more willing to open the substantive issues involved in some kinds of death penalty cases.

   1. In *Atkins v. Virginia* (2002), the Court concluded that states may not execute individuals found to be mentally retarded.

   2. In *Roper v. Simmons* (2005), the Court ruled that the death penalty may not be applied to minors under the age of 18.

   3. In *Herrera v. Collins* (1993), the Court considered a claim of "actual innocence," or a claim by a prisoner, in other words, that he could proffer real evidence of his actual innocence.

4. In rejecting the claim, the Court concluded, "A prisoner's claim of actual innocence standing alone is not sufficient grounds for relief, because federal courts do not sit to correct factual errors. They sit to correct constitutional violations."

B. What are we to make of the death penalty if, as seems likely, we sometimes execute individuals who are, in fact, innocent? Consider two additional quotes:

1. The first is an opinion by Justice Blackmun in *Callins v. Collins* (1994):

> From this day forward, I no longer shall tinker with the machinery of death. Rather than continue to coddle the Court's delusion that the desired level of fairness has been achieved, I feel morally and intellectually obligated simply to concede that the death penalty experiment has failed. The path the Court has chosen lessens us all. I dissent.

2. The second is a response, in the same case, from Justice Scalia: "Blackmun's opinion," he wrote, "often refers to intellectual, moral, and personal perceptions, but never to the text and tradition of the Constitution. It is the latter rather than the former that ought to control."

C. Finally, we should note that in many of the Court's most recent death penalty cases, the justices have begun to argue about when, if ever, our Court should draw on the constitutional jurisprudence of other countries.

1. Justice Breyer, for example, has seemed open to such inquiries.

2. On the other hand, Justices Scalia, Rehnquist, and Thomas have objected to the use of these kinds of interpretive materials.

Essential Reading:

Furman v. Georgia (1972).

Gregg v. Georgia (1976).

McCleskey v. Kemp (1987).

Atkins v. Virginia (2002).

Roper v. Simmons (2005).

Kommers, Finn, and Jacobsohn, *American Constitutional Law*, chapter 4, pp. 123–127.

Stuart Banner, *The Death Penalty: An American History*.

Supplementary Reading:

Hugo Adam Bedau, *The Death Penalty in America: Current Controversies*.

Walter Berns, *For Capital Punishment: Crime and the Morality of the Death Penalty*.

Charles L. Black, *Capital Punishment: The Inevitability of Caprice and Mistake*.

Austin Sarat, *When the State Kills: Capital Punishment and the American Condition*.

Questions to Consider:

1. In *Gregg*, Justice Brennan challenged the majority's deference to the people, noting, "This Court inescapably has the duty, as the ultimate arbiter of the meaning of the Constitution, to say whether 'moral concepts' require us to hold that the death penalty is cruel and unusual." Whose morals should prevail in such an inquiry, and why?

2. Is the Court the "ultimate arbiter" of the Constitution?

Lecture Seventeen—Transcript
Cruel and Unusual? The Death Penalty

In the past few lectures, we have explored issues that go to very heart of what it means to be a human being. In so doing, we have opened up questions that consider the relationship between self and society, between rights and responsibilities, and, indeed, questions that go to the very definition and meaning of life itself. In this lecture, we take up those issues in their most profound form: the death penalty. A majority of the Court has never come to the conclusion that the death penalty is, by definition, cruel and unusual, and. Hence, a violation of the Eighth Amendment. But if there is one distinguishing aspect of the Court's death penalty jurisprudence, it is the persistence and the intensity of disagreement over its constitutionality.

Among the issues we will consider in this lecture are the mechanics of the death penalty; what procedures must a judge or a jury follow in imposing the ultimate sanction? We will also consider questions concerning the actual application of the death penalty. Consider, for example, who gets the death penalty. We will consider the important case of *McCleskey v. Kemp* (decided in 1987), which concerned the possibility of racial discrimination in the death penalty. And we'll also open up—although only briefly—questions about the importance of actual innocence. We will conclude with two very important cases: *Atkins v. Virginia* (decided in 2002) and *Roper v. Simmons* (decided in 2005).

The Court's current death penalty jurisprudence starts where we should start, with the meaning of the Eighth Amendment itself; and I'd like to quote the Eighth Amendment because it is remarkably short and remarkably ambiguous: "The Eighth Amendment provides excessive bail shall not be required, nor excessive fines imposed, nor cruel and unusual punishments imposed."

If we were to take up the Eighth Amendment generally, we would find a welter of important and complicated questions. Consider briefly, for example, what does it mean to call a punishment "cruel"? What does it mean to call a punishment "unusual"? And then, of course, the residual question—or, I should say, the overarching question that we address in every lecture in this course—who gets to decide such questions? Are these questions that are primarily entrusted to the community, or are they questions that should be given over to the Court itself?

The Court's first important modern case was decided in 1972; the case is called *Furman v. Georgia.* In *Furman*, a sharply divided Court concluded that Georgia's death penalty system did violate the Eighth Amendment, but it could not agree upon why it violated the Eighth Amendment. Every single member of the Court issued an opinion. Two justices—Brennan and Marshall—concluded that the death penalty, by definition, is always unconstitutional. Please note that only two justices subscribed to that position. Three other justices—Justices Douglas, White, and Stewart—concluded that the Georgia system was unconstitutional for a single reason: it gave the jury—what we call "the jury authority"—too much discretion about when to impose the penalty and about why it should be imposed. The other four justices dissented, seeing (in the abstract, at least) no particular problem with the death penalty.

There are a number of important things we need to understand about *Furman*, but perhaps the most important is this ringing set of words from Justice Stewart, who wrote one of the concurring opinions. He wrote, "The penalty of death differs from all other forms of criminal punishment, not in degree, but in kind. It is unique in its absolute renunciation of all that is embodied in our concept of humanity."

Please understand that we do not need to concern ourselves directly with whether or not Stewart reached the correct opinion; and truthfully, I do not much care whether or not Justice Stewart reached the correct result or expressed the correct opinion in *Furman*. I quote him only to suggest what I suggested at the beginning of my lecture: that the Court in *Furman* has always recognized that there is something profoundly different about the death penalty from any other form of criminal punishment.

There is another opinion in *Furman* that is also worth considering, this one from Chief Justice Burger. Burger sounded a familiar theme—or at least a theme that should be familiar to us: "Since there is no majority of the Court, the future of capital punishment in this country is in limbo. If today's opinions demonstrate nothing else, they starkly show that this is an area where legislatures can act far more effectively than Courts." *Furman*, in other words, does an excellent job of reintroducing us to two important themes: themes about what it means to be a human being, themes about fundamental human dignity, the relationship of the individual to society; and a second theme, the relationship of the Court to the political process, more generally.

Furman's inability to construct a majority opinion meant, as a practical matter, that *Furman* left the states, as well as lower federal and state courts, without any clear guidance about when, if ever, the death penalty might be constitutionally acceptable. Following *Furman,* over 30 states adopted new death penalty laws, all of which shared certain characteristics, and all of which differed in important ways.

In 1976, in *Gregg v. Georgia,* the Court took up one of these new schemes. Once again, the Court could not find a majority voice. Writing for a plurality, Justice Stewart concluded that any mandatory death penalty scheme would be unconstitutional. Let me just stop there for a second—any criminal scheme that required the death penalty in any particular case, according to a plurality of the Court would be, by definition, unconstitutional.

Justice Stewart went on to conclude that the importance of the death penalty—remember in an earlier case, he had said, "death is different"—the differentness of the death penalty, nevertheless, means that there must be some set of limits on the death penalty. It might not mean that the death penalty is—as lawyers would say—"per se unconstitutional," but its differentness does mean that there are important limitations that must always restrict the state's ability to impose the death penalty.

"These restrictions," Justice Stewart argued, "are a consequence of the uniqueness of the death penalty because, or in the sense, that the death penalty, unlike other criminal punishments, somehow goes to the very heart of our understandings about human dignity."

That said, Justice Stewart did note that opponents of the death penalty must bear "a heavy burden" in attacking the "judgment of the representatives of the people." We can see here how Justice Stewart is struggling with the two dimensions that we identified earlier: the differentness, the solemnness of the death penalty, as well as the Court's relationship to the political process, more generally.

Just a quick word about what some of these conditions are, which impose or attach themselves to the death penalty. Perhaps the most important, certainly the best known, I believe, is the requirement from *Gregg v. Georgia* onward that death penalty cases have what are known as "bifurcated proceedings." By "bifurcated proceedings," the Court means only this one simple fact: there should be two sets of hearings in death penalty cases. The first hearing, unsurprisingly, should be directed simply to the question of guilt or innocence. A second hearing attaches to the process to decide the sentencing aspect of the decision. In other words, there must be one hearing just on guilt, and a second hearing that concerns whether or not the death penalty is the appropriate punishment once guilt has been established. And today, all death penalty cases have these kinds of bifurcated proceedings.

There were a number of important dissents. Perhaps the most impassioned was Justice Brennan's. Brennan's words go directly to one of this course's major themes. "This Court inescapably has the duty, as the ultimate arbiter of the meaning of the Constitution, to say whether 'moral concepts' require us to hold that the death penalty is cruel and unusual."

Imagine the power and the meaning of Justice Brennan's quote. Brennan asserts first that the Court is the ultimate, final interpreter of the Constitution. He suggests, secondly, that in its capacity as final, ultimate interpreter of the Constitution, the Court, at least in this arena of the Bill of Rights, has the authority, perhaps the obligation—the duty—to consider moral precepts.

In some ways, acknowledging that there is a moral dimension or component to the death penalty is not such a stretch. We have seen that the Court did as much in *Furman,* and it did so in earlier cases, as well. But to combine those two claims, there is a moral dimension that ought to influence our Eighth Amendment jurisprudence with the second claim that finally, in the end, the Court is possessed of that final authority, is a powerful statement about the relationship of judges to the political process, more generally; and one, of course, that is profoundly at odds, indeed cannot be reconciled with Justice Stewart's opinion for the plurality.

As happened as with *Furman, Gregg* initiated another round of state experiments with the death penalty. Together, *Furman* and *Gregg v. Georgia* teach us yet another lesson about constitutional theory. Whenever the judges find themselves engaged in a dispute about the proper relationship of judges to the majoritarian political process—whenever we see that dispute—we see also, usually, an ongoing dialogue about what the Constitution means. It is a mistake to think that, in a system such as ours, judges always do have the final word. Perhaps they should. That is a normative, prescriptive question that I leave to you to decide. But whether they should or not—typically what happens in these deeply controversial areas is that the Court is engaged in an ongoing dialogue. The Court announces an opinion; the states respond to that opinion; or other constitutional actors respond to that opinion. That is an ongoing dialogue about constitutional meaning; it's often a contentious dialogue; sometimes it's a civilized dialogue; but it's a dialogue that always occurs, and it's one that should remind us that constitutional meaning isn't settled, or wasn't settled in 1791, when the Bill of Rights was adopted. It's a constitutional dialogue that shows us that constitutional meaning is an ongoing part of the political process.

Now, almost any lecture on the death penalty has to address its actual application; not the mechanics of how it must be applied, but its actual application, in fact. Perhaps the best way to do that is to ask a simple, straightforward question. Here is the question: Who gets the death penalty? There probably is not a more important question to ask. I'm going to address this in two different ways. First, I'm going to talk about the racial dimensions of the death penalty; and then second, I'm going to talk about the question, or perhaps I should call it the problem, of innocence.

Who gets the death penalty? As far back as *Furman*, some justices had argued that the death penalty is racially biased. How do we get at that question? What kind of information do you need in order to begin to make sense of the claim that the death penalty is racially biased? Well, part of it is simply statistical, or at least we might start there.

So, in the year 2002, there were just over 300 persons on death row in the United States. Over 98 percent of those 300 individuals were male; 56 percent of them were white, 35 percent of them were African-American, 7 percent were Hispanic, and 2 percent were of other racial backgrounds. What, if anything, do these numbers tell us about the death penalty? I'm not sure, and scholars argue endlessly about what they mean.

©2006 The Teaching Company Limited Partnership

In a fantastically significant case, *McCleskey v. Kemp* (decided in 1987), the Court considered a rigorous academic study that concluded that African-Americans who murdered white victims were substantially more likely to receive the death penalty than whites who murdered African-American victims. What do you make of that?

The Court concluded, "…at most…the evidence presented indicates a discrepancy that appears to correlate with race." Let's stop here for a second again. There appears to be a discrepancy that correlates with race. The use of the word "correlate" here is precise and narrow. All it suggests is a correlation; it doesn't suggest causation.

The Court continues, "Apparent disparities in sentencing are an inevitable part of our criminal justice system." Now what does that mean? It means, presumably, that a simple correlation is not enough to establish a constitutional violation. As we'll see when we deal with equal protection issues later in the course, mere statistical evidence of discrimination is not, under the Eighth Amendment or under the equal protection clause, sufficient in the Court's view to establish a constitutional violation; in other words, sufficient to establish systemic or intentional racial discrimination.

And the Court suggested, in the latter part of the quote that I read to you that, because the death penalty is fundamentally a human institution, it will always be imperfect. There are, as the Court said, "inevitable discrepancies." The use of the word "inevitable" suggests, I believe, that we can't demand perfection. There will always be a risk. We should try to minimize it, to be sure, but we can never entirely overcome it, and some inherent error is an inherent part of the process. That inherent error, that inherent discrepancy, does not itself cause a constitutional violation.

Continuing, Justice Powell wrote, you'll recognize the theme again, that these are the kinds of arguments, these statistic arguments, these are the kind of "arguments that are best presented to legislative bodies." And here, again, we get the Court suggesting that there are some kinds of constitutional issues—I don't say "violations"; that prejudges the question—that should be left to the political process, more generally. Since *McCleskey,* the Court has refused to reopen questions that involve, perhaps, statistical displays of racial discrimination. And indeed, the Court has not directly addressed another claim of racial discrimination in the death penalty.

Before I continue, I want to make sure we understand precisely where we are, jurisprudentially. Since *Gregg v. Georgia*, the Court has refused to reopen the question, at bottom, of whether the death penalty is, by definition, unconstitutional. Perhaps some future Court will do that, but no Court has done it since 1976; and since 1987, the Supreme Court has refused to address in any detail the question about whether or not the death penalty is inherently discriminatory on the basis of race. On the other hand, in a series of cases, the Court has begun to address other kinds of death penalty claims. I just want to run through these very quickly.

In the year 2002, the Court decided a case called *Atkins v. Virginia*. In it, the Court concluded, overruling an earlier case, that states may not execute individuals who are found to be mentally retarded. And in *Roper v. Simmons,* decided in 2005, the Court ruled that the death penalty may not be applied to minors under the age of 18. That, I believe, is a reasonably comprehensive view of the Court's death penalty jurisprudence; but you'll recall earlier that I asked, "Who gets the death penalty?" And I promised that we would speak about race, which we have. And I promised that we would speak about another question, the so-called question of actual innocence. And I have left this to the last, because it is an important issue, but an easy one to resolve, at least as a matter of doctrine.

The Court addressed a claim of actual innocence in a case known as *Herrera v. Collins,* decided in 1993. In *Herrera v. Collins*, a prisoner had sought relief through a writ of habeas corpus. A writ of habeas corpus is simply a legal device used to claim that a prisoner, usually, is being held unlawfully, illegally, or unconstitutionally. It's a device—a legal device, a writ, a piece of paper—that a judge, if he or she is persuaded of the prisoner's case, will direct to the incarcerating authority; and that piece of paper, that letter, that judicial missive, will typically tell the incarcerating authority, "So-and-so is being held in your prison. So-and-so has claimed that the circumstances of his/her detention are illegal. Please, you or your representative, show up at a certain place and a certain time [in other words, "in my courtroom"] and demonstrate to me why the conditions of that incarceration, or why continued incarceration, are not constitutionally improper."

I should add, parenthetically, that the writ of habeas corpus is perhaps the oldest of all civil liberties. Indeed, it was of such significance to the Founders that it was one of the few civil liberties (property was the other one) that found actual protection in the Constitution reported out of Philadelphia before there was a Bill of Rights. Some individuals think that we can trace the writ of habeas corpus as far back as the Magna Carta. In any event, it is a cornerstone of Western common law legal systems. It is a cornerstone of the American constitutional system.

Now, in *Herrera v. Collins*, this prisoner wanted a writ of habeas corpus based on a simple claim. The claim was that he was genuinely, actually, innocent, and he might be able to proffer physical, real evidence of his innocence. His claim did not result in the granting of a writ of habeas corpus. The case worked its way through appeals up to the United States' Supreme Court, and a majority of the Court wrote, "A prisoner's claim of actual innocence standing alone is not sufficient grounds for relief, because federal courts do not sit to correct factual errors. They sit to correct constitutional violations."

In other words, according to a majority of the Court, a claim of actual innocence, at least in a death penalty case, is a factual claim, and not a claim about an inherent constitutional violation. Imagine what that means for a minute. If we execute an innocent prisoner, that is a factual error, not a constitutional error. The constitutional error concerns only the process, presumably, by which we sentence individuals to death, not whether or not we get it wrong. Where does that leave us with death penalty jurisprudence, more generally?

Few areas are as controversial in American law as the death penalty. Some of that controversy, we should be reminded, isn't simply about judicial opinions. So you may recall that Governor George Ryan of Illinois commuted a great many death penalty sentences in the state of Illinois, because, as he said in a speech, "I am persuaded that there are significant numbers of errors."

It isn't simply Courts that concern themselves with the imposition of the death penalty. Governors are always involved in the death penalty process, because they have, ultimately, the power of pardon, just as the president of the United States has the power. And, as a consequence, in most states, the governor's office has elaborate procedures and institutions set up to routinely review death penalty claims. What happens in these cases is an exchange of authority, or I should say, rather, a dance between two constitutional actors, Courts, and chief executives; and together, one hopes, these two partners reach the correct result in at least most of the cases. And we must wonder what to make of the undoubted fact that sometimes they do not reach the correct result.

As citizens of the Constitution, what are we to make of error in these cases. Who knows how many? Maybe it is a tiny percentage; maybe it is larger than that. What are we to make of that? I have asked you again and again to recall that constitutional doctrines, as obscure as they may seem, as complex as they may seem, ultimately are about human beings and individuals, and the death penalty cases, perhaps even more than our examination of *DeShaney,* ought to make that clear.

I have two other quotes that I would like to read to you, these from a case known as *Callins v. Collins,* decided in 1994. This is not actually a case. This case involved the Supreme Court deciding not to hear an appeal. Eight justices agreed that the case should not be heard. One justice, Justice Blackmun, thought that the Court should take up the case in *Callins v. Collins,* and he wrote dissenting from this decision:

> From this day forward, I no longer shall tinker with the machinery of death. Rather than continue to coddle the Court's delusion that the desired level of fairness has been achieved, I feel morally and intellectually obligated simply to concede that the death penalty experiment has failed. The path the Court has chosen lessens us all. I dissent.

Those are powerful words, and there are few, if any of us, I think, who are not moved by them in some important way. But, perhaps being moved by them is not the constitutionally appropriate response.

Blackmun's emotional confession prompted the following response from Justice Scalia: "Blackmun's opinion," he wrote, "often refers to intellectual, moral, and personal perceptions, but never to the text and tradition of the Constitution. It is the latter rather than the former that ought to control."

I said in an earlier lecture that to open up questions about the Bill of Rights is, in fact, to open up doctrinal questions; is, in fact, to open up cases. But I think I suggested, as well, that it is also to open up fundamental questions about the meaning of life, and about justice, equality, and human dignity.

I ask you now to put yourself in the position of Justice Blackmun or Justice Scalia; but start with Blackmun. You are a justice of the United States' Supreme Court, and you believe, perhaps for reasons you cannot fully articulate, that the death penalty is fundamentally unconstitutional. But you can't identify, constitutionally speaking—in the way that Justice Scalia would demand that you would identify, constitutionally speaking—precisely what the flaw is in these cases.

Perhaps the best you can do is to say, "I dissent because it is unjust." As a justice, as a citizen, as someone who has sworn allegiance to the Constitution, is the Constitution your highest obligation? Or do you have some other super-ordinate obligation; perhaps to justice, broadly defined? Perhaps to some other goal—human dignity, broadly defined? Does that higher obligation trump your obligation as a justice, sworn to uphold the Constitution, but to do no more? Does it trump your obligation as a citizen of the Constitution?

I have one final set of remarks that I would like to make about the death penalty. The death penalty cases in recent years have invoked a new dispute among the justices about when, if ever, it is appropriate to acknowledge the constitutional experience of other democracies; and the justices have fought viciously over this issue. With some justices—Breyer, Ginsburg—insisting that the constitutional experience of other democracies is directly relevant to our own; and others—such as Thomas, Rehnquist, and Scalia—insisting that we are Americans first, and the constitutional experiences of other democracies should not control our own. One final note: in 2001, 90 percent of all of the world's executions occurred in China, Iran, Saudi Arabia, and the United States of America.

Lecture Eighteen
The First Amendment—An Overview

Scope:

"Congress shall make no law … abridging the freedom of speech, or of the press." From these sparse words, the Supreme Court has created a huge and complicated jurisprudence. In this lecture, we consider what the Founders may have meant when they sought to protect speech and the equally important question of *why* they sought to protect speech. As we shall see, the answers to these questions are complex. And even if the historical record could show us precisely what the Founders meant by free speech and press, it is not so clear in the 21st century that attempts to restrict the interpretation of these terms to the meaning of the 18th century is possible or desirable.

Outline

I. "Congress shall make no law … abridging the freedom of speech, or of the press." From these sparse words, the Supreme Court has created a huge and complicated jurisprudence. In this lecture, we consider what the Founders may have meant when they sought to protect speech and the equally important question of *why* they sought to protect speech.

    A. Few areas in civil liberties cover as much ground, or are as complicated, as is the Court's First Amendment jurisprudence. Indeed, one aspect or another of the First Amendment will be the focus of our attention for the next 11 lectures, and even then, we can only hope to scratch the surface.

    B. What if the historical record could show us what the Founders meant by freedom of speech? Is it so clear in the 21st century that we should restrict the meaning of the First Amendment to an 18th-century understanding?

    C. As we have seen in nearly every lecture, the Constitution's meaning has changed over time, and with each change, the amendment—or, rather, its jurisprudence—seems to have become ever more complicated.

1. There are many reasons for this complexity, including the centrality of freedom of speech and religion to constitutional democracy, as well as the Constitution's relative silence on matters pertaining to speech.

2. As we have seen in earlier lectures, too, cases and conflicts concerning freedom of speech raise important and intractable issues about the nature of constitutional interpretation and the limits of judicial authority.

II. Why did the Founders single out speech and religion for special protection? There is no single answer to this question.

A. Some of the justifications advanced, both by the Founders and by courts charged with making sense of the First Amendment, include:

1. The close relationship between the free exchange of ideas and democratic self-governance.

2. The importance of free speech and thought to the self-realization and intellectual growth of free persons and citizens.

3. The importance of such freedoms to the pursuit and, perhaps, to the attainment of "truth."

B. The argument from self-government is premised on the claim that representative democracy would not be possible without the consent and participation of citizens.

C. The argument from self-realization regards freedom of speech as critical to the self-realization and intellectual growth of free persons, and perhaps, also, to notions of citizenship itself.

D. The argument from truth, derived in part from J. S. Mill's *On Liberty* (1859), rests on the assumption that truth is most likely to emerge in a free and open marketplace of ideas.

E. There are other, less grand justifications for expressive freedom, including the so-called *checking theory* and the *safety valve theory*.

III. We should take up each of the foregoing justifications for freedom of speech in more detail.

A. The first argument is premised on the demands of self-government.

   1. The claim, which might seem obvious, is that representative democracy would not be possible without the free exchange of ideas. This free exchange is partly about the ability of citizens to debate the merits of various public policies and matters of public import.

   2. But it is also critical to the free exchange of information between citizens and their representatives.

   3. It is important to note that this defense of speech—like all of the others we shall consider—does not extend, necessarily, to all forms of speech and expression. We might say, on this defense, that it is only "political" speech (however we define it) that must be protected.

   4. Consider a brief example—the case of *Moore v. City of East Cleveland* (1977) that we took up in the privacy lectures. It was clear that the case raised family/privacy issues, but it also raised issues that might fall under the rubric of freedom of association.

   5. One justice, Justice Stewart, argued precisely this and went on to note that freedom of association should extend only to associations that are political in nature.

   6. Of course, the obvious response to this line of argument is to open the question of definition. Is it clear that the family is not political?

B. The second argument for freedom of expression rests on its centrality to human personality and self-development.

   1. The idea here is that the development and flourishing of the human personality must mean that we are free to hold a wide array of ideas and beliefs, that we must be able to try them on, even if they are noxious to others.

   2. If there are ideas we may not hold or express, then there may be some avenues for self-development that are closed.

C. A third argument for freedom of expression is the argument from truth.

1. Many forms of this defense trace their origin to John Stuart Mill's *On Liberty* (1859). It rests on the assumption that truth is most likely to emerge from a free marketplace of ideas. The antidote for bad speech, it is thus said, is more speech.

2. There are, of course, a number of interesting questions that follow from this approach, such as: What do we do if we find truth?

D. There are a number of other defenses of freedom of expression that we shall see in the following lectures.

1. One is sometimes called the *checking theory*, or the idea that speech is a check against governmental power or bad speech.

2. A second is the so-called *safety valve theory*, which rests on the claim that freedom of speech acts as a safety valve for what might otherwise be violent action against the state or other persons.

IV. Of all these different justifications for freedom of expression, which did the Founders embrace?

A. The answer is that they embraced all of them, in various degrees and in various combinations.

B. It is important to remember, when we take up specific issues and cases, that, for the most part, we have very little evidence of what the Founders intended.

V. It is worth noting, too, that the First Amendment prohibits only laws curtailing freedom of speech, not speech itself.

A. The interpretive problems with the First Amendment, therefore, begin with an effort to determine the meaning of *freedom*.

B. For the sake of what values or interests would government be justified in limiting speech? The Constitution fails to answer these questions, at least directly; thus, we and the Court are left to the tricky business of interpretation.

C. Consider, for example, the familiar problem of shouting "Fire!" in a crowded theater.

D. Imagine another situation, such as threatening to kill the president.

E. And here is another problem: Should we tolerate speech that offends others, as opposed, in the earlier two examples, to putting them directly in harm's way?

F. A similar question is raised by prohibitions on hate speech or racially bigoted speech.

G. Consider, too, speech that makes derogatory remarks about public officials.

H. In each of the foregoing, we must balance our commitment to freedom of speech against our commitment to other principles, such as public safety, or equality, or the public welfare.

VI. The next 11 lectures will begin with 5 lectures concerning freedom of expression and be followed by 6 lectures concerning freedom of religion. .

Essential Reading:

Zechariah Chafee, Jr., *Free Speech in the United States*.

Harry Kalven, Jr., *A Worthy Tradition: Freedom of Speech in America*.

Cass Sunstein, *Democracy and the Problem of Free Speech*.

Supplementary Reading:

Walter Berns, *The First Amendment and the Future of American Democracy*.

Lee C. Bollinger, *The Tolerant Society*.

Thomas Emerson, *The System of Freedom of Expression*.

Leonard Levy, *The Emergence of a Free Press*.

John Stuart Mill, *On Liberty*.

David Rabban, *Free Speech in Its Forgotten Years*.

Questions to Consider:

1. Is freedom of speech really necessary for self-governance? If it is, does this tell us anything about what kinds of speech the First Amendment protects or what kinds of expression might not warrant protection?

2. Assume we can know precisely what the Founders meant by such terms as *speech* and *religion*. Should the meaning of the First Amendment be restricted to those 18th-century meanings? Is there a way to give these terms contemporary content while remaining faithful to the Founders' intent?

Lecture Eighteen—Transcript
The First Amendment—An Overview

"Congress shall make no law…abridging the freedom of the speech, or of the press." From these sparse words, the Court has created a huge and complicated jurisprudence. In this lecture—indeed, in the 11 lectures that follow—we consider what the Founders may have meant when they sought to protect speech and religion, and the equally important question of why they sought to protect them. As we shall see, the answers to these questions are complex. But consider for a moment: what if the historical record could show us precisely what the Founders meant by free speech and press? Is it so clear in the 21st century that attempts to restrict the interpretation of these terms to the meaning of the 18th century is possible? And if it is possible, is it desirable?

Consider, as we have seen in nearly every lecture, that the Constitution's meaning has changed dramatically over time. Should freedom of speech mean the same thing in our generation that it meant in the Founders' generation? That is not a trivial question. The Founders' generation had newspapers, but the Founders did not have the Internet; they did not have broadcast media. Our world is dramatically different than their world, and the speech provisions that they bequeathed us may have a radically different meaning for our time than they had for the Founders' time.

There are, of course, a number of reasons why we might seek, in the abstract, to protect freedom of speech. Most of these justifications—and we will run through a number of them—were available to the Founders for their generation just as they are available to ours. Let me quickly list a number of different justifications for the protection of speech, and then I would like to address each of them in a bit more detail.

Some of the justifications advanced by the Founders and by courts charged with making sense of the First Amendment include the following. First, the close relationship between the free exchange of ideas and democratic self-governance. That close relationship might require that we protect some degree of speech. A second reason why we might choose to protect speech: freedom of speech and thought are critical to the self-realization and intellectual growth of free persons, and perhaps, also, to notions of citizenship itself. Third, the importance of freedom of speech, of freedom of thought, of freedom to write and to communicate are probably critical to the attainment of truth, however we define truth. These three primary justifications for speech will appear in nearly every case we will read. At different times, one explanation, one justification for speech, will appear more prominent than another. At other times, they will interact with each other.

Let's go through each of them in a bit more detail. The first argument for protecting speech is the self-government argument. The argument from self-governance is premised upon the claim that representative democracy itself would not be possible without some notion of freedom of speech.

What does this argument mean? Is representative democracy possible without the free exchange of ideas? How could citizens deliberate between competing public policies if they did not have the authority, perhaps the obligation, to discuss the merits, the advantages and the disadvantages, of competing public policies? And, more fundamentally, how could representative democracy possibly function if there was not a protected degree of freedom of communication between the governed and their representatives, as well as the other direction?

Imagine, in other words, how one could possibly conduct electoral campaigns without some degree of freedom of speech. The argument from self-governance should remind us that we don't live in a majoritarian democracy; we don't live in a direct democracy; we don't live in a representative democracy. We live in a constitutional democracy. And I emphasize that it is a constitutional democracy, because the constitutional component of this polity points to the second reason why we might choose to protect some kinds of speech.

Before we get there, however, let's understand that each defense, each justification for speech, provides for the justification for the protection of a certain kind of speech, as well. Let me illustrate what I mean. If our justification for freedom of speech is that it is necessary for self-governance, then we ought to be able to ask ourselves the following kinds of questions: What kinds of speech promote representative democracy? Or, I should say, what kinds of speech enable democracy? Certainly, any speech that we might plausibly define as political in nature would have to be protected in such a system. But let's ask ourselves, is it possible—I mean is it intellectually possible—to carve out areas of human speech and to say, this area addresses questions of politics; this area does not? Some justices believe that that is possible. Some justices, in other words, think that the justification for speech, or a justification for speech that is grounded in democratic self-governance, protects so-called political forms of speech, but not necessarily nonpolitical forms of speech.

Perhaps it would be easier to understand this with an example. You will recall, from an earlier lecture (in those parts of the course where we dealt with privacy), a case called *Moore v. City of East Cleveland. Moore,* you will recall, we addressed when we looked at family rights, and whether family rights would be under the protection of the Fourteenth Amendment. *Moore* involved the case of a grandmother who wanted to live in a single dwelling with her two grandchildren who were first cousins to each other.

Obviously, that raises privacy issues, family right issues. Perhaps less obviously, it raises issues of freedom of association: with whom may we associate; under what conditions may the state limit the terms of that association. And at least one justice was prepared to decide the case on those grounds. That justice, Justice Stewart, wrote that there was, in fact, a freedom of association claim involved in the *Moore* case. But his understanding of the First Amendment was that it protected only political forms of association. This was a "familial" form of association, and as a consequence, that relationship, or that liberty interest—however one might describe it, as privacy or as expression of association—would not rise to the level of protection because, fundamentally, the choice made in that case was not about politics, it was about something else.

In other words, an argument for freedom of speech that is grounded in democratic self-governance might be limited to a set of protections for speech that is political in nature. And then the obvious question will be, under what conditions is speech genuinely political, and under what conditions might it be described as something else?

I want to continue just a little bit more with *Moore v. City of East Cleveland.* One potential response to this claim, that there was no form of political association involved in that case, would be to ask, what could possibly be more political than decisions about the nature of the family itself? Indeed, one might respond, just within the terms of *Moore,* that the city had chosen to politicize the definition of family by saying that only certain kinds of family could share a single dwelling. I hope you can see the potential problem here; there may not be a clear, bright line between political forms of speech or political forms of association and nonpolitical forms of association.

One final example—or really, I should say, one final rhetorical question—Is art political? I leave that to you to answer. That is the argument from democratic self-governance.

Consider a second argument—the argument, as I shall call it, from self-fulfillment. There is a long, Western political tradition that takes seriously the notion that government ought not to impede, at least, and perhaps ought to promote the development of human personality; that the point of "the good society" is to enable us all to live lives as flourishing, rational, cognizant human beings. In other words, in some Western philosophical traditions, the point of freedom of speech is not so much to enable self-governance as it is to enable the self to prosper, to flourish, to grow as a human being. Is speech, is freedom of speech, is freedom of association a necessary component of that growth, of that flourishing? It's hard to imagine how it could not be.

Part of the reason we value education—part of the reason I value a liberal arts education—is precisely because we believe that the pursuit of knowledge improves us, elevates us as human beings. How can we pursue knowledge without some notion of freedom of speech? But it is worth asking again if that is our justification for speech—self-promotion, not in the negative, petty sense, but in the most glorious of senses—if self-promotion is the point of speech, or the justification for speech, what kinds of speech must be protected, and what kinds of speech, if any, would fall outside the boundary?

We'll address this question in more detail when I pose a couple of hypotheticals about what kinds of speech should be protected in the constitutional democracy. But consider, just for now, and in brief, the following kind of problem.

As we prosper, as we grow as human beings, presumably there comes a point in our lives when we rethink who we were at an earlier time, when we reopen questions that were either settled at an earlier point in our lives, or which we did not realize were important questions. That growth of personality, presumably, enables us—

maybe it requires us, if we are truly sentient human beings—to rethink conceptions and beliefs that we held at an earlier point in our lives.

Let me rephrase the question a different way. Does the argument, does the justification for speech from self-fulfillment require in us all a certain degree of tolerance for speech we cannot stand or for speech we reject as harmful, untrue, or undignified? If individual self-fulfillment is, in fact, a critical part of the freedom to speak our minds, the freedom to believe what we will; then, presumably, we must embrace a notion of tolerance that allows others to adopt conceptions of themselves and ideas about their place in the world that we would find terribly offensive. If self-fulfillment is about testing ideas for oneself, then, presumably, we have to acknowledge that some individuals will embrace ideas, will embrace concepts that we ourselves would reject.

Is there anything in a constitutional democracy that individuals ought not to be allowed to speak about? And does shutting down speech mean, in effect, that some avenues to self-fulfillment, that some avenues to self-improvement, may be closed by the state? There is one way to make such an argument. The way to make such an argument is to pose the following problem: why should we, as a society, embrace the end of self-fulfillment?

Let's assume that the end state we want to achieve, the purpose we mean to achieve, isn't self-fulfillment, but rather is grounded in some notion of human dignity, more generally. Presumably, self-fulfillment is an instrumental value, not a value on its own. We value self-improvement or self-fulfillment, presumably because it takes us, or may take us, to some other place—a conception of human dignity. And if it is that ultimate value that we seek to promote through freedom of speech—the dignity of all human creatures—then maybe the state ought to shut down or regulate speech that is at odds with or fundamentally in tension with the reason why we have freedom of speech in the first instance: the protection of human dignity.

This is closely related to the third argument, the third justification for freedom of speech— the argument from truth. Many of you will recognize that this argument derives from John Stuart Mill's *On Liberty*. It rests on an assumption that truth is most likely to emerge in a free and open marketplace of ideas. This is a fascinating defense for speech. You have probably heard it expressed in one form or another. Here is a popular method of its expression: the antidote to bad ideas, the antidote to harmful speech, is "more speech on the theory that truth will out."

There is a series of questions here, and I don't mean them simply rhetorically; I mean these are serious questions that we need to develop answers to. Why should we care about truth? If we are simply concerned with the polity, with making government work on a day-to-day basis, who cares what truth is? Maybe we should be more concerned with efficiency. And if we take truth seriously, then what are we to make of individuals who, in their quest for self-fulfillment, embrace things that we know not to be true?

Alternatively, what are we to do if we find truth? Imagine society settles upon a truth; is it at that point that we shut down speech that promotes falsehood? If we reach truth, then why isn't that sufficient to say, "The marketplace is closed. We are where we wanted to be"? And if the answer to that is, "We don't know truth when we see it;" or "We can't be sure of truth if we see it;" or "We can't even be sure if there is truth, period;" perhaps on the assumption that, as liberals with a small "l," we are all committed to the good society, but also committed to a society in which nobody can identify precisely, and for anyone else, what the "good life" is; then why pursue truth at all?

In some ways, truth might be antithetical to freedom of speech. There are a number of other justifications advanced for the freedom of speech as well; perhaps not so grand in expanse, but important nonetheless. I won't spend a great deal of time with them, but it is at least worth going through two of them quickly. The first is the so-called checking theory; and much like the argument from the marketplace, the idea here is that speech checks other speech, or perhaps that good speech will check bad speech. A second theory is the so-called safety valve theory. The argument here is that every society has dissent. There are positive, perhaps nonviolent ways to express dissent—say, through speech—because that is a safety valve. A safety valve for what? In the absence of the safety valve, perhaps the speech explodes into violence. If dissent will always out, perhaps we should give it an out that is grounded in nonviolent speech, rather than in violent, political action.

Now, stepping back for a second, which of these theories of speech did the Founders embrace? All of them; or if you prefer, not a single one of them, but all of them in combination, in various combinations. We don't have reliable evidence about what the Founders intended for most of our speech questions. In your recommended and required reading, or essential reading, I have tried to give you a number of sources that address specifically the questions about what the Founders meant by speech. As you read through those materials, you will see that there are as many opinions about what the Founders sought to achieve, or meant by speech, as there are books and articles written about the subject.

Now permit me, please, to change direction for just a second. If we go back and take the words of the First Amendment seriously, and we shall see that some justices have insisted that we take them literally, we will note that the First Amendment doesn't protect speech. It protects freedom of speech. Is there a meaningful difference between these two positions? I think perhaps the best way to get a handle on that question is to consider a number of hypothetical issues, or hypothetical questions. I call them "hypothetical," only because I will not attach them to a specific case; but as we will see in subsequent lectures, there are specific cases that raise each and every one of these questions.

For example, consider this first issue: does freedom of speech, or should freedom of speech, include comments, words—spoken or written—that put other individuals in harm's way? The most famous version of this problem is one that most of you will have encountered in one form or another—Justice Holmes's famous aphorism that, "You have freedom of speech, to be sure, but you may not shout 'Fire!' in a crowded theater."

This is an easy case. The aphorism has a certain kind of appeal to it at the level of rhetoric, but as a constitutional problem, it poses no difficulty at all. The reason you can't shout "Fire!" in a crowded theater (unless, of course, there is a fire in a crowded theater) is because we fear that people will be harmed as they try to escape the theater. Perhaps they will be trampled underfoot. Perhaps they will be pushed and harmed in some way. The reason you can't shout "Fire!" in a crowded theater is not necessarily because it's false, but because there is the direct and immediate potential for harm to other human beings. I say this was an easy case—not so easy, really.

Imagine another situation in which harm might result from speech. What if I threaten to kill the president? That is speech that not only threaten harm to another, but might directly cause harm to another human being. As we shall see when we take up the cases, part of what's involved here in our assessment of the case, or part of what will be involved when the Court assesses the case, is how immediate and direct the threat is. If it appears to a reasonable observer that I am genuinely inciting someone else to harm the president, or genuinely threatening—directly, immediately, imminently—the president myself, then clearly my speech rights do not cover that situation.

On the other hand, if I speak about harming the president as an abstraction, and no reasonable observer could imagine that the president is genuinely in fear for his life, or that I am not immediately counseling somebody else to harm the president, that is likely to be resolved, assessed, in a dramatically different way. When we talk about speech that puts others in harm's way, we are engaged in a series of judgment calls; and that's the easy set of cases.

Does freedom of speech, or should freedom of speech, invalidate speech that offends others, as opposed to putting them in harm's way? Imagine I say something truly offensive—offensive not only to you personally, but offensive to a larger group of individuals. Now, it might seem immediately obvious to you that harm in this case, if there is harm, is dramatically different than the physical kind of harm that we dealt with in the Holmes example. But why should that difference between physical harm and emotional harm—for lack of another phrase—why should that difference be constitutionally relevant?

And I'm not sure we can answer that question without going back to first principles and asking ourselves, why do we protect speech in the first instance? And you'll recall that I said if we protect speech because it is a key component of an individual's growth over time; if it is a key component to self-fulfillment, to self-realization; then maybe what we need to say is, "We have to allow that speaker to speak." Or maybe we take refuge in the larger principle that I alluded to, that of human dignity, and maybe we say, "There is no constitutionally relevant distinction between threats or harms that are physical in nature and the harms that are spiritual or emotional in nature; both offend our core sense of human dignity."

Consider, alternatively, derogatory remarks about the particular racial or religious minorities. Are those different in kind? Are they even different in character from speech that offends more generally? One might argue that there are good constitutional reasons why speech directed at historically disfavored minorities are, in fact, different in kind; maybe if only because the Constitution itself, through the equal protection clause, suggests a distinct classification here.

Or alternatively, maybe what we want to say is that those kinds of classifications are fundamentally incompatible with notions of equality more generally; and that, in that case, it must be a violation of the First Amendment, too, to carve out speech as protected or not protected, depending upon whom, or depending upon which group the speech is directed to.

And then one final problem: What about speech that makes derogatory remarks about public officials? One might argue that public officials ought to have thick hides; that that is the point of speech—to promote representative democracy; and only robust speech will produce a robust republic; and if you choose to run for office, then you choose to suffer any insult to your character.

Or maybe you want to make a slightly smaller claim. Maybe your justification for speech is, "We are a representative democracy, and so we might say, any kind of speech, no matter how derogatory, directed against the public official must be constitutionally protected, so long as it is directed to that public official's public life." But claims directed to, or speech directed to, a representative's, or a governor's, or a senator's, or a president's private life must be out of bounds; because here we need to reconcile our commitment to a theory of speech premised on human dignity and a theory of speech committed on its necessity to representative democracy. These are the kinds of issues we shall have to encounter.

Now again, just to shift direction just for a minute, issues concerning the First Amendment take up nearly one-third of this course; and I want to give you just a brief overview of the kinds of issues we'll be taking up in the next eleven lectures. Five of those lectures following this one will concern themselves directly with freedom of speech; and the latter six will concern themselves with a latter First Amendment problem concerning freedom of religion.

In our next lecture, we will take up perhaps the most profound of speech problems, the problems of subversive speech, or speech that somehow implicates the nation's internal security. This issue was alive for the Founders. It expressed itself in the Alien and Sedition Acts of 1798, and it is just alive for our time. Consider, for example, the war on terrorism, which clearly yields issues that concern themselves with speech.

Following that, we'll take up issues of symbolic speech and expressive conduct. Clearly, if I say, "Hello" to you, that means "Hello." If I wave without saying anything, clearly I have communicated. And as I mentioned in an earlier lecture, what if I sleep as a form of political protest, but say nothing at all? Those are the kinds of issues we take up.

After that, we'll take up the intractable problems of indecency and obscenity. I think I'll leave indecency and obscenity right there and then proceed to the next issue. What about hate speech and fighting words?

And then, finally, we'll consider something that may not seem as obvious as these obvious problems: under what conditions, if any, does the Constitution, through the First Amendment, protect our right not to speak, not to believe, not to associate, not to assemble? Those are the kinds of topics that we will address in the next five lectures.

There are also some themes that we will consider in the next five lectures. In particular, I want to consider again what different theories of constitutional interpretation the justices have used to try to resolve these questions; and, by way of foreshadowing, I think I can describe three very briefly. We will see, perhaps more than in any other area of the course, justices making appeals to Founders' intent or to originalism. We will also see appeals to the purpose of the clause, and we will also see or encounter a new method of interpretation known as "definitional balancing." Definitional balancing refers simply to those instances where the Court tries to balance one set of societal interests against another set of societal interests. Those are the kinds of issues that we will take up in the following lectures.

Finally, we will want to consider the importance of the First Amendment itself. Some justices, for example, have called the First

Amendment the most preferred of amendments; thereby suggesting that, when the First Amendment collides with other liberties, it is the values of speech and religion that we must protect.

Lecture Nineteen
Internal Security and the First Amendment

Scope:

As we saw in the last lecture, the reasons we protect speech are complex. Are there times when we might not want to protect it? When is the nation entitled to protect itself against speech that advocates illegal action or, arguably, endangers the security of the United States? As we shall see in this lecture, the United States has wrestled with this question from its inception, beginning with the Alien and Sedition Act of 1798, through the Espionage Act of 1917, and most recently, in the USA Patriot Act. We begin with the well-known case of *Schenck v. United States* (1919), in which the Court penned the famous "clear and present danger" test. Over the years, the test has undergone various formulations, from the "bad tendency" test in *Gitlow v. New York* (1925) to the "incitement" test elaborated in *Brandenburg v. Ohio* (1969), but in all of them, the underlying issues have been the same: How deep does our commitment to freedom of speech run, and who should balance the competing demands of the First Amendment and national security?

Outline

I. As we saw in the last lecture, the reasons we protect speech are complex. Are there times when we might not want to protect it? When is the nation entitled to protect itself against speech that advocates illegal action or, arguably, endangers the security of the United States? Are there times when, the First Amendment notwithstanding, we should not protect any and all forms of speech? This question has plagued the nation since the Founding.

   A. Some scholars, for example, have argued that the Founders intended to prohibit the prior censorship of the press but perhaps not seditious libel or a written communication critical of the government or the state.

   B. The Alien and Sedition Acts of 1798 illustrate the longstanding tendency of the state to seek to stifle criticism, as well as the intense controversy and backlash that such efforts typically generate.

II. The Court's consideration of such issues starts with the important decision in *Schenck v. United States* (1919).

    A. In *Schenck*, the Court upheld the Espionage Act of 1917, which made it illegal for individuals, in this case, to distribute pamphlets that encouraged resistance to military proscription.

    B. Sometimes the Court insists that there are different kinds of speech, and some kinds are of greater constitutional weight.

        1. The Court has often suggested, for example, that political speech goes to very core of the First Amendment and, thus, warrants great protection.

        2. If that is true, then consider the kind of speech at issue in this case: Schenck is protesting perhaps the most political of actions—war—and making an argument based upon the Constitution itself.

    C. *Schenck* is critical to the development of First Amendment doctrine because it introduced the well-known "clear and present danger" test. Holmes wrote:

> The character of every act depends upon the circumstances in which it is done. The question in every case is whether the words are used in such circumstances and are of such a nature as to create a clear and present danger that they will bring about the substantive evils that Congress has a right to prevent. It is a question of proximity and degree.

    D. It is worth noting that the clear and present danger test is not necessarily a standard that protects speech; instead, the test is largely contentless.

        1. In *Schenck*, for example, the defendants were convicted simply for distributing pamphlets—it is difficult to imagine that there was much of a substantial threat to proscription in particular or to the war effort in general.

        2. The critical question, then, is less the test than who gets to apply it.

III. In later cases, the Court continued to reformulate the clear and present danger test, sometimes in ways that were more protective of speech and, at other times, more sympathetic to governmental regulation.

A. In *Gitlow v. New York* (1925), the Court relaxed the test, transforming it into the so-called "bad tendency" test. The Court sustained the application of a New York criminal anarchy law to political strikes.

> **1.** In so doing, the Court simply accepted the judgment of the New York legislature that certain words, in and of themselves, tended to present a danger. The Court wrote: "A single revolutionary spark may kindle a fire that, smoldering for a time, may burst into a sweeping and destructive conflagration."

> **2.** In an important dissent, Justices Holmes and Brandeis argued that the clear and present danger test required an actual and immediate threat.

B. In *Whitney v. California* (1927), Justice Brandeis, writing for the Court, argued in contrast to *Gitlow*: "The fact that speech is likely to result in some violence is not enough to justify its suppression. There must be the probability of serious injury to the State."

[**Supplementary note**: On the other hand, in the midst of the Cold War, the Court seemed to reassume the deferential posture it had adopted in *Gitlow*. In *Dennis v. United States* (1951), for example, the Court ruled that the First Amendment does not make the government helpless "in the face of preparation for revolution," no matter how far off it might be.]

C. Finally, in *Brandenburg v. Ohio* (1969), the Court, following suggestions in *Yates v. United States* (1957) and *Noto v. United States* (1961), reformulated the clear and present danger test once again. In its current formula, the test prohibits the suppression of speech "except where such advocacy is directed to inciting or producing imminent lawless action and is likely to incite or produce such action."

IV. Although the decision seems more protective of speech than some of the Court's earlier efforts, *Brandenburg* is not without its own difficulties.

  A. Such terms as *advocacy*, *incitement*, and *likely to incite* are sufficiently vague to require interpretation, and judges may vary on how much emphasis they give to one part of the test or another.

  B. The illegal advocacy cases, therefore, raise the perennial issues of when the state may act to protect itself and how far it may go in restricting civil liberty in the pursuit of security.

  C. These issues did not die with the end of the Cold War. Instead, they are the heart of current conflicts surrounding parts of the USA Patriot Act and the war on terrorism.

V. The illegal advocacy cases raise familiar issues about how to weigh competing interests in constitutional cases and about when judges should defer to majoritarian judgments. These issues extend well beyond the illegal advocacy cases.

  A. Consider a hypothetical set of issues: What if a political party challenged the very legitimacy of the government of the United States?

  B. In other words, imagine a political party committed to the destruction of representative democracy in the United States but one that denunciates violence.

  C. Can we prohibit such speech—unquestionably political in content—without running afoul of the First Amendment?

  D. The Supreme Court has yet to decide such a case, but we might have the doctrinal tools necessary to resolve the issue. Should we apply the clear and present danger test? If we do, what should be the result?

  E. In addition to the doctrinal issues, there are larger issues of constitutional theory involved. Does a constitutional democracy have the right to defend itself?

1. Some constitutional states, such as the Federal Republic of Germany, have adopted a concept called the *fighting* or *militant democracy*, or the concept that a democracy—even one committed to freedom of expression—need not tolerate speech committed to the destruction of democracy.

2. Something like the logic of the fighting democracy is partly behind several of the provisions in U.S. antiterrorism legislation, such as the USA Patriot Act.

Essential Reading:

Schenck v. United States (1919).

Gitlow v. New York (1925).

Whitney v. California (1927).

Dennis v. United States (1951).

Yates v. United States (1957).

Brandenburg v. Ohio (1969).

Kommers, Finn, and Jacobsohn, *American Constitutional Law*, chapter 7, pp. 366–367.

Supplementary Reading:

Pnina Lahav, "Holmes and Brandeis: Libertarian and Republican Justifications of Free Speech," 4 *Journal of Law & Politics* 451 (1987).

J. C. Miller, *Crisis in Freedom: The Alien and Sedition Acts*.

James Morton Smith, *Freedom's Fetters: The Alien and Sedition Laws and American Civil Liberties*.

Questions to Consider:

1. These cases raise important issues about the relationship between security and freedom. Does the Constitution say anything about which branch of government should have primary responsibility for weighing the balance? In *Dennis*, the Court seemed to defer to legislative assessments, but *Brandenburg* seems to envision a Court more inclined to decide for itself. Is there a constitutional reason to prefer one approach to the other?

2. Does a decision by the state to restrict speech and expression betray a lack of faith in the idea that truth will always win out in the marketplace of ideas?

3. Consider this quote by Justice Holmes, writing in *Gitlow*: "If, in the long run, the beliefs expressed in proletarian dictatorship are destined to be accepted by the dominant forces of the community, the only meaning of free speech is that they should be given their chance and have their way." Do you agree?

Lecture Nineteen—Transcript
Internal Security and the First Amendment

As we have seen, the reasons why we protect speech are many and complex. Consider, for example, the argument that we developed in an earlier lecture that speech might be necessary for the full development of human personality. Or, alternatively, speech might be necessary because representative democracy itself depends on the free exchange of ideas in order for democracy to fulfill its final and its foremost ambition: that of political accountability. On the other hand, there may well be times when speech is not the highest value that we ought to achieve, or ought to seek to achieve as a political community. Or, to put it more bluntly, are there times when it may be in our collective self-interest not to protect speech, or at least not to protect certain kinds of speech?

This is a question that has plagued the democracy from the beginning, from its earliest foundations. Consider, for example, the Alien and Sedition Acts of 1798. Those acts criminalized a wide variety of simple forms of political dissent. Almost any form of criticism of the standing government might well have been prosecuted under the Alien and Sedition Acts; and its constitutionality was a critical question at the time of the Founding, although not one that was ever decided by the Supreme Court itself.

These kinds of questions about when society may seek to dissent or to squash dissent have plagued our democracy since the beginning, but they are also remarkably current. Many of you, for example, will know that certain forms of political dissent are, if not prohibited, at least inhibited by the USA Patriot Act, passed just a few years ago.

We will begin our examination of these issues, not so much with the Alien and Sedition Acts—as I said, the Court never got around to making a decision—but rather with the important case of *Schenck v. United States,* decided just after the conclusion of World War I in 1919. *Schenck* is a fascinating case, both factually and legally. The facts are these: Charles Schenk, a general secretary of the United States Socialist Party, had sent over 15,000 pamphlets to individuals who were likely to be drafted for the war. In these little pamphlets, he argued that forced conscription violated the Thirteenth Amendment of the United States' Constitution; and you'll recall that the Thirteenth Amendment is the one that prohibits slavery. So you can see the argument here. As clumsy as it might be, it's straightforward, at least—forced conscription is a kind of involuntary servitude prohibited by the Thirteenth Amendment.

Now, before I go into the Court's opinion, there is one thing I want to stress about this. Sometimes, as we have seen, and as we shall continue to see, sometimes the Court insists that there are different kinds of speech, and that these different kinds of speech may be rank ordered in terms of their importance to the society at large. Whenever the Court does this, it always agrees on at least one basic proposition, and that basic proposition is this: some forms of speech may be of lesser value, some forms of speech may be of higher value; but always, the highest order of speech is political speech.

I mention that because it harkens back to one of the rationales for speech. Speech may be a necessary component of any representative democracy. But I mention it also because of the concept of the *Schenck* case, it has a special meaning, and the special meaning is this: if any speech must be considered political, surely speech that argues that some form of governmental conduct, that some governmental policy violates a constitutional amendment, has to be ranked as political speech. And the Court has never actually suggested this, but one might continue—if political speech is of the highest value, surely within that range of ideas, speech that goes to the heart of the Constitution must be of the highest order. So, one might argue that if we're going to protect any kind of speech at all, speech that alleges unconstitutionality should surely deserve high protection. That is arguably what was at stake in the *Schenck* case.

Schenck is also critically important to First Amendment jurisprudence, because it is the origin of a test that many of you will know, known as the "clear and present danger test." We will have to spend a little bit of time in this lecture talking about its initial formulation in *Schenck,* and then we'll trace what happened to the "clear and present danger test" in subsequent decisions. Let me start, however, with the opinion by Justice Holmes. I'm going to read a long quote, and I don't normally like to read at this length, but this one is important. Holmes wrote:

> The character of every act depends upon the circumstances in which it is done. The question in every case is whether the words are used in such circumstances and are of such a nature as to create a clear and present danger that they will

bring about the substantive evils that Congress has a right to prevent. It is a question of proximity and degree.

Now let's just back off for a second. There is the test—we'll parse it in a few minutes—but first let's ask ourselves the following question: what "substantive evil" did Congress seek to prevent in passing this act, the Espionage Act of 1917? Presumably, a kind of treasonous evil; an evil, presumably, that goes to the very ability of the government to prosecute the war.

This then leads us to a second question: if that is the evil that Congress sought to prevent, if the reason Schenck was arrested was because his speech might somehow inhibit the ability of the government to prosecute the war, should we not also ask—following Holmes' insistence that it is always "a question of proximity and degree"—the following question: was there really any danger that Schenck's 15,000 pamphlets would seriously impede the government's ability to prosecute the war?

Presumably, Holmes demands that somebody asks and answers that question. If "it is a question of proximity and degree," then I do not see how we can fail to inquire into the likelihood of any real harm flowing from Schenck's activity. Is it really likely that a single individual was going to resist the draft because he had read, apparently for the first time, that a military proscription might violate the Thirteenth Amendment? And even if one individual suddenly reached that conclusion off the strength of Schenck's pamphlet, would that really harm the government's effort? At what point do we have enough individuals who might conclude that there's a genuine risk here to their constitutional rights, and as a consequence, might resist the draft?

But even that, I suspect, is not the real, important issue in *Schenck*. The critical question in *Schenck,* as it has been in so many others of our cases, must be, who gets to weigh that question? If "it is a question of proximity and degree," if the words must be "of such a nature as to create a clear and present danger that they will bring about a substantive evil," who gets to decide whether the words have that kind of meaning, whether they will bear that kind of weight or have that kind of consequence? Unfortunately, the majority opinion in *Schenck* does not actually address those subsequent questions at any great level of detail. Presumably, it must ultimately be, at least in part, a judicial "question about proximity and degree." In other words, the "clear and present danger test" must give some measure of authority to judges to decide; but it doesn't say under what conditions, or even how precisely or how far, that authority must run.

It is also worth noting, finally, in *Schenck,* that the defendants were convicted. The clear and present danger test sometimes seems to students to be a great measure of protection for speech, but it need not necessarily be so. Indeed, there was very little protection for speech in *Schenck.* One must understand that the "clear and present danger" test hasn't got any independent content to it. It is simply a verbal formula—an equation, if you prefer—that may be weighed more heavily or less heavily, depending on who uses it, when they use it, and depending ultimately on how they value behind that the twin commitments we must have as a democracy to freedom of expression; and also to our physical integrity, to our ability to survive any crisis. The clear and present danger test is simply a shorthand formula without any independent content that allows judges to weigh these different values in different kinds of ways.

In subsequent cases, over a long period of time—beginning, say, in 1925 and ending not until the 1960s—the Court continued to tinker with the clear and present danger test, and at times, the test was more protective of speech, usually in the hands of judges who were more sympathetic to speech. And at other times, the test we use was used in ways that tended to favor governmental interest; again, depending upon which justice utilized the test; and frankly, depending also on larger social and political phenomenon.

In *Gitlow v. New York*, for example, decided in 1925, the Court seemed to relax the test considerably. Indeed, some scholars have gone on to say that what happened in *Gitlow* was that the clear and present danger test was transformed into something called "the bad tendency test," and I'll explain that in a second. But first, in *Gitlow*, the Court sustained the application of a criminal anarchy law to political strikes, and presumably, also, to labor strikes as well.

What was "the bad tendency test"? The Court argued that any speech might be shut down if it had a tendency to bring about the substantive evil that government had a right to prohibit. In other words, it didn't necessarily have to lead to that bad judgment; it didn't have to necessarily cause the bad consequence that might follow from negative speech or from subversive or "bad" speech.

Instead, it needed only to tend in that direction; hence, the "bad tendency test."

In utilizing this test, the Court simply announced that the judgment of the New York State legislature about which words were likely, in and of themselves, to bring about the substantive evil, the Court simply announced that it was essentially a legislative decision that it was required to defer to. Here is a quote from an opinion by Justice Sanford in *Gitlow* writing for the majority. And before I read the quote, I think it is worth noting that, perhaps more than in any other area of civil liberties, judges tend to write with extreme flourish, with extreme rhetoric; perhaps there is something about the First Amendment itself that gives rise to the best kind of writing and speech, at least on the part of judges. Hence, this quote, which is remarkable in its own right: "A single revolutionary spark may kindle a fire that's smoldering for a time may burst into a sweeping and destructive conflagration."

A labor strike? One might imagine that certain kinds of strikes, labor or political, or some other kind of strike, may indeed spark a revolutionary wildfire. That could happen. But why should judges assume that legislators are more likely to know when that will happen than judges will? And when we put the test in such (if you'll pardon the pun) inflammatory language, don't we necessarily prejudice how we think about the case? If we are worried that every tiny spark may cause a forest fire, then don't we necessarily suggest to ourselves—at least, even if only implicitly—that, in weighing the balance between speech and our physical integrity, our very survival, we must weigh survival more heavily always, independent of how serious the threat to our survival actually is? Again, it is worth noting that the clear and present danger test, at least as articulated in *Schenck*, did not provide for a great deal of protection for speech; but it certainly provided for more protection than its reformulation as the bad tendency test in *Gitlow,* which, one might conclude, offers very little, if any, protection for speech at all.

On the other hand, two years later in 1927, in *Whitney v. California*, Justice Brandeis wrote in direct contrast to *Gitlow,* "The fact that speech is likely to result in some violence is not enough to justify its suppression. There must be the probability of serious injury to the State."

Look at how different these two formulations are. In *Gitlow*, a bad tendency is enough to suppress speech. In *Whitney* however, even the probability, or at least the possibility of violence is not enough to shut down speech. The test, again, I say, is that there must be a "probability of serious injury to the State." Not a likelihood; a "probability"; and not simply injury, "of serious injury to the State." And again, the rhetoric is extraordinary. Here is Brandeis writing in *Whitney*: "Fear of serious injury cannot alone justify suppression of free speech and assembly. It is the function of speech to set men free from the bondage of irrational fears." Then he continues, "Only an emergency can justify repression."

Now, there's this second issue here, hinted at in *Schenck*, hinted at in *Gitlow,* and, unfortunately, not resolved explicitly in *Whitney;* and that is: who can decide if there really is an emergency? Who can decide if something more than serious injury is likely to result if we don't shut down speech? In *Schenck*, the Court seemed to defer to the legislative process. In *Gitlow*, the Court seemed to defer to the New York state legislature. In *Whitney,* however, the Court seemed to carve out for itself a somewhat more aggressive role. Presumably, there is some role for Courts to play, or for any single Court to play, in justifying or in considering whether or not there truly is an emergency involved.

I say this because, again, Justice Brandeis wrote about "irrational fears." Presumably, a fear that is not irrational, a rational fear of some genuine threat to society, or to the state, will justify some repression of speech. Where does irrationality make itself felt in the political process? My suspicion is that Brandeis thought that irrationality was most likely to present itself in the form of the legislative process, and that there must be a judicial check on that kind of irrational behavior.

That's *Whitney*. *Whitney* doesn't end the Court's tinkering with the clear and present danger test. The Court took it up again in the important cases of *Yates v. United States* (decided in 1957) and *Noto v. United States* (decided in 1961); but the most important formulation followed those cases in *Brandenburg v. Ohio* (decided in 1969).

In the current *Brandenburg* formulation, the test is straightforward, at least, again, at the level of doctrine. In its current form, the test prohibits the suppression of speech, "except where such advocacy is directed to inciting or producing imminent lawless action and is likely to incite or produce such action." This is sometimes called "the incitement test." It is simply a verbal formulation, or variation, on the clear and present danger test. Under the *Brandenburg* test—which seems, to many scholars and judges, to be a very protective test for speech—only an emergency can, in fact, justify repression.

How do we know when there is an emergency? We must distinguish between mere advocacy of harmful speech, or of harmful ideas, and the actual incitement to treason, to revolution, to insurrection, to violence, more generally.

On the other hand, terms like, "advocacy," "incitement," "likely to incite," are sufficiently vague to require constitutional and judicial interpretation; and judges, of course, are likely to vary in terms of how much emphasis they give to one part of the test or to another. There isn't any real likelihood, in other words, that the *Brandenburg* variation of the clear and present danger test is going to actually provide much guidance to courts or to citizens about what forms of speech may be prohibited and about under what conditions they may be prohibited.

We call these "the illegal advocacy cases," and they constitute a nice, concise, constrained set of cases. Judges like to use them because they constitute a clear line of precedent. Scholars like to teach them because they illustrate nicely for students how a verbal formula, how a particular method of constitutional interpretation—that of doctrinalism and the appeal to precedent—plays itself out over time. And scholars like myself like to use them because they illustrate also, I think, like most forms of constitutional interpretation, that appeals to precedent or to doctrinalism, doesn't really resolve the underlying constitutional issues. They simply give tools for judges to reach one decision or another without actually having to constrain judicial decision making in any particular way.

The illegal advocacy cases, however, are also deeply misleading, because they are narrow in an important sense. There are a range of issues surrounding so-called subversive speech that do not simply appear, do not only appear in the clear and present danger test; and I'd like to spend a little bit of time talking about them.

The illegal advocacy cases raise the perennial issue of how competing interests should be assessed. The competing interest, on the one hand, say, being freedom of speech; the other competing interest being our collective security. And secondarily, they raise the issue of who should balance them. As we have seen, those two questions get treated differently in different kinds of cases. But imagine those same questions outside of simple cases of illegal advocacy.

I want to deal with another couple of other kinds of examples, very briefly. First, consider the following kind of case. What if a political party forms—we'll call this party the "Treason Party of the United States," so that its aims are without question; and the Treason Party of the United States argues the following: The United States' government (not its people, just its government) is corrupt to the core. And the reason it is corrupt to the core is not because money has polluted the political process. The reason it is corrupt to the core is because representative democracy is itself a bourgeois, outdated, capitalistic concept, and completely opposed to the true flourishing of human beings. In other words, the Treason Party of the United States advocates a particular method (treason) in search of a larger goal—finding a form of political community for us all that does not corrupt the human spirit in the way, say, that representative democracy supposedly does.

I want there to be no misunderstanding about my hypothetical here. I am talking about a political party that is committed to the destruction of representative democracy in the United States, but is willing to do so without using violence.

So, imagine a political program, a platform adopted by this party, that says, we shall use the means of representative democracy itself to destroy representative democracy. We will use the ballot and not the bullet. In fact, we abhor violence. Instead, we intend to conduct a political campaign that urges people, that persuades people, to adopt a benevolent dictatorship. So, in the next presidential campaign, we will run representatives for the House of Representatives, we will run candidates for the Senate, who are pledged to the destruction—the peaceful destruction—of those two institutions. And our presidential candidate will be Professor Finn, who promises to run kindly, gently, but with complete, absolute, unquestioned authority.

This is not simply a hypothetical issue. Those of you who are students of history will know that such campaigns have been run in the past. Such a campaign was run in Weimar, Germany. Does a political community, does our political community, does our Constitution require us to tolerate speech, purely nonviolent in nature; that is, nevertheless, opposed to the existence of the constitutional document that allows such speech to occur in the first instance?

The Supreme Court of the United States has yet to address, clearly and unequivocally, the kind of specific constitutional question raised by my hypothetical; and that specific constitutional question is this: Can we ban a political party simply because we don't like its underlying political message? Can we pick and choose which elements of a political program we will accept as a legitimate part of democratic debate, and which ones we must reject as being fundamentally inimical to representative democracy? This is an issue that has been addressed in other constitutional democracies; and in several of them—Germany for one, Israel for another, Turkey for yet another—Supreme Courts have decided that the political commitment of representative democracy does not actually require those states to accept or to tolerate political ideas and political actions that seek to dismantle democracy itself. That is the fundamental issue that I am talking about with my hypothetical program. And although our Court has never decided it, it is worth asking ourselves, do we have the kinds of doctrinal tools available to us that would allow us to answer this question?

So let's go back to the clear and present danger test. Imagine that you are a Supreme Court justice, and you have in front of you a political party committed to the nonviolent destruction of this representative democracy. Presumably, you ask yourself, following *Schenck,* is there a clear and present danger of such a nature that it will bring about the substantive evil that Congress has the right to prevent? And now I hope we can begin to see what one of the biggest problems is with the *Schenck* test, with the clear and present danger test, more generally. Does Congress have the right to prevent this substantive evil?

Schenck does nothing to tell us what the answer to that question must be. In other words, *Schenck* is just a mechanical formulation; it's a verbal equation. It doesn't help us in any meaningful way to address the underlying issues, about under what conditions, if any, a democracy might seek to protect itself. In those democracies—I have mentioned a few—where this kind of suppression of political dissent is permitted, there is usually made reference to a doctrine known as "fighting democracy," or "militant democracy"—and the terms, I think, are wonderfully instructive. A fighting democracy, or a militant democracy, is a democracy that takes seriously the idea that it can be committed to the preservation of itself; and there's something wonderfully admirable and noble about that.

Some scholars like to say if Weimar, Germany, had been more committed to the proposition that democracy itself had a stake in its own existence, then perhaps Weimar would not have fallen. That seems to me to be overly optimistic. But there can be no doubt that democracies must take seriously the idea that there are threats to their own well-being, threats to their very existence. It is that kind of logic that inheres in the USA Patriot Act, which has several provisions that intrude, either directly or implicitly, on First Amendment freedoms.

Without going into the specifics of the Patriot Act, because those will change over time—some will be repealed, some will be modified, some will be enhanced—it is important to understand the logic behind such provisions; because it is only by understanding the logic behind those provisions that we can really assess constitutionally whether the threat they present to civil liberties is a threat that we should embrace, or whether it is a threat that we should reject as unfounded. The logic behind the Patriot Act, and its provisions that implicate speech, is the logic of the fighting democracy, or the logic of the militant democracy. it is the logic, in other words, that says that we all have a stake, not simply in our physical survival, but in the maintenance of those constitutional ideals, those constitutional values that define us every bit as much as our physical natures define us.

In other words, the illegal advocacy cases and the hypothetical cases that I have drawn up for you show us that the most important issues, with regard to the internal security cases, are not issues about doctrine, not issues about how a verbal formulation changes over time, but instead, issues that force us to ask the most basic question, the question we started with in this lecture; indeed the question we started with when we began to take up the First Amendment materials, more generally: Why do we value speech at all? Is it possible that sometimes we should sacrifice our commitment to freedom of expression, not simply because we want to maintain our physical selves, not simply because we want to protect the state in its most physical forms of manifestation, but also because we want to maintain our commitment to democracy itself? Ironically, are there times when speech is inimical to the values of speech? That is the question that our Court has yet to take up in my so-called hypothetical cases; but the Court certainly will take it up at some point in the future.

Now there's one final thing I'd like to talk about with regard to the internal security cases. I have suggested that if there is a conflict here, that conflict might be understood as a conflict between our desire for freedom of speech and other First Amendment liberties and physical survival. I've also suggested that the conflict might be between our desire for free speech and our desire to protect other constitutional values, such as the maintenance of democracy itself; but there may be yet another way to understand what the conflict is.

Perhaps the conflict is between our commitment, not simply to constitutional ideals, and not simply to physical ideals; but our commitment to a way of life, to a form of political community that can survive the ravages not only of war, but of time. And the reason I mention this is because I think it is worth understanding, or worth recalling, I should say that it is in the very first of *The Federalist Papers,* where Publius writes: "It has been left to the people of this good country to decide whether or not human beings, human communities, can overcome time and chance." In other words, these conflicts illustrate the most fundamental sorts of conflicts that drive the constructional order—fundamental conflicts of the sort that the *Federalist Papers* address not early on, but immediately.

Lecture Twenty
Symbolic Speech and Expressive Conduct

Scope:

The last two lectures concentrated on the rationale for protecting speech. Should those reasons also influence how we define *speech*? In the next four lectures, we take up thorny questions about the meaning of speech and expression, about what we might include in the ambit of the First Amendment, and what we might choose to leave unprotected because it is not "really" speech. The Court has long recognized that the distinction between conduct and content can be elusive, particularly when "speech" and "nonspeech" elements unite in a single course of action. Any action, such as burning a draft card or a flag, or hanging an effigy, or wearing an armband, might be motivated by an expressive purpose. In this lecture, we consider how the Court has handled symbolic speech and expressive conduct. In *United States v. O'Brien* (1968), the Court developed a four-part test for determining the validity of governmental actions that regulate expressive conduct. As we shall see, however, the test is not always easy to apply and does little to help us understand the most vexing of issues: What is *speech*, what is *conduct*, and what is the difference?

Outline

I. In our last lecture, we saw that the *Schenck/Brandenburg* line of cases is very complicated doctrinally. But at no point did anyone argue that the cases did not involve speech at all. In other words, in *Schenck*, *Brandenburg*, *Gitlow*, *Dennis*, *Yates*, and that entire line of internal or illegal advocacy cases, we all agreed, without even really having to ask, that there was actually speech involved in those cases.

   A. In the next four lectures, however, we take up thorny and difficult questions about the very definitions of *speech* and *expression*, or about what we might want to include in the ambit of the First Amendment and what we might choose to leave unprotected because it is not "really" speech, whatever *speech* means.

B. The Court has long recognized, as we shall see in this lecture, that there is a distinction between conduct and content, and that that distinction can be elusive, particularly when there are "speech" and "nonspeech" elements that unite in a single course of action.

II. Many definitional issues haunt the First Amendment. Perhaps the most intractable of these definitional issues is misleadingly straightforward: What is *speech*? This is a topic that will occupy us for several lectures.

A. In this lecture, we consider the question in its most basic sense: Is there a difference, constitutionally, between speech and conduct?

B. The Court has long held that some things that seem plainly to be speech, such as obscenity, are sometimes not protected. On the other hand, some things that might seem to be conduct, such as sleeping in a park, might be expressive and, thus, protected.

C. And there are the cases in which the distinction is blurred— such as wearing an armband to protest a war or carrying a placard in a union strike. In these cases, the conduct, or activity, seems motivated by an expressive purpose.

III. The Court has created a complicated set of tests to govern the area of *symbolic speech* or *expressive conduct*. In the leading case of *United States v. O'Brien* (1968), the Court developed a four-part test for reviewing the constitutionality of legislation regulating expressive conduct.

A. *O'Brien* involved a person who had burned his draft registration card in a public protest against the Vietnam War. A federal statute made it a crime to destroy a draft card.

B. According to the Court, the statute at issue was content neutral. Its primary purpose, in other words, was to protect the integrity of the registration system, not to suppress speech. The Court tries to distinguish between *content-based* and *content-neutral* restrictions on conduct.

C. Because the legislation was content neutral, the Court did not subject it to strict scrutiny. Instead, the Court offered a multi-pronged test. A content-neutral law is constitutional:

1. If it is otherwise justifiable as within the legitimate powers of the state.

2. If it furthers an important governmental interest.

3. If that interest is unrelated to the suppression of speech and if the incidental restriction on speech is no greater than necessary to further that interest.

D. The basic test, then, is this: If a governmental action regulating conduct is intended to suppress the message, the restriction must be subjected to strict scrutiny.

1. There are difficulties with this test. The most obvious is that it is often difficult to determine legislative intent or purpose.

2. Another difficulty is definitional: How can we know whether the activity or behavior is expressive?

3. The Court addressed this question at least in part, noting: "We cannot accept the view that an apparently limitless variety of conduct can be labeled 'speech' whenever the person engaging in the conduct intends thereby to express an idea."

E. There is another difficulty with *O'Brien*. The Court ruled that the government's stated purpose in maintaining the integrity of the draft system was sufficiently important to overcome the speech interest. The Court also hints that a part of its conclusion rests on the idea that there were other methods of communication open to the plaintiff. The Court will begin to build on that suggestion in later cases.

F. Finally, the *O'Brien* Court should remind us of the doctrine of comity. *Comity* is the principle that one branch of government owes the other branches a great deal of respect. How is it involved in *O'Brien*?

1. The government stated that it had no hostility to O'Brien or his message. Comity holds that the Court must respect this claim, absent any direct evidence that would contravene it.

2. Why is comity important? The principle is grounded in larger considerations of separation of powers.

IV. The *O'Brien* test is not always easy to apply. More troublesome, however, is that it does little to help us understand the most vexing of issues: What is *speech*, what is *conduct*, and what is the difference? The Court's consideration of subsequent cases may help us to get a handle on the distinction.

A. In *Tinker v. Des Moines* (1969), the Court considered a case in which several students at a public school were suspended for wearing black armbands to oppose the war in Vietnam.

B. In his opinion for the Court, Justice Fortas described this conduct as "akin to pure speech."

C. Consequently, "In order for the State to justify the prohibition of a particular expression of opinion, it must be able to show that its action was caused by something more than a mere desire to avoid the discomfort and unpleasantness that always accompany an unpopular viewpoint."

D. Fortas concluded by noting, "In our system, state-operated schools may not be enclaves of totalitarianism."

E. The case generated an impassioned dissent by Justice Black, who wrote: "Assuming the Court is correct in holding that the conduct of wearing armbands for the purpose of conveying political ideas is protected by the First Amendment, the crucial remaining questions are whether students and teachers may use the schools at their whim, as a platform for the exercise of free speech."

F. *Tinker* suggests a wide range of First Amendment freedoms for students in public schools, but, in recent years, the Court has been more sympathetic to the claims of school officials who argue that limits on expression are necessary to maintain school discipline and the integrity of the curriculum.

V. Two years later, in *Cohen v. California* (1971), the Court considered the case of young man who entered a courthouse wearing a jacket with the slogan "F--- the Draft" imprinted on the back.

    A. Writing for the Court, Justice Harlan ruled that the conviction violated Cohen's freedom of speech, noting, "It is, nevertheless, often true that one man's vulgarity is another's lyric. In fact, words are often chosen as much for their emotive as their cognitive force."

        1. Recall our discussion of *O'Brien*. Should we ask if Cohen had available another means, nonvulgar, of expressing his idea?

        2. Do we want judges to decide whether "Damn the Draft" is equivalent to "F--- the Draft"?

    B. In dissent, Justice Blackmun argued, "Cohen's absurd and immature antic, in my view, was mainly conduct and little speech."

VI. Finally, consider the interesting case of *Clark v. Community for Creative Nonviolence* (1984).

    A. In this case, protesters wanted to camp overnight in Lafayette Park to bring attention to the plight of the homeless. The Park Service refused to issue permits for overnight stays. The protesters sued, claiming that their desire to sleep in tents was a form of symbolic expression protected by the First Amendment.

    B. Following *O'Brien*, we should ask: What is the governmental policy or interest at play, and is it content neutral? If so, we apply the *O'Brien* test, as did the Court. The Court had little difficulty concluding that the restriction passed the constitutional analysis.

    C. Unfortunately, the *Clark* case fails, as have all others, to do much to address the underlying question about whether and when there is a constitutionally relevant distinction between speech and conduct.

Essential Reading:

United States v. O'Brien (1968).

Tinker v. Des Moines (1969).

Clark v. Community for Creative Nonviolence (1984).

Kommers, Finn, and Jacobsohn, *American Constitutional Law*, chapter 7, pp. 364–365.

Supplementary Reading:

Mark R. Arbuckle, "Vanishing First Amendment Protection for Symbolic Expression 35 Years after United States v. O'Brien," 25 Communications and the Law 1 (2003)

Joshua Waldman, "Symbolic Speech and Social Meaning," 97 Columbia Law Review 1844 (1997).

Questions to Consider:

1. Why did the Founders fail to define *speech* in the First Amendment? Is the search for a definition a necessary part of the Court's effort to interpret the First Amendment? Is such a search destined to failure?

2. Should a person's intent matter in trying to determine if conduct is sufficiently expressive to warrant First Amendment protections? What if a person intends to communicate, but the audience fails to comprehend the message or even to understand that there is a message?

3. The Court typically distinguishes between content-based and content-neutral restrictions on symbolic speech and conduct. Why? In either case, isn't the effect to chill speech?

Lecture Twenty—Transcript
Symbolic Speech and Expressive Conduct

In our last lecture, we took up the so-called "illegal advocacy" cases. You'll recall that we spent some time with the "clear and present danger" doctrine, and one thing we learned, or at least I think we learned, is that the meaning of that doctrine has tended to change from case to case. One thing that was not especially at issue in those cases, however, or I should say perhaps instead, that throughout the entire line of the *Dennis*, *Yates*, *Schenck*, *Brandenburg* cases, there was always one unspoken assumption, one point of agreement, and that point of agreement was simply this: No one, at least to my recollection, ever argued in any one of those cases that there was not actually speech involved in the particular set of issues at question. We all agreed at every point through those line of cases that we had a speech problem. We weren't sure how to resolve it and the mechanism for resolving it changed from case to case, but at least we knew what kind of a problem we had.

In the next four lectures, we take up thorny questions about the meaning of speech and expression, or about what we might include in the ambit of the First Amendment; and what we might choose to leave unprotected because it is not really speech.

The Court has long recognized that the distinction between conduct and content can be elusive, especially when speech and nonspeech elements unite in a single course of action. Any action, such as burning a draft card or a flag, or hanging an effigy, or wearing an armband, might be motivated by an expressive purpose.

In this lecture, we consider how the Court has handled the doctrines of symbolic speech and expressive conduct. We will consider two cases in particular. First, we will take up *United States v. O'Brien* (decided in 1968), and then secondly, we will take up the interesting case of *Cohen v. California* (decided in 1971). We shall see in those cases that the Court has developed a four-part test for determining the validity of governmental actions that regulate expressive conduct. As we shall see, however, the test is not always easy to understand and does little to help us to understand the most vexing of issues: what is speech, what is conduct, and what is the difference?

Let's start with that *O'Brien* case. In *O'Brien*, the Court started off with a series of non-problematic and non-controversial propositions.

The most simplistic of these, the easiest to understand, is simply this: if a governmental action regulating conduct is intended to suppress some kind of message associated with that conduct, and that is the very purpose of a governmental regulation, then we have a simple, straightforward test to apply. That governmental conduct, that governmental policy, must be subjected to the "strict scrutiny" test.

We have encountered this test before. All it means is that that governmental action, this governmental policy, will be subject to the most intense, searching form of judicial scrutiny, and it will only be upheld if there is some overwhelming, compelling reason why the government ought to have the authority to shut down this speech, or, I should say, this conduct. This is a simple test. Unfortunately, in the real world, it is not often the case that we know unequivocally that some governmental policy is intended to suppress speech, particularly when the speech is a kind of expressive component of conduct, more generally.

And consider another difficulty. How do we know whether the activity or the behavior or the conduct is, itself, expressive? Is it enough, for example, that the speaker—I use that word loosely—intends to convey a message? If I have an armband, is it necessary that I mean for that armband to express some political or other kind of message? What if I choose the armband because I think it makes me look cool? What if I choose an armband because it expresses opposition to a war? Is my intent what is critical? Or, alternatively, do we need to assess whether there is a communicative component based on whether or not there is an audience that can comprehend that I'm even intending to send a message? The Court has rarely, if ever, resolved these questions, at least clearly and unequivocally.

One other sort of thing we need to know before we actually get into *O'Brien*: the Court tries to distinguish between what it calls "content-based" restrictions on speech and "content-neutral" restrictions on speech, or restrictions on conduct. A content-based restriction on speech or conduct means just what it sounds like; that the whole point of the regulation, the whole point of the governmental policy is to shut down that message; hence the regulation is, as the Court says, "content-based." The nature of the regulation is directly tied to the nature of the content of the speech or the conduct. "Content-neutral," however, refers to a governmental policy that doesn't care about the message, but cares only about the underlying conduct, and for reasons that have nothing to do with the nature of the message. And we'll see a great case later on, *Clark v. Community for Creative Nonviolence,* where the Court tried to elaborate on that distinction.

Now, to go to *O'Brien. O'Brien* involved a very interesting set of facts. A young man stood on the steps of the courthouse and burned his draft card in opposition to the Vietnam War. As it turns out, there was a federal statute that made it a crime to destroy a draft card. Before we go further, it's important to understand what governmental policy might be advanced by such a rule or by such a statute.

The Court, in its opinion, indicated that there was a perfectly good, content-neutral reason why the government might seek to have such a rule. The very integrity and efficiency of the draft-system, the government argued, required that everybody who was drafted have such a card, and that they keep it on their person and that they maintain it. In other words, the efficiency of the draft itself depended on such cards being maintained.

That is, if it is true, a classic example of a content-neutral regulation. The regulation prohibiting the destruction of a draft card has nothing to do with the government's sense of the underlying message—in this case, opposition to the Vietnam War. If the government had shut down just this activity, and had done so because it disagreed with the young man's message about the war; or if it had shut it down for the reasons it was shut down in *Schenck*—some feared that harm would be done to the military conscription—that would be different. That would be a content-based regulation. But this is content-neutral, and as a consequence, "We do not have to apply," the Court said, "the strict scrutiny" that I mentioned earlier.

Before we get to the actual test, it is worth understanding, however, or inquiring into, how the Court knew that there was any speech here at all. Here's what the Court said: "We cannot accept the view that an apparently limitless variety of conduct can be labeled 'speech' whenever the person engaging in the conduct intends thereby to express an idea." You can see the Court's fear. If every time we act, we intend to express an idea, then we have multiplied the universe of First Amendment protections exponentially.

But one might ask the Court: why can't we accept that view? Shouldn't we accept the view, instead, that every time we mean to express ourselves, whether through speech or action, presumptively, the First Amendment ought to apply, because sometimes words don't speak as loudly as actions?

The Court actually doesn't proffer a set of explanations about why it cannot accept that view. One suspects that the Court does not accept it because it worries that it will turn the Court into a perpetual censor; that it will turn the Court's business from constitutional adjudication to social regulation.

That said, some forms of conduct are sufficiently imbued with expressive purpose that they do warrant First Amendment protection; and now we really have a problem. The Court tells us that not all forms of conduct that are meant to be expressive should be protected, but some should. And the obvious question is, which ones? Why? And then, secondarily, who should get to decide? Nothing in *O'Brien* tells us the answers to those questions; but we do have a test, and it is important to understand the test.

Because the statute, the legislation, was "content-neutral," the Court did not subject it to strict scrutiny. Instead, a law that is content-neutral that applies to a course of conduct that has an expressive component is constitutional. The Court wrote:

> If it is otherwise as justifiable within the legitimate powers of the State, if it furthers an important governmental interest and if that interest is unrelated to the suppression of speech and if the incidental restriction on speech is no greater than is necessary to further the government's interest.

That test is not easy to apply. And, as I said before, it suffers from a fundamental problem in that it does nothing to resolve the underlying question: which forms of speech will we protect? Which forms of conduct will we protect? And which forms of conduct fall outside the ambit of the First Amendment? Nevertheless, the Court continues to apply the test, and part of what I want to do in this lecture is give you a sense of the different kinds of cases that have been brought up, and the way the Court has tried to apply the *O'Brien* test.

There is one other sort of part of the *O'Brien* test, though, that we need to address before we move on to its subsequent application. In

O'Brien, the Court ruled that the government's avowed interest in maintaining the integrity of the conscription system was sufficiently important—it furthered an important governmental interest—to warrant or to be upheld as constitutionally acceptable.

There are hints—there are no more than hints, but there are hints—in the opinion that part of the Court's inquiry is grounded in yet another factor; one that doesn't rise to the level of a formal test, but which will appear in subsequent cases; and that additional factor is this: the Court seems to put some reliance on the fact that there are other methods of communication that the young man might have adopted, which would nevertheless get his message across. In other words, the existence of an alternative mode of communication that would get across the fundamental, underlying message seems to be, at least implicitly, an important part of the *O'Brien* test. And we'll see the Court begin to develop that subsequently.

And then one final other thing about *O'Brien*. We have not yet encountered this doctrine except obliquely, but now is the time, I think, to express it explicitly. In every area of civil liberties, there is a doctrine known as comity. "Comity" refers to the respect that one branch of government must have for other branches of government. The doctrine, again, is perhaps only implicit in *O'Brien,* but it's important.

Many students are deeply suspicious about the governmental action in *O'Brien*. So, when I said that the government's purported interest was the maintenance and the integrity of the conscription system, many students will often say, "How do you know that to be true? Did the government arrest everybody who lost a draft card, or who accidentally sent one through a washing machine? Did it only pick out people who are expressing some sort of public opposition to the war?" The Court didn't really inquire into that question, and part of the reason it did not was because to do so was to come dangerously close to suggesting that the government was acting on the basis of an illegitimate, improper motive. The Court is always reluctant to inquire into motive. There are good reasons for doing so. The most important of those is this doctrine of comedy, or respect for another branch of government.

There are other reasons as well. How could the Court possibly know why the young man was arrested? It's difficult to get evidence of motive. It's difficult to inquire into a person's state of mind, and to get any genuine evidence—authentic, reliable evidence about why a person, or government official, in this case, may have acted the way he did.

And assume for a minute that, like most individuals, the person effectuating the arrest in this case is complicated; might well have agreed with the government's position that, "This is opposition to the war, and it's fundamentally treasonous, or, at least, awful." But he might also have thought, "This is my job and I don't inquire into why I'm told to do what I do." Or he might also have thought that, "It doesn't matter whether I agree or not. I am simply charged with upholding the law."

Many of us, perhaps all of us, usually act, especially in complicated and difficult cases, on the basis of several motives. Sometimes those motives are inconsistent with each other and can't be reconciled. What is the Court to do when faced with that complex range of motives? Is it to pick out the bad one and to say, "Well the presence of a bad motive offsets all the other appropriate, legitimate motives?" For these reasons, for reasons of application, as well as for reasons of principle, the Court refused to inquire into *O'Brien* about whether or not the government was really acting with some sense of opposition to the young man's message.

Now, consider some subsequent cases. Just one year later, in 1969, in a case called *Tinker v. Des Moines*, the Court considered the armband case that I hinted at earlier. A number of students wore black armbands to school in opposition to the Vietnam War. They were suspended. In a seven-to-two opinion for the Court, Justice Fortas began by noting that the wearing of the armbands was, "Akin to peer speech." I have no idea what that means. It's either peer speech or it's not; or it's "akin to peer speech," which means it's like peer speech; but presumably, if it's like peer speech, we would want to know in what precise ways is it like peer speech, and in what ways, if any, is it more akin to something else, like, not speech, conduct. The underlying issue in *O'Brien*—how do we know which forms of expressive conduct warrant First Amendment protection and which ones don't—is left again unresolved in *Tinker* just a year later. Instead, we get this verbal flourish, "Akin to peer speech."

In his opinion for the Court, Justice Fortas wrote the following:

In order for the State to justify the prohibition of a particular expression of opinion, it must be able to show that its action was caused by something more than a mere desire to avoid the discomfort and unpleasantness that always accompany an unpopular viewpoint.

In other words, if the government, acting through the institution of a public school, is going to shut down students' speech, it must do so based on some other factor than mere distress or discomfort about the nature of the speech.

Before I continue with Justice Fortas's opinion, it's probably worth asking, what would count as a good reason for shutting down speech? And the majority suggested, for example, that, if the speech was genuinely disruptive of school discipline; or, alternatively, if it really disrupted the school curriculum, then that might be a good reason for shutting down speech. In the Court's opinion, there was no evidence of that happening in this case. Indeed, other students had worn t-shirts with different kinds of messages, and they had not been shut down. As the Court noted, there appeared to be a substantial threat that the school would be disrupted in any material way. There was only the sense that this might be "unpleasant."

Continuing, Justice Fortas wrote, "In our system, state sponsored schools may not be enclaves of totalitarianism." It's a wonderful quote. One wonders how applicable it is here. I mean, telling students they can't wear an armband doesn't necessarily transform school authorities into totalitarian dictators. Nevertheless, it does suggest the underlying concern that the Court brought to the case, and that underlying concern is that school officials sought to shut down this speech simply because they were afraid of the controversies associated with the Vietnam War.

There is a passionate dissent in *Tinker*. That dissent was written by Justice Hugo Black. Before I go into his dissent, this is the place, this is the time to say a few words about Justice Black. Justice Hugo Black came to the Court from the United States Senate. During his time on the Court, he developed a reputation as a great civil libertarian, and much of that reputation was founded on Black's view of the First Amendment. Black is sometimes called an "absolutist," is perhaps better described as a "literalist" in his approach to the First Amendment. I say "literalist," because he insisted that the First Amendment should be taken literally. So when it begins, "Congress shall make no law…," Black was of the opinion that that meant, "no law." And one can see, I think, how this might result in a great variety, a wide expanse of protection for First Amendment freedoms, and yet Justice Black dissented in *Tinker*. He wrote:

> Assuming the Court is correct in holding that the conduct of wearing armbands for the purpose of conveying political ideas is protected by the First Amendment, the crucial remaining questions are whether students and teachers may use the schools at their whim, as a platform for the exercise of free speech.

What an extraordinary quotation! "Assuming the Court is correct…," which he's clearly only willing to do for purposes of argument. But how could the Court not be correct, unless one is prepared to say that there is, in fact, a firm, constitutional—and perhaps practical—distinction between conduct and speech?

So, one would want to ask Justice Black, what if the students had politely, quietly, without causing a disruption, not worn armbands, but instead chanted, "We are opposed to the Vietnam War"? And you'll realize how genteel my version of this argument is. I haven't given you the more prolific, colorful forms of opposition to the war that start with, "Hey, hey, hey, LBJ…" and many of you will be able to supplant the rest of it. That would clearly be speech. We wouldn't have to have Justice Black say, "assuming it's speech;" it would be, "it's speech." And then where would Justice Black go?

"The crucial remaining questions," he wrote, "are whether students and teachers may use the schools at their whim, as a platform, for the exercise of free speech." One might respond, "Well, why not?" Unless he wants to say (and I assume he does) that, "Yes, you have speech rights, and no, Congress may make no law; but your speech rights don't apply everywhere and in everyplace;" that, presumably, there is something different about the schoolhouse—in this case, at least—that takes it out of the orbit of First Amendment protections; or at least reduces the range of First Amendment protections.

He concluded: "I have never believed that any person has a right to give speeches or engage in demonstrations where he pleases and when he pleases." How can one possibly reconcile that with the First Amendment, taken literally, that says, "Congress shall make no law…."? Unfortunately, Justice Black doesn't elaborate. He can't take refuge here in the speech/conduct distinction because he doesn't make it himself.

Tinker suggests a wide range of protections for students in schools; and this is not a theme that I intend to elaborate on at any length, but I think it is important to note that *Tinker* probably represents the high-water mark for protection of student speech. Since *Tinker,* and through the 1980s and the 1990s, the Court has been more inclined to accept the Black point of view.

I don't mean the Black point of view that one can't speak wherever or however one wants. I mean to suggest, instead, that the Court has adopted, or at least been more deferential to, more sympathetic to, another aspect of Justice Black's dissent. And that aspect is this: Black insisted, time and time again, in his *Tinker* dissent, that what the Court was involved in and what the majority had done was to supplant its level, its sense of expertise about how schools should be run for local school administrators.

Black believes, in other words, that one of the fundamental errors in the *Tinker* opinion was the Court's willingness to override the judgments of local officials about what was actually necessary to maintain the curriculum, or to maintain school discipline. Subsequent courts have been more inclined to adopt that perspective. In other words, subsequent courts have been less eager to oversee school officials, and to invest themselves, or to inject themselves, into the day-to-day operation of school regulations.

Now, that's *Tinker.* Remember, *Tinker* was decided in 1969, one year after *O'Brien.* Another two years later, in 1971, the Court considered the case of a young man who walked into a municipal courthouse in Los Angeles with a leather jacket, and on the back of his jacket was a slogan that read, "F--- the draft." He was arrested for violating, in essence, local breach of peace ordinances. This is an extraordinary case.

Justice Harlan wrote for the majority. Now recall, this is 1971. This is Justice Harlan's last year on the Court, and, as it turned out, Justice Black's last year on the Court, as well. At this point in time, Harlan is legally blind; he can't read what was written on the jacket; and he was sufficiently squeamish that at no point during any of the Court's hearings, at no point during the drafting of his opinion, will he ever actually use the word involved in this case. He doesn't use it until he actually sets out to write the majority opinion.

Harlan begins with the following proposition. Noting that there is a fine line between speech and conduct; between what's acceptable in a democratic society or what's acceptable in polite society; and what is, as he says, "It is, nevertheless, often true that one man's vulgarity is another's lyric. In fact, words are often chosen as much for their emotive as their cognitive force." And surely, if that sentiment is applicable to any case, it is applicable to this case.

Remember, I mentioned in *O'Brien* that there was some hint that the young man who had burned his draft card had alternative means of expression open to him. It is worth asking in *Cohen,* is there an alternative means of expression open to Cohen? He might say, "What?" Instead of "F--- the draft," perhaps he says, "I think the draft is unseemly;" or perhaps he says, "I think the draft is unconstitutional;" or perhaps he says, "Damn the draft!" Do any of those sentiments express the same thing as "F--- the draft"? If they don't, then a governmental decision to criminalize this particular form of expression goes to the heart of First Amendment freedoms.

This might seem like an important question, particularly because I have just given it such power; but it might not be a question we want to ask, and here is why: do we want judges engaged in this kind of picking apart of speech? Do we want judges to decide whether or not "F--- the draft" means the same thing as "Damn the draft"? What would give judges any special competence to decide whether or not one kind of expression is more or less the same thing as another kind of expression?

So you'll recall, when we did the abortion cases and the right-to-die cases, that Justice Scalia once wrote in dissent, "The nine judges of this Court have no more knowledge about this issue than nine members chosen at random from the Kansas City phone book." Why is the same not true here? Let me be really obnoxious about this. Nine old men and women are going to tell the rest of us that "F--- the draft" is functionally the same thing as "Damn the draft"? I think I'd rather ask nine people chosen at random from the MTV audience. I don't understand where the Constitution entrusts such kind of expertise to judges.

In dissent, Justice Blackmun, joined, in part, by Justice Black, wrote, "Cohen's absurd and immature antic, in my view, was mainly conduct in little speech." "Mainly conduct in little speech"—how do we know? I suppose, literally, it was "little speech," but it was conduct that clearly had an expressive purpose. Even more than the armband cases, this is conduct that expresses a message. It's right there on the back. How can you miss it? Once again, the underlying problem is, how do we distinguish between speech and conduct? The majority says little about it, and the dissenting opinions simply assume what is in question.

Now, one final sort of case that I alluded to at the very beginning. In a very interesting case, decided in 1984, the Court considered a case that I have alluded to on at least two occasions now: *Clark v. The Community for Creative Nonviolence.* The question in this case is, does sleeping overnight in Lafayette Park constitute a form of protected expressive conduct? And you will recall from my earlier mention of the case that what happened here is that a number of activist groups decided to camp out on the Mall and in Lafayette Park to protest homelessness in Washington, D.C. Their argument was simple: that nothing conveys the sense of the homelessness problem like sleeping out. The park police, on the other hand, assumed that camping out would, arguably anyway, threaten the integrity of the Mall and of Lafayette Park itself; and it violated a number of regulations designed to keep people from camping in certain kinds of national parks.

Let's go all the way back to *O'Brien.* What is the governmental policy designed to protect the integrity of the parks? Is that content-neutral or content-based? Clearly, in this case, it was content-neutral, at the level of theory, anyway. But one suspects, like we did in *O'Brien,* that there may have been a political purpose behind the government's decision to shut down speech. In this case, the Court had no difficulty concluding that the park service regulation passed the four-part test that we described in *O'Brien.* Unfortunately, the Court did not resolve the underlying question about whether it was speech or conduct.

Lecture Twenty-One
Indecency and Obscenity

Scope:

In the past few lectures, we have struggled with a series of classic First Amendment problems. For example, in Lecture Nineteen, we explored the so-called internal security or subversive speech cases, and in Lecture Twenty, we took up the problems of symbolic speech and expressive conduct. In both areas, as we saw, the Court has constructed a complicated jurisprudence, a jurisprudence that centers on a variety of doctrinal tests, such as the clear and present danger doctrine or the four-part *O'Brien* test for regulating symbolic speech. And implicit in both areas of inquiry was also a problem of definition: What is *speech*? What isn't?

We will follow the same course in this lecture, where we ask: Is pornography speech? This is, in many ways, also a question of definition. And the Court's efforts to provide such a definition have similarly resulted in a set of doctrinal tests that we will need to consider. In *Miller v. California* (1973), the Court provided some support for the efforts of state and local governments "to maintain a decent society," developing a three-part test designed to distinguish between protected speech and the "crass commercial exploitation of sex." Since *Miller*, the Court has continued to struggle, however, with the problem of definition. As we shall see, too, the Court's recent efforts to define pornography and indecency have been further complicated by the rapid advance of technology. Thus, in *Reno v. American Civil Liberties Union* (1997), the Court found unconstitutional two key provisions of the Communications Decency Act of 1996 designed to prevent minors from indecent and patently offensive communications on the Internet. In *Ashcroft v. Free Speech Coalition* (2002), the Court struck down a part of the Child Pornography Protection Act that regulated "virtual child pornography." Finally, we will conclude by returning to the question that undergirds every First Amendment case: What do we do if the values that inform the First Amendment conflict with other values, such as equality or human dignity?

Outline

I. The Court's modern obscenity jurisprudence begins with *Roth v. United States* (1957), in which the Court reaffirmed the rule that obscenity is unprotected by the First Amendment.

    A. The justices on the *Roth* Court, however, could not agree on a definition of *obscenity*.

        1. In his majority opinion, Justice Brennan wrote: "All ideas having even the slightest redeeming social importance … have the full protection [of the First Amendment]…. But implicit in the history of the First Amendment is the rejection of obscenity as utterly without redeeming social importance."

        2. Critics object: Who is the Court to determine which kinds of speech have "redeeming social importance"? Where does the Constitution give the Court any guidance about which kinds of speech merit protection and which do not?

    B. In a separate opinion, Justice Harlan accused the majority of begging the question. What question was that? The definition of pornography itself, we might say.

        1. Justice Harlan wrote: "We deal with highly emotional, not rational, questions. To many, the Song of Solomon is obscene. I do not think we, the judges, were ever given the constitutional power to make definitions of obscenity. If it is to be defined, let the people debate and decide by a constitutional amendment…."

        2. Note here how Justice Harlan has combined the question of definition with another of the themes that runs throughout our course—the power of judges to decide constitutional questions and the issue of what should be left to the political process or to the people themselves.

    C. Consider what might happen if we followed the course suggested by Justice Harlan; that is, consider a constitutional amendment that prohibits pornography and obscenity.

        1. Is it clear that the Court would be out of the business of considering whether and when certain kinds of pornography or obscenity violate the First Amendment?

2. What about a pornographic work that is simultaneously political?

3. Feminist legal theory has argued that all forms of pornography are deeply political because they embrace the subordination of women.

4. A new constitutional amendment prohibiting pornography and obscenity would come in conflict with the First Amendment freedom of speech, and a court would eventually have to rule whether (and, if so, how) to reconcile the new amendment with the First Amendment or whether some constitutional values are even more important than freedom of expression.

D. Finally, in *Roth*, Justice Douglas, dissenting, likewise rejected the majority's formulation, arguing, "I reject too the implication that the problems of freedom of speech … are to be resolved by weighing against the values of free expression the judgment of the Court that a particular form of that expression has 'no redeeming social importance.'"

E. In this and other cases, we can fairly ask: How does the test work in practice?

1. Following *Roth*, the Court found almost all forms of obscenity, except for hard-core pornography, protected by the Constitution.

2. The *Roth* definition simply failed to give lower courts the kind of guidance that would be necessary to provide for a workable test.

II. In *Miller v. California* (1973), the Court again picked up the issue of definition.

A. As in *Roth*, some kinds of pornography are not protected by the First Amendment. The Court began by acknowledging that state and local governments may take steps to "maintain a decent society."

B. The majority in *Miller* rejected the *Roth* test in favor of a new three-part standard for determining obscenity.

C. Under the new test, a work is obscene if:

1. The average person, applying contemporary community standards, would find that the work, taken as a whole, appeals to the prurient interest;

2. The work depicts or describes, in a patently offensive way, sexual conduct specifically defined by the applicable state law; and

3. The work, taken as a whole, lacks serious literary, artistic, political, or scientific value.

D. Let's look at each part of this three-prong test.

1. The average person, applying contemporary community standards, would find that the work, taken as a whole, appeals to the prurient interest.

   a. Who is the average person? It is the job of the jury to speak for the average person.

   b. What is the relevant community?

   c. What is prurient interest? Courts have defined this as "shameful" or "sinful" interest in sexuality.

2. The work depicts or describes, in a patently offensive way, sexual conduct specifically defined by the applicable state law.

   a. The state law must define such conduct with a certain level of detail; otherwise, citizens can't know what is prohibited.

   b. "Patently offensive representations or descriptions of ultimate sexual acts, normal or perverted, actual or simulated, or alternatively, patently offensive representations or descriptions of masturbation, excretory functions, and lewd exhibition of the genitals."

3. The work, taken as a whole, lacks serious literary, artistic, political, or scientific value.

   a. What if the work in question violates prongs one and two but satisfies prong three?

   b. And who decides? Remember, it is the same jury, representing the community, that took up prongs one and two.

4. This suggests that *Miller* sets out a process for resolving pornography cases but doesn't really get to the underlying, fundamental question, just as Justice Harlan suggested in *Roth*: When, if ever, should some kinds of pornography merit protection as speech, and when and why, if ever, should other kinds of social interests and concerns outweigh freedom of expression?

E. Notwithstanding the seeming precision of the new test, since *Miller*, the courts have continued to struggle with basic definitional issues, even as they have seemed to warm to suggestions that obscenity and pornography sometimes debase "family life, community welfare, and the development of the human personality," as the Court noted in *Paris Adult Theatre I v. Slaton* (1973).

F. In some recent cases, for example, the Court has begun to consider the doctrine of the secondary effects of pornography in the community, suggesting, for example, that in areas where there are pornographic bookstores and theaters, there may be secondary effects, such as increased crime rates and an increase in prostitution.

G. One of the best examples of this new approach is in the case of *Barnes v. Glen Theater*, decided in 1991.

1. In this case, the Court sustained an Indiana public decency statute as applied to nude dancing as a form of entertainment.

2. Three justices—Rehnquist, Kennedy, and O'Connor—were willing to admit that nude dancing might well have an expressive dimension, though they did not inquire directly into the nature of the message that might be communicated.

III. The Court's efforts to construct obscenity jurisprudence have also been hampered by the rapid advance of technology, especially as evidenced by the Court's cases involving the Internet.

A. Thus, in *Reno v. American Civil Liberties Union* (1997), the Court found unconstitutional two key provisions of the Communications Decency Act of 1996 designed to prevent minors from exposure to indecent and patently offensive communications on the Internet.

B. In his majority opinion, Justice Stevens ruled that a federal law prohibiting intentional transmission of obscene or indecent messages to minors is unconstitutional. In distinguishing the case from others involving indecent material on television and radio, the Court observed that the Internet is "a unique and wholly new medium of worldwide communication."

    1. The first key question would seem to be: In what ways is the Internet unique? Is it unique because, unlike some other broadcast media, the resource is "unlimited"?

    2. Is it unique because it transcends state or national boundaries?

C. More recently, in *Ashcroft v. Free Speech Coalition* (2002), the Court struck down a part of the Child Pornography Protection Act that regulated "virtual child pornography."

    1. Of course, a central problem here was the inherent ambiguity in such a prohibition.

    2. However, the state's efforts to protect children on the Internet might survive in other contexts if the government can overcome that ambiguity.

D. One similarity in these two cases is that the government sought to restrict expression in order to advance another interest—in both of the cases, obviously, the asserted interest was to protect children in society.

IV. Another important area in the fight against obscenity involves the effort to define pornography as a violation of the civil rights of women.

A. Catherine A. MacKinnon and Andrea Dworkin, who drafted an anti-pornography statute adopted by the city of Indianapolis, spearheaded much of the early impetus for these efforts.

B. The statute prohibited "trafficking" in pornography and provided that anyone injured by someone who had seen or read pornographic materials could sue the maker or seller of the materials.

C. In *American Booksellers Association, Inc. v. Hudnut* (U.S. Court of Appeals, 7th Circuit, 1985), a circuit court ruled the statute unconstitutional.

    1. Judge Easterbrook wrote, "Indianapolis justifies the ordinance on the ground that pornography affects thoughts…. [W]e accept the premises of this legislation. Depictions of subordination tend to perpetuate subordination."

    2. The judge also noted, though, that "this simply demonstrates the power of pornography as speech."

    3. Precisely because pornography can influence some people (in this case, men) to harm others (in this case, women and children), it is speech—and not just speech but consequential speech—and, therefore, must be protected by the First Amendment.

V. Judge Easterbrook's quote is a nice place to end, because it reminds us that a robust commitment to freedom of expression means that we may sometimes have to see, hear, and read things that are deeply offensive or that assault our good sense.

A. When, if ever, is that assault not only on our sensibilities but also on basic constitutional values, such as dignity and equality?

B. That was the logic of the Indianapolis statute, and that is the topic raised by the decision in *Hudnut*: When, if ever, must we regulate or moderate our commitment to freedom of speech simultaneous with our commitment to protecting human dignity?

C. We will take that question up in our next lecture, when we consider the problems involved with hate speech and fighting words.

Essential Reading:

Roth v. United States (1957).

Miller v. California (1973).

Reno v. American Civil Liberties Union (1997).

Ashcroft v. Free Speech Coalition (2002).

American Booksellers Association, Inc. v. Hudnut (U.S. Court of Appeals, 7th Circuit, 1985).

Kommers, Finn, and Jacobsohn, *American Constitutional Law*, chapter 7, pp. 372–375.

Supplementary Reading:

Donald A. Downs, *The New Politics of Pornography*.

Lawrence Lessig, "Reading the Constitution in Cyberspace," 45 *Emory Law Journal* 869 (1996).

Catherine A. MacKinnon, *Only Words*.

Nadine Strossen, *Defending Pornography: Free Speech, Sex, and the Fight for Women's Rights*.

Questions to Consider:

1. Why should the First Amendment protect only those works that have redeeming social value, or serious artistic, literary, political, or scientific value? What theory or understanding of the purposes of the speech clauses would support such a rule?

2. The tension between liberty and community looms large in the obscenity cases. But exactly what do these terms mean? What, precisely, is the liberty interest in producing or having access to pornographic materials? And precisely what interests does the state advance when it prohibits them? Having identified these competing interests, is there a clear constitutional rule for balancing them?

3. Consider another aspect of this problem: In *Miller*, the Court does try to identify the sorts of interests a state or community might have in prohibiting certain kinds of pornography and obscenity. What reasons does the Court offer for entrusting such decisions to smaller local communities instead of the nation as a whole?

Lecture Twenty-One—Transcript
Indecency and Obscenity

In the past few lectures, we have struggled with a series of classic First Amendment problems. For example, in Lecture Nineteen, we explored the so-called internal security or subversive speech cases, and in Lecture Twenty, we took up the problems of symbolic speech and expressive conduct. In both areas, as we saw, the Court has constructed a complicated jurisprudence, a jurisprudence that centers on a variety of doctrinal tests, such as the clear and present danger test or the four-part *O'Brien* test for regulating symbolic speech. And implicit in both areas was also a problem of definition: What is *speech*? What isn't? We will follow the same path in this lecture.

In this lecture we ask: Is pornography speech? This is, in many ways, a question of definition. And the Court's efforts to provide a definition have resulted in a set of doctrinal tests that we will need to consider. So, we will take up the case of *Miller v. California*— decided in 1973, where the Court asked, "Is pornography speech?" and answered with a resounding, "Sometimes." *Miller* provided some support for the efforts of state and local governments to maintain what the Court called "a decent society" and, in so doing, that *Miller* Court offered a three-part test designed to distinguish between what must be protected speech and what is sometimes, the Court called, "the crass commercial exploitation of sex." Since the *Miller* case, the Court has continued to struggle with the problem of definition. Those struggles have been further complicated by the rapid advance of technology. Thus, we will take up two cases: *Reno v. American Civil Liberties Union*, decided in 1997, and a second case—*Ashcroft v. Free Speech Coalition*, decided in 2002, where the Court considered the complicated intersection of Internet pornography and the protection of minors. After we conclude with those two cases, I want to end the lecture by taking up the question I think is hidden behind every First Amendment inquiry we have taken up and that is certainly hidden in today's cases. That question is simply this: What are we to do as a constitutional community if the values that inform the First Amendment, such as freedom of expression and the development of autonomy, what do we do if those values seem to conflict with other constitutional values, such as equality or human dignity?

To begin, as I suggested, the Court's jurisprudence concerning pornography goes back some time. Perhaps the first important case the Court considered was *Roth v. United States*, decided as far back as 1957. Before we unpack that decision, I want to make it clear that in *Roth* the Court held plainly without question that obscenity is not protected by the First Amendment. Sadly, that one bit of clarity is probably the *only* bit of clarity that exists in *Roth* or, indeed, in any of the Court's subsequent cases. Although the Court in *Roth* concluded that obscenity is not necessarily constitutionally protected, it could not agree upon a definition of obscenity proper. In his majority opinion for the Court, Justice Brennan wrote, and here I want to quote him: "All ideas having even the slightest redeeming social importance…have the full protection [of the First Amendment].… But implicit in the history of the First Amendment is the rejection of obscenity as utterly without redeeming social importance." I strongly suspect that many of you have heard that phrase "utterly without redeeming social importance" at one point or another. It is worth asking, first, "What does it mean?" and, second, "How could one ever come to any clear constitutionally grounded understanding about what kinds of speech actually *do* have social importance?"

I want to concentrate just briefly on that second question. A number of critics of the *Roth* Court have raised a single objection. That single objection—it is an important objection—is this: Who is the Court to determine which kinds of speech have "redeeming social importance"? I think you can see the problem here. The difficulty for most of us is that it appears to set the Court on a course of inquiry, on a course of the exploration into the value of the speech itself. I'm not sure we want any Court to assess whether speech should be protected on the basis of whether the Court thinks the speech is important or with value. Consider just this one aspect of the problem: Where does the Constitution give the Court any guidance about which kinds of speech are sufficiently important to merit protection and which kinds of speech are just so without value that no one ought to care about them? We have explored consistently throughout this course the difficulties that surround judicial decision-making when that decision-making process cannot rely on the constitutional text for any clear or coherent guidance, and that seems to be precisely the kind of difficulty that is raised by this inquiry into redeeming social importance.

In a separate opinion, Justice Harlan accused the majority of begging the question. What question was that? The definition of pornography itself. So, Justice Harlan wrote—and again I want to quote from his opinion—"We deal with highly emotional, not rational, questions. To many, the Song of Solomon is obscene. I do not think we, the judges, were ever given the constitutional power to make definitions of obscenity. If it is to be defined, let the people debate and decide by a constitutional amendment...." Note here how Justice Harlan has combined the question of definition with another of the themes that runs throughout our course—the power of judges to decide constitutional questions. Here, he has said explicitly that the obscenity—or the definition of obscenity—is precisely the kind of question that ought to be left to the political process or to the people themselves. Consider what might happen if we followed the course suggested by Justice Harlan. Consider, in other words, a constitutional amendment that prohibits pornography and obscenity, and does so with a certain degree of care and detail so that we might have some real guidance about what is obscene and what is not. Is it clear that the Court would have no role to play once the people have spoken?

Imagine a situation where some kind of pornographic work is also a political work. Now, I don't actually want to do that for you. I will leave it to you to imagine some situations in which pornography might be simultaneously political. But, if you have difficulty doing that, it wouldn't hurt to go out, for example, and to consider feminist legal theory, which has argued, for example, on many occasions, that all forms of pornography are deeply political because they embrace the subordination of women. So, imagine something that falls into that category. It seems to me that we might say, in such a case, that our new constitutional amendment prohibiting pornography is in fundamental tension with the First Amendment requiring freedom of speech or protecting freedom of expression. Somebody, presumably a court, will eventually have to open up the question about whether or not the second amendment—not the Second Amendment concerning arms, but my second hypothetical amendment prohibiting pornography—can be reconciled with the underlying provisions of the First Amendment concerning speech or whether or not there is some set of constitutional values represented by the rejection of pornography that is more important, even more important than freedom of expression. It is precisely that problem to which I will return at the end of this lecture.

Finally, just quickly, there was also a dissent in *Roth*—a dissent by Justice Douglas—who likewise rejected the majority's formulation of the "utterly without redeeming social importance" test. He said, and I quote: "I reject too the implication that the problems of freedom of speech...are to be resolved by weighing against the values of free expression the judgment of the Court that a particular form of that expression has 'no redeeming social importance.'"

One question we might fairly ask every time the Court proposes a test is simply this: How does the test work in practice? So, let's ask that question. What happened to *Roth*? Or, I should say, what were the constitutional politics surrounding obscenity following *Roth*? I think I can give you a fairly straightforward answer in this case. Following *Roth*, the Court found almost all forms of obscenity, except the most hard-core pornography, to be protected by the Constitution—or I should say, in particular, by the First Amendment. That's the practical result. There is a second practical result. The *Roth* definition of pornography "utterly without redeeming social importance" simply failed to give lower courts the kind of guidance that would be necessary to provide for a workable test.

So, in 1973, in the leading case of *Miller v. California*, the Court again picked up the issue of definition. Before we actually get to the Court's definition of obscenity, I want to stress one point of continuity between *Roth* and *Miller*. Remember, in *Roth*, the ultimate holding was that some kinds of pornography are not protected by the First Amendment. The Court continued that theme in *Miller*, arguing that the state, the community, that "we the people," sometimes do have a legitimate interest in maintaining what the Court called "a decent society." That is the premise; there are times when it is okay for the state, for the community, to prohibit pornography because such prohibitions advance a larger social interest. That's where the Court begins; it then develops its famous three-part test.

I want to just briefly describe the three parts for you, and then I'll spend a little bit of time talking about each of them. But, I just want to run through the three parts first. Under the new *Miller* three-part test, a work is obscene and may be constitutionally prohibited if, number one, the average person, applying contemporary community standards, would find that the work, taken as a whole, appeals to the prurient interest. Prong two: A work may be described constitutionally as obscene if the work depicts or describes, in a patently offensive way, sexual conduct specifically defined by the applicable state law, and if that state law is sufficiently precise to give citizens some specific guidance about what patently offensive works are. That's prong two. Then, prong three: A work may be taken to be obscene if the work, taken as a whole, lacks serious literary, artistic, political, or scientific value. So, what does *Miller* give us? *Miller* gives us this three-part test and what happens—in the abstract—is that any particular potential pornographic or obscene work must be measured in accordance with these three prongs.

I want to say just a brief word or two about each of the prongs, and I'm going to do them more in the form of rhetorical questions than questions that I really want to answer at any length. Consider the first prong: The average person, applying contemporary community standards, would find that the work, taken as a whole, appeals to the prurient interest. Question A: Just who is the average person? My overly brief answer is simply this: The average person is the person who speaks through the jury. The average person is actually a collective institution. It is the job of the jury to speak for the average person. Then, we have to ask, "What is the relevant political community?" Remember that average person has to apply contemporary community standards. What is the community? You can imagine why we want to ask this question, can you not? The community that has these applicable standards might well be very different if we are speaking about Peoria, Illinois, and Hollywood, California. Then, finally, "What is a prurient interest?" Here, the Court has said repeatedly that a prurient interest is an interest that appeals to the "shameful" sides of sexuality; it appeals to our "shameful" or "sinful"—I'm a little reluctant to describe it as sinful, but some courts have—our "sinful" interest in sexuality.

Consider prong two: The work depicts or describes, in a patently offensive way, sexual conduct specifically defined by the applicable state law. The impetus here is straightforward. The act must tell the community at large, must tell us as citizens, with a certain degree of detail, what is actually prohibited and what is acceptable. The Court has gone on to say that this is typically the level of detail that is necessary—and here I want to quote—the state law might, for example, describe "patently offensive representations or descriptions of ultimate sexual acts, normal or perverted, actual or simulated, or alternatively, patently offensive representations or descriptions of masturbation, excretory functions, and lewd exhibition of the genitals." That's what this applicable state law must do.

Then, finally, there is the third prong of the *Miller* test: The work, taken as a whole, lacks serious literary, artistic, political, or scientific value. I want to give you *my* opinion on this. I want to stress that it is *my* opinion, that the Court has yet to fully or squarely decide this, but I am of the opinion that prong three, this third inquiry under the *Miller* test, by definition trumps the first two prongs. Here's what I mean: What if the pornographic work in question does violate the average person's sense of what appropriate community standards are? In other words, we could ban the act under prong one. What if the work does depict, in a patently offensive way, appropriate sexual conduct defined specifically by state law? Imagine, in other words, a pornographic work that we can plainly ban under prongs one and two, but then somebody says, "Wait, that act, nevertheless, has some kind of serious literary, artistic, political, or scientific value." Is it not the case, I would ask, again only rhetorically, that the saving grace of prong three must mean that even truly awful, patently offensive works of sexuality that clearly violate the average person's sense of a community's standards must, nevertheless, be constitutionally protected because somebody thinks that it has serious literary, artistic, political, or scientific value?

My inquiry—and it really is just an inquiry; I don't know the answer to it—suggests a more fundamental question surrounding this complicated three-part test. It suggests the same kind of question we had with *Roth*. It suggests, in other words, that the Court has yet to give us any clear sense about how to resolve the underlying, fundamental question. That question is, again: When, if ever, should some kinds of pornography merit protection as speech, and when and why, if ever, should other kinds of social interests and concerns outweigh freedom of expression? I would propose to you that there is nothing in the *Miller* test itself that directly tackles that fundamental, underlying question. Since *Miller*, you probably will not be surprised to hear, the courts have continued to struggle with the most basic of definitional questions here. However, although they continue to struggle with the very definition of pornography and obscenity, the courts have seemed, as a collectivity, to begin to warm to arguments, to warm to suggestions, that obscenity and pornography sometimes, as the Court once said, debase "family life, community welfare, and the development of the human personality." That Court was the Court speaking in *Paris Adult Theatre I v. Slaton*, decided also in the year 1973, the same year as *Miller*. I mention that case because it harkens us back to the fundamental premise of *Roth* and to the fundamental premise of *Miller*. Notwithstanding our complicated inquiry into the test, there is also a fundamental truth that emerges from those two cases, which emerges from cases also like *Paris Adult Theatre*, and that is simply this: There are times when the state does have a legitimate interest in shutting down pornography.

In very recent cases, the Court has called that collection of interests the doctrine of the secondary effects of pornography. Here's what the Court means by that: In an area, for example, where there are pornographic bookstores or theaters, the Court has said there may be secondary effects, such as increased crime rates or increases in prostitution. The Court has also said that the community's interest, the government's interest, in responding to those secondary effects is sometimes strong enough to shut down whatever speech might be involved in pornography. Perhaps the clearest expression of this logic occurred in the case of *Barnes v. Glen Theater*, decided in 1991. In this case, *Barnes*, the Court sustained an Indiana public decency statute as applied to nude dancing as a form of entertainment. Three justices—Kennedy, O'Connor, and Rehnquist—were willing to admit that nude dancing might well have an expressive dimension to it, although they did not inquire directly into the nature of the message that might be communicated. They went on to conclude, however, that notwithstanding the expressive component that might be involved in this activity, the state's interest, our community's interest, in responding to the secondary effects of such establishments is sufficiently important to outweigh the First Amendment claim involved in that case. The Court's efforts to construct its obscenity jurisprudence in other words—in recent years, at least—have been profoundly influenced by the Court's willingness to inquire into the kinds of interest that the state might advance to regulate pornography.

I now want to switch emphasis just for a second to talk about one of the more specific kinds of interests that the state might want to advance. Consider, for example, our undoubted, collected interest in protecting minors from exposure to pornography or to obscenity more generally. The Court addressed this interest in two important cases that I want to spend just a little bit of time on. In the first of these, *Reno v. American Civil Liberties Union*, decided in 1997, the Court found unconstitutional two key provisions of the Communications Decency Act of 1996. That act was designed to prevent minors from exposure to indecent and patently offensive communications on the Internet. The Court had no doubt that that was a legitimate state interest. Nevertheless, Justice Stevens, writing for the majority, declared that a federal law prohibiting the intentional transmission of obscene or indecent messages to minors was unconstitutional.

There was one other dimension to this case that is worth exploring, just briefly. Justice Stevens sought to distinguish this case from other Supreme Court cases involving indecent material on the television or on radio. Here, the Court observed that the Internet is "a unique and wholly new medium of worldwide communication." I think it is important to say: In what ways is the Internet unique from these other forms of communication? I suspect the answer is the following: The Internet is unique because, unlike other forms of broadcast media, the resource is "unlimited." It is unlimited in the sense that nearly everyone may have exposure to it or can gain access to it, and it is unlimited and unique because, as a medium, it transcends national, or state, or domestic boundaries, which makes the problem of regulation infinitely more complicated, according to Justice Stevens.

More recently, in *Ashcroft v. Free Speech Coalition*, decided in 2002, the Court struck down a part of the Child Pornography Protection Act that regulated what it called "virtual child pornography." Without going into any great length on this case, I think you can see immediately what the constitutional difficulty is. It is profoundly ambiguous to talk about "virtual child pornography." One might imagine, however, that the state's efforts to protect children on the Internet might survive in other contexts if the government can overcome that problem of ambiguity, can overcome that problem of vagueness.

Now, in these two cases—*Reno* and *Ashcroft*—we could say that the government sought to restrict expression to advance another important interest—in both cases, obviously, the asserted interest was the protection of children in society, of undoubted importance. I want to continue this examination of the kinds of interests that the state might advance or want to protect as a reason for overcoming speech rights in a slightly different area. The area I want to take up now involves the fight against obscenity defined in a particular way—defined, in other words, as a means of protecting the civil rights of women. This is an important and extremely complicated area. As far back as the 1970s, some feminist theorists had begun to argue that pornography might be best considered as a civil rights violation of women. That kind of academic argument was transformed into real political action in the late 1970s, early 1980s. In particular, I am thinking of the work of Catherine A. MacKinnon and Andrea Dworkin, who drafted what they called an "anti-pornography statute." This statute was adopted by the city of Indianapolis. The statute in question prohibited what it called "trafficking" in pornography, and it provided that anyone who had been injured by someone who had read or seen pornographic materials could sue the maker or the seller of the materials.

I want to make sure we understand what's going on here. The civil rights violation consists presumably of two parts—actual, physical harm done to the individual and, secondly, harm that was caused by that individual having had exposure to pornographic materials. Now, the Supreme Court never took up this case, but the 7th Circuit did. In that case, *American Booksellers Association, Inc. v. Hudnut*, Judge Frank Easterbrook, writing for the 7th Circuit in 1985, concluded that the Indianapolis statute was unconstitutional. I want to quote a little bit from his opinion. He began by saying: "Indianapolis justifies the ordinance on the ground that pornography affects thoughts…. [W]e accept the premises of this legislation. Depictions of subordination tend to perpetuate subordination." The judge continued, however, and again I quote by saying that "this simply demonstrates the power of pornography as speech." Think about what this means here. The premise behind the legislation was that sometimes pornography may have the power to influence some of us to harm others. In this case, it may influence some men to harm women and children. The Court, speaking through Frank Easterbrook, accepts that proposition, saying, "Yes, that may absolutely be true, but it is precisely because it *is* true that it tells us that pornography is speech. It's not just speech but consequential, important speech." Then you can see what the next step in the logic will be: It is precisely because it is speech that it must be protected by the First Amendment. That 7th Circuit Court went on to conclude that the civil rights legislation involved in this statute was, in fact, unconstitutional because it infringed on First Amendment values.

Judge Easterbrook's opinion is a nice place to end this lecture, because it reminds us, at least in part, that a robust commitment to freedom of expression means that sometimes we may have to hear, see, and read things that are deeply offensive or that assault our good sense. When, if ever, is such an assault not only upon our sensibilities as human beings but also upon basic constitutional values, such as human dignity and equality? That was the logic of the Indianapolis statute, and that is the topic raised by the decision in *Hudnut*: When, if ever, must we regulate or moderate our commitment simultaneously to freedom of speech and to protecting human dignity? We will take that up in our next lecture, when we consider the problems involved with hate speech and fighting words.

Lecture Twenty-Two
Hate Speech and Fighting Words

Scope:

Consider the following: Should a liberal society suppress racist propaganda or hate speech directed at particular groups? Should it regulate the use of epithets or words that offend, hurt, or simply shock those who hear the message? These questions are important because they highlight the tension between our commitment to freedom of expression and our collective interest in protecting such values as civility, social morality, and public order. We begin with *Chaplinsky v. New Hampshire* (1942), in which the Court ruled that fighting words "contribute nothing to the expression of ideas or truth." We conclude with *Texas v. Johnson* (1989), the infamous flag-burning case, and *R.A.V. v. City of St. Paul* (1992), in which the Court struck down a Minneapolis ordinance banning certain kinds of hate speech.

Outline

I. When, if ever, may society limit speech because the expression in question is racist, bigoted, or hateful? May society limit speech because it offends or tarnishes cherished national symbols, such as the flag? The Supreme Court has struggled with each of these issues in the last few decades, and like its work in other First Amendment issues, the decisions highlight the tension between liberty and community.

II. Although such concepts as *hate speech* may seem of recent vintage, the Court has a long history in such areas. In two early cases, for example, the Court tried to balance speech rights against a community's interest in prohibiting offensive speech. One of these was *Chaplinsky v. New Hampshire*, decided in 1942. However, I begin with a later case, *Beauharnais v. Illinois* (1952), because it dealt with racially offensive speech. As it turns out, the Court's most recent hate speech cases also often involve race, so I think it best to begin and end on that topic.

A. In *Beauharnais v. Illinois* (1952), the Court considered the constitutionality of a statute that made it a crime to defame any class of persons based on race or creed as "criminal, unchaste, or lacking in virtue...."

    1. In upholding the statute, the majority noted that it would be "arrant dogmatism" for the Court to deny a state legislature the authority to protect society against such attacks.

    2. It is important to note that we might describe the conflict here as between our commitments to freedom of speech and to equality, as well as between individual and community.

    3. In this case, then, the Court weighed the balance in favor of community, but it recognized that in other cases, the balance might be struck differently.

    4. In an important dissent, Justice Douglas wrote: "Intemperate speech is the distinctive characteristic of man. Hotheads blow off and release destructive energy in the process. So it has been from the beginning, so it will be throughout time. The Framers of the Constitution knew human nature as well as we do." This seems to recall the safety valve defense of freedom of expression that we considered in an earlier lecture.

B. I mentioned an earlier case that laid some of the groundwork for *Beauharnais*. In the important case of *Chaplinsky v. New Hampshire* (1942), the Court considered a New Hampshire statute that forbade the use of "any offensive, derisive, or annoying word to any other person ... with an intent to deride, offend, or annoy him."

    1. The facts involved a Jehovah's Witness, Chaplinsky, who made a series of inflammatory remarks in public in Rochester, New Hampshire.

    2. A local police officer arrested Chaplinsky, who had called the officer a "God-damned racketeer" and a "fascist."

C. In his opinion for the Court, Justice Murphy noted that the First Amendment does not protect "fighting words," or words that tend "by their very utterance" to injure or to "incite to an immediate breach of the peace."

1. What would it mean to say that a word "by its very utterance" tends to injure or incite a breach of peace?

2. Justice Murphy elaborated: "There are certain well-defined and narrowly limited classes of speech, the prevention and prohibition of which have never been thought to raise any constitutional problem. These include the lewd and the obscene, the profane, the libelous, and the insulting or 'fighting' words...."

3. The Court noted that fighting words "contribute nothing to the expression of ideas or truth" and that their value is outweighed by society's interest in "order and morality."

4. In this case, then, the Court explicitly measured the speech against a particular theory about why speech is valuable in a democracy. It measured it, too, against our collective interests in other values, such as "order and morality," the prevention of harm to others, or perhaps, the promotion of human dignity.

5. Finally, we should ask if there is some standard that allows us to distinguish fighting from nonfighting words. The Court suggested that context would be a critical part of such a test.

III. Context was also important in our next case. In *Texas v. Johnson* (1989), the Court considered another kind of offensive expression—the burning of an American flag.

   A. In a 5–4 opinion, a divided Court struck down a Texas statute that prohibited the "desecration of venerated objects," such as a U.S. flag. In this case, a man had burned the flag in protest at the Republican National Convention in Dallas.

   B. In his opinion for the Court, Justice Brennan overturned the conviction because, in seeking to preserve the integrity of the flag as a symbol of national unity, Texas had tread directly on the content of the intended message: "If there is a bedrock principle underlying the First Amendment, it is that the government may not prohibit expression of an idea simply because society finds the idea itself offensive or disagreeable."

C. In dissent, Chief Justice Rehnquist denied that the flag burning was an "essential part of any exposition of ideas" and, indeed, compared it instead to "an inarticulate grunt." In addition, the Chief argued that the act conveyed nothing that "could not have been conveyed and was not conveyed just as forcefully in a dozen different ways."

D. In a separate dissent, Justice Stevens noted, "the value of the flag as a symbol cannot be measured."

E. It is important, too, to consider a part of Justice Kennedy's extraordinary concurring opinion. What is important is not so much what it has to say about the First Amendment, but rather what it says about one of the great themes—or, if you prefer, one of the great unanswered questions—of this course: Do the justices just make it up? Justice Kennedy wrote: "The hard fact is that sometimes we must make decisions we do not like. We make them because they are right—right in the sense that the law and the Constitution as we see them compel the result."

IV. The Court revisited *Chaplinsky*'s fighting words doctrine in the important case of *R.A.V. v. City of St. Paul* (1992), a case that recalls, in some ways, *Beauharnais*.

A. In this case, the Court addressed the constitutionality of a St. Paul ordinance that forbade placing "on public or private property a symbol, object, appellation, characterization, or graffiti, including, but not limited to, a burning cross or Nazi swastika, which one knows or has reasonable grounds to know arouses anger, alarm, or resentment in others on the basis of race, color, creed, religion, or gender."

B. The Court was unanimous in striking down the law, but the Court could muster only a bare majority of 5–4 in favor of an opinion by Justice Scalia that found the statute unconstitutional as *viewpoint discrimination*. In Justice Scalia's opinion, the statute was unconstitutional because it prohibited only certain kinds of fighting words but not all fighting words.

    1. This amounted to a kind of censorship, Justice Scalia wrote. Again, we sometimes refer to this as *viewpoint discrimination*.

    2. There is, also, a principle of equality implied by a prohibition on viewpoint discrimination.

    3. Finally, Justice Scalia also argued, "An ordinance not limited to the favored topics … would have precisely the same beneficial effect."

C. In a subsequent case, *Virginia v. Black* (2003), the Court upheld a Virginia statute that provided for enhanced criminal penalties in cases involving racial "hate crimes." The difference between that case and *R.A.V.*, wrote Justice O'Connor, was that the statute in *Virginia* was directed to conduct, not speech.

    1. Justice O'Connor wrote: "The First Amendment permits Virginia to outlaw cross burning, because burning a cross is a particularly virulent form of intimidation."

    2. One might respond that this does not squarely face up to Justice Scalia's opinion in *R.A.V.* or to the question of whether such actions should be considered speech, no matter how offensive.

V. These cases remind us that speech may not be shut down simply because it offends or shocks. But they may also show that the traditional rationales for protecting speech may be less persuasive when the point is not so much about the communication of ideas and is instead more about the vilification and intimidation of others.

Essential Reading:

Chaplinsky v. New Hampshire (1942).

Texas v. Johnson (1989).

R.A.V. v. City of St. Paul (1992).

Wisconsin v. Mitchell (1993).

Kommers, Finn, and Jacobsohn, *American Constitutional Law*, chapter 7, pp. 370–372.

Kent Greenawalt, *Fighting Words*.

Supplementary Reading:

Richard Abel, *Speech and Respect*.

Donald A. Downs, *Nazis in Skokie: Freedom, Community, and the First Amendment.*

Questions to Consider:

1. Assume that some speech is deeply offensive, perhaps because it is racist or bigoted. What understanding of the purposes of the First Amendment requires the community to tolerate such speech? Does the argument that freedom of speech is a necessary mechanism for the discovery of truth require such tolerance, for example? Do the speech rights of individuals necessarily outweigh another's interest in human dignity or society's interest in civilized discourse?

2. Is the integrity of the community at issue in the flag-burning case? One might argue that the flag is a visible symbol of social integrity or that it shelters the memory and character of our shared community. Doesn't the protection of the flag ensure, or help to ensure, that the community will exist over time, beyond the lives of the individuals that comprise it? Alternatively, is the meaning of America, which the flag also symbolizes, our freedom to disagree on or about any institution, idea, convention, or symbol, no matter how sacred or cherished?

3. What constitutional value or values, if any, trump freedom of expression?

Lecture Twenty-Two—Transcript
Hate Speech and Fighting Words

Should a liberal society suppress racist propaganda or hate speech directed at particular groups? Should it regulate the use of words or slogans that offend, hurt, or simply shock those who hear the message? These questions are important because they highlight the tension between our commitment to freedom of expression and our collective interest, our undoubted interest, in protecting values such as civility, social morality, and even public order. In this lecture, we will begin to take up these questions, starting with such cases as *Beauharnais v. Illinois* and *Chaplinsky v. New Hampshire,* where the Court considered whether or not these words should be banned because they offended these fundamental values of human dignity or public decency, or public order, more generally.

Although concepts like hate speech may seem like they are of fairly recent vintage, in truth the Court's work dates back at least from the 1940s, and the Court's first decision was in *Chaplinsky v. New Hampshire* (decided in 1942). However, that is not where I'm going to begin.

I'm going to begin with a somewhat later case, the case of *Beauharnais v. Illinois* (decided in 1952). And I take up these cases in reverse chronological order for a substantive reason. As we shall see, *Beauharnais* dealt largely with questions of racially offensive speech, and the Court's most recent work in cases such as *RAV v. St. Paul* or *Virginia v. Black*, the Court has returned to that theme. So, I hope to come full circle in this lecture by starting with racially offensive words and ending with racially offensive words; or, more generally, with hate speech that may be grounded on questions of race or, perhaps, sometimes creed, ethnicity, and gender.

So let's begin with *Beauharnais v. Illinois*. This is an important case because, in it, the Court, for the first time, considered what might be called a statute that tried to criminalize not simply thoughts, but speech. It's a very interesting statute. The statute made it a crime to defame any class of persons, based on race or creed as, "criminal, unchaste, or lacking in virtue…."

I think it's worth stopping for a moment and thinking about what that statute does. It says that, if you criticize another human being based on his or her race or his or her creed; and you call that person "unchaste," or you defame them, or you suggest that they lack in virtue; that that itself is a crime. You need not do anything to another individual; you need only criticize that individual based on one of these outlawed criteria. That is a fascinating statute, one that would seem obviously to implicate First Amendment freedoms. Perhaps it's less obvious, but it also implicates our commitment to equality as a society as well; and this is the first time in this course that we've had an opportunity to consider a direct conflict between our commitments to freedom of expression and our commitments to equality as well.

Now in upholding the statute, the majority noted that, "it would be arrant dogmatism," for the Court to deny a state legislature the authority to protect the society against such attacks. There was an important dissent in *Beauharnais* by Justice Douglas, and I want to read from his dissent. He said:

> In temperate speech is the distinctive characteristic of man. Hotheads blow off and release destructive energy in the process. So it has been from the beginning, so it will be throughout time. The Framers of the Constitution knew human nature as well as we do.

And that's the end of Justice Douglas' dissent. In other words, he wants to suggest that "in temperate speech," of the kind prohibited by this statute, is an inevitable characteristic and an irreducible characteristic of the human condition; and it is folly to try to prohibit it. But I think he means more than simply folly. I think he means also that it is probably dangerous for the state to try to prohibit it as well; hence, the use of the phrase, "hotheads blow off steam." I think the suggestion here is that, without recourse to speech, hotheads may well resort to violence or to other forms of socially unacceptable behavior. Speech may be the least of our problems with such individuals.

Now, we started with the *Beauharnais;* but there was, as I suggested, an earlier case, *Chaplinsky v. New Hampshire* (decided in 1942). The decision in *Chaplinsky* really provides the bedrock foundation for what happened in *Beauharnais*. *Chaplinsky* is among my most favorite of cases. In 1942, Chaplinsky, a Jehovah's Witness, traveled to Rochester, New Hampshire; and there on the public green, began to give a set of speeches. It is probably too polite to call them speeches. With a bullhorn, he shouted amazingly offensive things, largely about other religions, largely about Roman Catholics. But he didn't limit himself to Roman Catholics. He was an equal opportunity bigot. He said all sorts of terrible things about everybody who came into his path, including a police officer who was sent there to investigate charges that a riot was about to occur. And in the course of dealing with the police officer, Chaplinsky called him "a goddamned racketeer" and "a fascist." Those might not seem as though they are the most terrible fighting words or hate speech as one has ever heard, but they were sufficiently noxious to have violated what surely must be one of the most interesting statutes ever passed by a state legislature.

New Hampshire had passed a statute that forbade the use "of any offensive, derisive, or annoying word to any other person…with an intent to deride, offend, or annoy him." What an extraordinary statute. One might easily understand why it would be in the state's best interest to prevent fighting words, whatever those mean; but to prevent words or sounds that simply annoy another individual— that's an extraordinary position on speech, but not necessarily a bad one. If I were king, I would happily make that among my first items of business. Surely, the world would be a better place if other people were not allowed to say things that annoy me. I know I would be a happier person.

It's a fascinating case for a lot of other reasons as well, in part because Justice Murphy noted that the First Amendment does not protect so-called fighting words; and then he offered up a definition of "fighting words." Fighting words are words that tend "by their very utterance," he said, to injure or to "incite to an immediate breach of the peace." And, again, I'd like to stop here before we continue with his opinion.

What would it mean to say that a word "injures," or by its "very utterance" tends to breach the peace? I want to continue with this quotation. I want to round it out a bit more to try to get a sense of how Murphy would answer these questions. He wrote:

> There are certain well-defined and narrowly-limited classes of speech, the prevention and prohibition of which have never been thought to raise any constitutional problem. These include the lewd and the obscene, the profane, the libelous, and the insulting or fighting words….[And here's

where the definition comes in] those by which their very utterance inflict injury or tend to incite an immediate breach of the peace.

What kind of a word, through its "very utterance," tends to inflict injury? Now, I will leave this to your imagination, but we can probably all think of words that are profoundly obnoxious; words that insult at the core of one's being. But to say that they cause injury is to assume what counts as an injury. There are no words, I think, that physically harm simply through their utterance; so we must be talking about a different kind of harm; and that should force us to think more carefully about what interests society is truly trying to protect here. I can only think that it might be the kind of equality interest that is later articulated in *Beauharnais v. Illinois*; or, perhaps, it's some larger interest in social morality, or social dignity, or social quietude. Maybe it suggests, in other words, that, in addition to our commitment to freedom of expression—and indeed, part of our commitment to freedom of expression—is also our commitment to ourselves as human beings entitled to a certain core measure of human dignity.

There's another, more straightforward interest, however, and that would be Murphy's insistence that some of these words "tend to incite an immediate breach of the peace." Again, what an extraordinary thing to say, which doesn't suggest necessarily that he was wrong or incorrect, but think of words that might incite a breach of peace. And, probably, we can think of words, or at least slogans, or speech, more generally (as opposed to specific words) that might actually incite others to harm. We considered that when we did the illegal advocacy cases just a few lectures ago.

Now, a couple of other things about this opinion. It's one thing to suggest that these words may harm or may cause injury, and quite another to suggest that, even if they do, we may, nevertheless, have to protect them. That is one possible understanding of the First Amendment; that some words may, in fact, injure, but our commitment to freedom of expression might be so deep, might be so profound, that we have to go ahead and say we're going to protect them anyway. That was not the majority's conclusion.

The majority noted, again, writing through Frank Murphy, that these fighting words "contribute nothing to the expression of ideas or truth, and their value is outweighed by society's interest in order and morality." If this is the case, then, in which the Court specifically, explicitly measured the value of speech against other kinds of social values, and concluded that those other social values trump the value of speech.

One more thing about "fighting words:" context is critically important. When I teach this case, I often ask myself, and I always ask my students the following: What was so terribly obnoxious about calling a police officer a "racketeer" or a "fascist"? Surely, we expect police officers to have a skin that is thick enough to tolerate those kinds of abuses and certainly much worse; but maybe those kinds of abuses were much worse in 1942. It's one thing to call somebody a fascist now. That is a charge that gets traded liberally (perhaps too liberally in our society); but it might have meant something quite different in 1942, just as calling somebody a "racketeer" might have meant something different in 1942.

And Murphy continued by saying that, "it isn't simply the words that are important. It is the way in which they are used, and the overall context in which they are spoken or written." It matters, in other words, what the speaker intends to say; and it matters, to some extent, what the hearer of the words imagines him or herself to be hearing. It is one thing for me to walk up and to call you a fascist; quite another, Murphy would have suggested, for me to walk up and call you a fascist with a broad smile on my face, and to slap you on the back and say, "How are you, old friend, you old fascist?" Those words are disarmed, so to speak, by the context in which I've delivered them and the manner in which I have spoken them. It becomes critically important in all fighting words cases to examine this sense of context.

Context is also critically important in a much later case, in a deeply controversial case, known as *Texas v. Johnson,* decided in 1989. Here we have a different kind of offensive expression—the burning of an American flag. And it is probably worth noting, again, just a little bit, about what the context was. In this case, the young man burned a flag outside the Republican National Convention in Dallas—probably not the smartest place to burn a flag.

In overturning the young man's conviction, Justice Brennan, speaking for the Court, struck down a Texas statute that prohibited, "the desecration of venerated objects," such as the United States flag.

Justice Brennan argued that, "in seeking to preserve the integrity of the flag as a symbol of national unity, Texas had tread directly on the content on the young man's intended message."

He doesn't actually go into any length about what the context of the message is, but one must assume that it's political speech—the burning of a flag outside a political party convention—and that the speech itself must be deeply political in the sense that it's critical, either of the United States government or of the Republican Party, or perhaps of some more specific set of proposals advanced by the Republican Party.

Brennan continued by saying, "The government may not prohibit the expression of an idea simply because society finds the idea itself offensive or disagreeable." I want to stop here for a second. It's possible, I think, to imagine that a flag desecration statute could be upheld as constitutional if it had no intention of shutting down the underlying content. So, if we have flag desecration statutes that are geared only to the proper disposal of a flag, and they had nothing to do with shutting down the underlying message that might be involved in a protest, that would be a different kind of case; but that's not the case we have here. Or, at least, Brennan didn't think that was the kind of case we have here.

In dissent—in a powerful dissent, I should add—Chief Justice Rehnquist denied that flag burning was, "the essential part of any exposition of ideas." Indeed, he said that it was, "an inarticulate grunt." I want to stop here. Assume it was "an inarticulate grunt;" it would still convey meaning, or at least one could argue, and that an "inarticulate grunt" might, nevertheless, be understood by the audience as conveying a particular kind of message. Presumably, "an inarticulate grunt" could be ripe with meaning; and if it is ripe with meaning, then one can't dismiss it as speech by saying it was "inarticulate" or a "grunt." The idea must be, does the activity, does this "inarticulate grunt," have an expressive component to it? And if it does, you can't dismiss it as easily as saying it's inarticulate. One might wonder if that kind of claim is, in itself, deeply elitist.

On the other hand, there's another part of Chief Justice Rehnquist's dissent that I think carries more weight, and which is going to be important as we continue in our lecture. The Chief argued that there was nothing conveyed in the flag burning, "that could not have been conveyed and was not conveyed just as forcefully in a dozen different ways."

Now, think about what the meaning of this proposition is—that we can shut down this mechanism for speech, and it doesn't much matter if we do. It certainly doesn't rise to the status of a constitutional violation, so long as the individual speaking has some alternative methods, some alternative mechanism, for making the same point. This is an important part of the Court's jurisprudence, and a deeply controversial one.

Consider, for example, the following kind of criticism: Is anything really going to convey the same kind of disgust, or angst, or distrust of government that this young man presumably meant to express as burning the flag? Will it be the same speech if, instead of burning the flag, he now is forced to carry a picket sign, which expresses the same underlying message? Perhaps it is. The question becomes, how much can you distinguish the message from the mechanism for the message? And one might argue that, in point of fact, it ought to be a choice that the speaker makes; that that is, itself, a part of the freedom of expression involved, or that ought to be protected—not simply the choice of the underlying message, but the choice for the means of expression of that message.

In a separate dissent, Justice Stevens noted simply, "the value of the flag as a symbol cannot be measured." And presumably the claim here is that some things—just as in *Beauharnais* and *Chaplinsky*— some things are so overwhelmingly important to our collective identity, to our collective experience as Americans, that they trump speech. Now, the difficulty here is that he may well be right. We have to ask ourselves, does the Constitution give us any calculus for knowing when these other values should trump speech, or when speech should be more important? We didn't ask that question in *Beauharnais*, though we should have. We should have asked it in *Chaplinsky,* as well. And I think we need to ask it here.

Assuming there are values like equality or collective identity that are more important than speech, how do we know? What source of constitutional meaning allows us to weigh this balance, and to know that we are weighing the balance in accordance with a constitutional instruction, as opposed to simply weighing them on the basis of our personal preference? I use the phrase, "weighing them on the basis of our personal preference," because that raises a final issue in *Texas v. Johnson*, one not directly relevant, one not only relevant to freedom of speech cases, but relevant to a question we have struggled with throughout this entire course: are judges simply making these opinions up or are they grounded in some objective source of meaning such as the Constitution?

I can't resist saying just a few words about Justice Kennedy's concurring opinion in this case. It's truly a moving opinion. It's a concurring opinion, and he wrote the following: "The hard fact is that sometimes we must make decisions we do not like. We make them because they are right—right in the sense that the law and the Constitution as we see them compel the result."

I hope you are as moved by that quote as I am. He is telling you, as bluntly as any judge knows how, that it is hard work being a Supreme Court justice, and that part of the hard work is the consequence of having to make decisions that you might find personally revolting. It is clear throughout Kennedy's opinion that he finds the speech that is protected in this case deeply offensive. He is deeply troubled by the idea that anybody might burn the flag, but, nevertheless, compelled, or at least he thinks, to argue that it is constitutionally protected. What an extraordinary set of opinions!

Now, *Texas v. Johnson* was decided in 1989. Interestingly, that is roughly the same period of time in which "hate speech" became a new constitutional issue. Hate speech, as a constitutional issue, probably originated in the efforts of the nation's university to pass speech codes; and, to the lesser extent, on the part of employers to pass speech codes, as well.

I use "speech codes," assuming everybody knows what they are. That is not a smart assumption. A speech code, broadly speaking, is a set of provisions that indicate what kinds of words, what kinds of speech patterns, what kinds of phrases are so noxious that they ought to be prohibited in the interest of maintaining some other value in the universities of this country. For example, that other value may be their commitment to freedom of academic inquiry; or alternatively, to equality; or alternatively, to social quiet. The same may well be true of the nation's employers, as well; or in the employment context.

The Court's first real consideration of the fighting words/hate speech doctrines occurred in the important case of *R.A.V. v. The City of St. Paul,* decided in 1992. The facts of this case, as they are so often, are not happy. A number of young teenagers trespassed on somebody's property, and on that property, erected a burning cross. And we all know how fundamentally offensive that kind of speech, if speech it is, might be. In this case, the young men were not arrested for trespass, though they might well have been. They were not arrested for breach of peace, although they might well have been arrested for that, as well. Instead, they were arrested for violating a municipal ordinance that forbade placing on private property—or even public property, I should add—a symbol, an object, an appellation, a characterization, or graffiti, including, but not limited to, a burning cross or a Nazi swastika, which, according to the statute, "one knows or has reasonable grounds to know arouses anger, alarm, or resentment in others," and then—this is an incredibly important part of the statute—"on the basis of race, color, creed, religion, or gender."

Now, I suppose the first thing we ought to be thinking about in *R.A.V.* is that this case doesn't look too terribly different than the old *Beauharnais* case that I started with. Indeed, that was the reason why I started with *Beauharnais* earlier in the lecture. There are similarities, both factually and legally, in the sense that the statutes, while not precisely the same, presumably are involved with both the same set of public interests: public order, public quiet; also, human dignity, equality, and a sense that there are some things that so offend the community that they ought to be prohibited, even if they really do constitute expression.

The Court was unanimous in striking down this law, but it could only find a bare majority of five-to-four supporting an opinion by Justice Scalia that found the statute unconstitutional as a kind of viewpoint discrimination. Here's what he means by "viewpoint discrimination." I'll give you a quick definition, and then I want to try to elaborate on it.

According to Justice Scalia, there is viewpoint discrimination, and viewpoint discrimination is unconstitutional in the following sense: this statute didn't prohibit all forms of hate speech; it didn't prohibit all fighting words; it picked out certain categories—and again, those categories were race, creed, gender, you'll recall. Presumably, hate speech that is grounded or centered on some other kind of human characteristic—let's say sexual orientation or sexual preference; or, perhaps, employment. (One could imagine hate speech being directed against lawyers, for example; or some other human occupation) Those kinds of hate speech were not criminalized by the St. Paul community ordinance. In other words, certain forms of hate speech, the state believed, were sufficiently important that they warranted special criminal penalties. Other forms of hate speech, presumably, didn't fall into that category.

That is a viewpoint. That is the state's viewpoint, that some forms of hate speech are more noxious, and hence should be criminalized to a greater extent than other forms of hate speech. That's viewpoint discrimination. "That's unconstitutional," Justice Scalia argued, because in that case, or in this instance, what has happened is that the state has picked out certain kinds of topics and said, "These are disfavored; others, less so." That also represents an intrusion into the content, or a particular kind of viewpoint adopted by the state that is then turned into a kind of viewpoint monopoly that citizens cannot challenge without running afoul of the criminal law itself.

There is, in other words, a kind of equality argument, or an equality principle, hiding behind Justice Scalia's position; and I want to quote it again here: "The statute," Justice Scalia said, is unconstitutional because the ordinance only limits fighting words, "that insult or promote violence on the base of race, color, creed or religion or gender. The First Amendment does not permit St. Paul to impose special prohibitions on those speakers who express views on disfavored subjects."

Now, as I said, *R.A.V.* was a unanimous decision; but there was so much criticism of this particular line of argumentation by Justice Scalia that four other justices wrote very long, separate opinions arguing that *R.A.V.* should be unconstitutional for substantially different grounds than the ones advanced by Justice Scalia.

R.A.V. was followed—or I should say, perhaps, reaffirmed; or maybe modified; or maybe it was just completely blown out of the water— by a subsequent case known as *Virginia v. Black*, decided in 2003. Now, I have deliberately waffled about what the effect of *Virginia v. Black* was on *R.A.V.* because I don't think it's clear to anybody involved. *Virginia v. Black* also involved the statute that addressed cross burning. In this case, however, in *Virginia v. Black,* the Court went ahead, in an opinion by Justice O'Connor, upholding the Virginia statute that prohibited cross burning, and picked out specific enhanced criminal penalties for cases involving hate speech and cross burning.

One might think immediately that a Virginia statute, or a statute passed by any state, that picks out cross burning as an especially offensive form of hate speech would immediately run up against the prohibition in *R.A.V.* Recall, Justice Scalia said if you're going to ban fighting words, you can't pick out some of them as being worse than others; you have to prevent or prohibit them all. That's not what *Virginia* did. *Virginia* did the exact opposite. It picked out cross burning, and said, this one is especially bad, and we want to enhance criminal penalties for it.

On the first level it might seem different to reconcile those. I want to stress how difficult it might be at this level by adding to our criticisms of *R.A.V.* an additional criticism, which is the following: assume for a minute that Justice Scalia's opinion is the correct constitutional opinion in *R.A.V.* You can't pick out some forms of hate speech and make them worse, criminally speaking, than others. What's your alternative?

Well, one alternative, of course—perhaps it is the one intended by Justice Scalia—is to say that the state may never pick out hate speech. And perhaps, Scalia's opinion, if that's where he means it to go, is deeply reminiscent of Douglas' dissent in *Beauharnais;* that hate speech is something we must tolerate in a society, and there are good reasons why we must tolerate it.

But that's not the only possible implication of Justice Scalia's opinion. Here is a different implication. One might say that, "Okay, we can prohibit hate speech, even consistent with Scalia's opinion in *R.A.V.,* if we simply take care to prohibit all forms of hate speech. We won't discriminate between which ones are especially bad and which ones less so. We'll simply prohibit them all." The difficulty with that, of course, is that, how are we going to identify and advance all of the different forms of hate speech that we might be able to identify? Surely, human beings are too inventive, too creative, and language itself, too pliable to be able to really do that. Any list we could hope to elaborate will inevitably be incomplete. Time alone will render it incomplete and ineffective.

On the other hand, if we simply ban fighting words, period, the statute is likely to be unconstitutional because it is too vague; because no one would really know which words are fighting words and which ones are not. That problem is complicated by our earlier insistence that we only know fighting words—or at least, usually, we only know fighting words, at least as defined by *Chaplinsky*—in a specific factual context; and we're not going to be able to anticipate all those specific factual contexts. If those are the only two options open to us after *R.A.V.*, it is again difficult to understand what we should do with *Virginia v. Black*, where we have just the cross-burning statute.

Interestingly, O'Connor wrote the opinion, and not Scalia. Scalia couldn't find a majority this time. O'Connor wrote, "The First Amendment permits Virginia to outlaw cross burning, because burning a cross is a particularly virulent form of intimidation."

Now, let's think about that for a minute. She may well be correct. It may be an especially noxious, terrible form of intimidation. But that doesn't address the underlying question of whether or not it's speech; and there's nothing in *Virginia v. Black* to suggest that the cross burning isn't expressive. It clearly has an expressive component. That's what makes it so noxious on some level. It isn't seeing a cross burn; it is the implicit message about racial inferiority, about racial violence, that makes the cross burning so terribly obnoxious.

I urge you to think back to an earlier lecture, where we discussed the obscenity statute that was passed by the city of Indianapolis, which made pornography a crime against women. And you'll recall that Judge Frank Easterbrook, writing for the Seventh Circuit, concluded that pornography may, in fact, have an underlying message that teaches about the inferiority and the subordination of women. He argued that that was part of why pornography was so powerful; that it did express the underlying message that those statute writers had intended to prohibit. He went on to conclude that that was what made the statute itself unconstitutional; because, in other words, the statute simply disagreed with the underlying message that pornography sends.

Think about that in the context of *Virginia v. Black*. The statute prohibiting the cross burning is one that expresses the state's—our—collective repudiation of the message. But, in doing so, that is viewpoint discrimination. That suggests that you can only say certain kinds of things, and only if we like them. *Virginia v. Black* can probably only be justified on the same grounds that *Beauharnais v. Illinois* was justified—that sometimes speech is so noxious that, even if it is speech, there are other values, such as racial equality, or social quiet, or human dignity, that must trump it. And that is a good place to end this lecture. It is worth reminding ourselves that freedom of speech may be important, but it may not be the most important value in a constitutional democracy.

Lecture Twenty-Three
The Right to Silence

Scope:

Does freedom of speech include the right not to speak? In *Talley v. California* (1960), the Court considered a variant of this question in finding unconstitutional a Los Angeles ordinance that restricted the distribution of anonymous handbills and flyers. In this lecture, we also take up two important cases in which the Court addressed the constitutionality of state laws that required schoolchildren to recite the pledge of allegiance. In *Minersville v. Gobitis* (1940), the Court upheld such a requirement. But just three years later, in *West Virginia v. Barnette* (1943), the Court changed its mind, concluding that a compulsory pledge "invades the sphere of intellect and spirit which it is the purpose of the First Amendment ... to reserve from all official control." More recently, in *Wooley v. Maynard* (1977), the Court ruled that the state of New Hampshire could not prosecute an individual who had masked over the phrase "Live Free or Die" on the license plate of his car.

Outline

I. We typically think of freedom of speech as involving the right to speak our minds, to say or express what we believe. But should it also include the right to be silent—not in the criminal sense, but in the sense that the state may not compel us to say what we might not believe?

    A. Such cases arise more frequently than one might imagine. Every day, thousands of students recite pledges as school begins. Many of us take certain kinds of oaths—such as loyalty oaths or oaths to testify truthfully in a court of law—as a matter of routine.

    B. Sometimes such oaths implicate freedom of religion issues, as we shall see in Lectures Twenty-Five through Twenty-Seven, but they also raise freedom of speech claims, as well.

II. Before we take up these issues, this is an appropriate point to reflect on fundamentals.

   A. We began our study of the First Amendment by considering the different justifications we can advance for protecting freedom of expression.

   B. We then moved to a discussion of some specific First Amendment issues, such as illegal advocacy, pornography, and hate speech.

   C. We can say, I think, that no matter what the specific issue, some basic themes or principles are always present.

   1. First, there is the problem of definition.

   2. Second, we confront a wide variety of doctrinal tools and formulas, though we may wonder how much they assist in reaching decisions.

   3. Third, specific issues and doctrines notwithstanding, there are always present larger questions about how we reconcile tensions between our commitment to expression and other social values.

   D. There is, too, yet another difficulty, especially prominent in this lecture. This is what we might call the problem of decisional authority, and we have seen it before. The problem is: Which branch of government should be entrusted with such weighty matters?

III. In *Talley v. California* (1960), the Court considered a variant of this question in finding unconstitutional a Los Angeles ordinance that restricted the distribution of anonymous handbills and flyers.

   A. The plaintiffs in *Talley* challenged the prohibition on anonymous flyers. In this case, they had distributed flyers and handbills urging a boycott of merchants who allegedly discriminated against their employees on the basis of race.

   B. The Court ruled for the plaintiffs, noting that a requirement of identification would tend to restrict speech.

   C. Justice Black wrote that "persecuted groups and sects from time to time throughout history have been able to criticize … either anonymously or not at all."

D. We need to understand the rationale behind this opinion. Justice Black stressed the point that without anonymity, some speech might never be voiced or heard. But we should consider, too, what kinds of interests might lie behind a governmental regulation prohibiting anonymous speech.

IV. The Court's most famous cases involving compelled speech, however, have not addressed the question of anonymous speech but, instead, have considered the constitutionality of state laws requiring schoolchildren to salute the flag and recite the Pledge of Allegiance.

> **A.** In the first of these cases, *Minersville v. Gobitis* (1940), the Court upheld the constitutionality of the flag salute as an exercise of the state's use of the police power to promote patriotism among the students. The Gobitis children, Jehovah's Witnesses, were expelled after they refused to say the pledge.
>
> **B.** Writing for the Court, Justice Frankfurter agreed that "every possible leeway should be given to the claims of religious faith" but nevertheless upheld the school's requirements.
>
> > **1.** Frankfurter noted, "The state's interest is inferior to none…. National unity is the basis of national security."
> >
> > **2.** Frankfurter also struck a familiar chord about the necessity for judicial deference to legislative authority as a central feature of democratic self-governance.
>
> **C.** *Gobitis* unleashed a wave of persecution against the Witnesses; the Justice Department, for example, recorded several cases of lynching and castrations.
>
> **D.** The Court reopened the issue three years later in the case of *West Virginia v. Barnette* (1943). This time, the Court changed its mind, concluding that a compulsory pledge "invades the sphere of intellect and spirit which it is the purpose of the First Amendment … to reserve from all official control."
>
> **E.** In his opinion for the Court, Justice Jackson began by noting, "One's right to life, liberty, and property, to free speech, a free press, freedom of worship and assembly, and other fundamental rights may not be submitted to vote. They depend on the outcome of no election."

1. This claim is fundamentally at odds with the claim made by Felix Frankfurter, writing for a majority in *Minersville*.

2. Jackson continued: "The freedom asserted by these appellees does not bring them into collision with rights asserted by any other individual. Nor is there any question in this case that their behavior is peaceable and orderly. The sole conflict is between authority and the rights of the individual."

F. Justice Jackson has described the conflict in a particular way. But we might remember that the community does have an interest in this case—the promotion of patriotism, for example—and we might wonder if the First Amendment gives us any real guidance about how to weigh the balance.

G. It is here that we see the importance of Jackson's insistence that: "The very purpose of a Bill of Rights was to withdraw certain subjects from the vicissitudes of political controversy, to place them beyond the reach of majorities…."

H. Jackson continued: "Freedom to differ is not limited to things that do not matter much…. The test of [freedom] is the right to differ as to things that touch the heart of the existing order." The case, he wrote, "is made difficult not because the principles of its decision are obscure, but because the flag involved is our own."

I. In a strongly worded and emotional dissent, Justice Frankfurter (who had written the majority opinion in *Minersville*) began, "One who belongs to the most vilified and persecuted minority in history is not likely to be insensitive to the freedoms guaranteed by our Constitution."

1. Frankfurter also noted, in the same vein, "Were my purely personal attitude relevant, I should wholeheartedly associate myself with the general libertarian views in the Court's opinion."

2. Why tell us that? Why does it matter what his personal opinion would be? Justice Frankfurter reminds us that there is a difference between a judge's appeal to his or her own personal identity or personal set of beliefs and the obligation to interpret the Constitution.

J. Coming to the merits, Frankfurter argued, "The state is not shut out from a domain because the individual conscience may deny the state's claim...."

K. In *Wooley v. Maynard* (1977), the Court ruled that the state of New Hampshire could not prosecute an individual who had masked over the phrase "Live Free or Die" on the license plate of his car.

1. *Wooley* involved a Jehovah's Witness who objected to the phrase "Live Free or Die" on his New Hampshire license plate. In his majority opinion, Chief Justice Burger compared the case to *Barnette*, noting, "Here, as in *Barnette*, we are faced with a state measure which forces an individual as part of his daily life—indeed constantly while his automobile is in public view—to be an instrument for fostering public adherence to an ideological point of view he finds unacceptable."

2. Chief Justice Burger argued also that freedom of speech "includes both the right to speak freely and the right to refrain from speaking at all" as equal parts of a comprehensive "individual freedom of mind."

Essential Reading:

Talley v. California (1960).

Minersville v. Gobitis (1940).

West Virginia v. Barnette (1943).

Wooley v. Maynard (1977).

Kommers, Finn, and Jacobsohn, *American Constitutional Law*, chapter 8, pp. 467–468.

Supplementary Reading:

Peter Irons, *The Courage of Their Convictions: Sixteen Americans Who Fought Their Way to the Supreme Court*, pp. 13–36.

Questions to Consider:

1. As we saw earlier, there are several different justifications for freedom of speech. Do all of them support a conclusion that freedom of speech must also include a right not to speak or not to be compelled to speak?

2. What explains the different opinions in the two flag-salute cases? Do they turn on different claims about the purposes of the First Amendment? Do they turn, instead, on different definitions of speech? Do they rest on different estimates about the importance of the state's interests? Do they embody different understandings about the limits of judicial power?

3. Does the First Amendment point, as Chief Justice Burger suggested in *Wooley*, to "an individual freedom of mind"? What would be the limits on such a right, if any?

Lecture Twenty-Three—Transcript
The Right to Silence

In this lecture, we conclude our sprint through the First Amendment by considering a question that is perhaps a little unusual; certainly not the ordinary kind of question one would approach or consider in this kind of a course. That question is simply this: Does the First Amendment include a right not to speak? We'll consider a number of different versions of this question. We'll first take it up with the Supreme Court case of *Talley v. California,* decided in 1960, where the Court considered the problem of anonymous speech. Then we will move quickly to the Court's two flag salute cases, among the most important and controversial cases decided in the 20th century. And we'll conclude with a more recent case, *Wooley v. Maynard,* decided in 1977.

Before we get to those cases, however, which, as I mentioned, are extremely controversial and will require a great deal of our attention, it might be the appropriate time now to think about where we have been so far. We began our study of the First Amendment by considering the different kinds of rationales and justifications that rest behind our commitment to freedom of speech. We saw that there are many reasons why we might choose to protect speech; and we saw, also, that many of those reasons are extraordinarily complex.

We then moved quickly to a series of discussions about more specific First Amendment problems, such as the problem of illegal advocacy, pornography, or obscenity. And we saw that, no matter what the specific issue involved, there were always two or three basic themes that were present. The first of those, I think, we might describe as the problem of definition. In other words, we were concerned to ask: What is speech? What is protected, what isn't protected, and why?

Secondly, we were concerned with trying to decide and to examine what kinds of tools the Court has at its disposal to decide such issues. So, to some extent, of course, we had to discuss precedent; and also, we had to discuss the various kinds of doctrinal devices that the Court has managed to construct over the last century or so. We saw, as we have often seen, that those doctrines themselves are very complex; but their complexity does not mean, necessarily, that they lead easily or inevitably to simple conclusions.

Thirdly, we considered, more generally, the relationship between individual freedom and the various kinds of social or collective interests that sometimes seem to conflict with speech. As we have seen, with speech, and with every other liberty we have so far considered, no right is ever absolute. There are always conflicts between other kinds of constitutional values; in this case, constitutional values such as dignity, for example, or equality, that will sometimes conflict with our commitment to speech.

And then, finally, we considered an issue that is, again, hardly unique to our First Amendment inquiry. When should judges, if ever, choose to defer to the democratic process in valuing—I should say, in balancing—these various kinds of constitutional interests and constitutional liberties? That issue, which I think we might call the issue of decisional authority—where does decisional authority rest?—is an issue highlighted by the cases in today's lecture.

Let's begin, as I suggested, with the Court's decision in *Talley v. California* (again, decided in 1960). Now, *Talley* is not as well known as many of the cases we will consider, but it does provide for a very interesting set of little problems. In this case, the Court considered the constitutionality of a Los Angeles ordinance that restricted the distribution of anonymous handbills and flyers. The plaintiffs in *Talley* challenged that prohibition on anonymous flyers. In this case, they had distributed handbills urging a boycott of various merchants who had allegedly discriminated against their employees on the basis of race.

The Court ruled for the plaintiffs, noting that a requirement of identification—in other words, the prohibition on anonymity—would tend, in the abstract, and also in the concrete case, to restrict speech. And the rationale here, I think, is very interesting. Justice Black wrote, "persecuted groups and sects, from time to time throughout history, have been able to criticize…either anonymously or not at all."

Now, before we move off of *Talley,* I think it's important we understand the rationale behind the majority's opinion. The idea here is that anonymity makes it possible, in some instances, for some individuals to speak. There is an individual interest that we mean to protect here; but there is also a social interest. All I mean by that is simply that Justice Black, again, writing for the Court, seemed to understand that society has a value in hearing certain kinds of speech that might not otherwise make it to the marketplace if we insist upon identifying the speaker. He certainly has a point here.

But I think it's probably also important to think about what kinds of communal or social interests might have rested behind the Los Angeles decision to prohibit anonymous speech. That, perhaps, is not so easy to do. One might imagine, for example, that there was a littering interest; we don't want, as a city or as a community, thousands of handbills and flyers littering our streets.

But that hardly seems enough of an interest to justify whatever the potential restriction is on speech. Could the state—or in this case, could the city—have come up with another rationale for why it would prohibit anonymous speech? Well, perhaps not with regard to this particular law, or at least to this particular factual situation; but in the abstract, there might be perfectly good reasons why the state might sometimes want speech not to be anonymous. What might those reasons be?

Well, if one of the social values we want to protect would be the dignity of other human beings, or the civility of social discourse, one might argue that anonymity, while it sometimes makes other kinds of speech possible that we not would otherwise have the opportunity to hear, also might encourage irresponsibility. And one of the few things that we have failed to cover in this course is the possibility that constitutional liberties might somehow be associated also with constitutional responsibilities. It might be the case, in other words, that the prohibition on anonymity cleanses the public sphere and makes speech, or imposes upon speech, a certain kind of responsibility, and that might not be such a terrible social interest.

Talley, however, as I suggested, is not among the better known of the Supreme Court cases; and the issue it raised, in particular, has not come up that often. I propose now that we turn to two other cases that are much better known, and which, at least at first appearance, seem to have much more significance for our day-to-day lives. I should add that these two cases, as I mentioned before, are extraordinarily controversial. In part, they are controversial because the Court rarely, if ever, reverses itself in the span of three years. But this Court did with these two cases; and for that reason alone they are important and significant. But the underlying issues are issues that, as Americans, all of us, at some point, wrestle with. And if you pay any attention to current politics, you will recognize in these cases hints of controversies to come.

Let me begin with the first of these two cases: *Minersville v. Gobitis*, decided in 1940. *Minersville* involved the constitutionality of the flag salute as an exercise of the state's police power. And you will recall that the police power is the power of the state to protect the health, safety, welfare, and morals of the community. *Minersville* is a tiny little town located in coal country, Pennsylvania. And in the late-1930s—remember we are on the cusp of World War II—America was overcome—or at least we could say that *Minersville* was overcome—with a profound concern for the promotion of patriotism. The Minersville school board, and later, at city council, reacted to this concern by requiring children to say the Pledge of Allegiance and to salute the flag every morning.

Now, to some of you, that may seem perfectly innocuous. Before you reach that conclusion, it might be well to remember that the pledge that these children spoke is not precisely the same pledge that schoolchildren today make in the morning. Nor is the flag salute precisely the same kind of flag salute that I, at least, learned as a child. As far as I know, the flag salute that is said by millions of children every day involves the placing of one's hand over one's heart.

That is not the flag salute that the Gobitis children, members of the Jehovah's Witness religion, were asked to perform. They were asked to perform a different kind of flag salute. It wasn't different at the time—I mean it was different than our own. The flag salute required in Minersville was the same flag salute that was required by a thousand other school districts in the United States; and that flag salute involved the upraising of one's right hand, palm open, and the recitation of the pledge.

Now many of us, of course, will have an instinctive kind of emotional reaction to that particular pledge, because it seems deeply reminiscent of pledges we associate, for example, with Nazi Germany. We do not need the benefit of 40 or 50 years of hindsight to make that connection; even at that time, there were objections to the flag salute based on precisely those grounds. The Jehovah's Witness Church, for example, objected, in part, because the gesture seemed too eerily similar to these other kinds of gestures. And, more generally, the Jehovah's Witnesses—in this case, the Gobitis family—objected to the flag salute because it seemed to them to violate a basic principle of their religious faith, that "thou shalt not worship a graven image."

Writing for the majority, Justice Frankfurter agreed, "that every possible leeway should be given to the claims of religious faith." Nevertheless, he upheld the requirements, noting, "The state's interest is inferior to none…. National unity is the basis of national security." Frankfurter also struck a familiar chord about the necessity for judicial deference to legislative authority as a central feature of democratic self-governance; and, as I reminded you at the beginning of this lecture, that is a recurrent theme, not only in Justice Frankfurter's jurisprudence, but in the jurisprudence of civil liberties, more generally.

I could, of course, go on at great length about this decision. I could, as I did so many times, try to parse it, sentence by sentence, and tell you the various kinds of academic criticisms that one might address against Felix Frankfurter's opinion. I don't think it's necessary to do that here. I would prefer to concentrate on the larger social and political reaction to the Court's opinion. Within two weeks of *Minersville*—think about that—the Department of Justice received hundreds of reports of violence directed against the members of the Jehovah's Witness Faith. Some of those reports, as awful as it sounds, involved the lynching of Jehovah's Witnesses, and there are even recorded cases of castrations directed against Jehovah's Witnesses.

What an extraordinary reaction! How do we explain such a reaction? I am not confident of any explanation that I could offer you. I don't think the Court's decision caused such violence. Before I reached that conclusion, I would want to know, for example, how much violence, if any, had been directed against Jehovah's Witnesses before the decision. Perhaps it seemed to a community deeply concerned about the possibility of war, deeply concerned about the state of the nation's sense of pride and patriotism. Perhaps Jehovah's Witnesses would have come in for violence in any event. But clearly, something about the Court's decision seemed to spark—or, at least, add to—this sense of outrage directed against members of this particular faith.

Just two years later, in 1942, three justices, in a case unrelated really to *Minersville,* called *Jones v. Opelika*—those three justices were Justices Black, Douglas, and Murphy—announced that they had erred in *Gobitis.* Now, we have not spent a great deal of time in this course talking about the niceties of the Supreme Court's jurisdiction. But it is a truism amongst scholars and judges that courts are passive/reactive institutions. Unlike Congress, which can charge a hearing whenever it wants to, to consider any pressing, social problem; unlike the president, who can command the airwaves at his own initiative, the Court may only react to cases that are brought to it. That is the truism. This case, however, suggests that, while the Court may have to wait for others to act, it can, at least, prod them into action.

The dissent—or I should say, the opinion—by Black, Douglas, and Murphy, that they had erred in *Minersville* was, of course, an open invitation for somebody else to bring a case that would give the Court an opportunity to reconsider its decision. That opportunity came about in the case of *West Virginia v. Barnette,* decided in 1943.

Now, again, in *Barnette,* we have a statute that requires the recitation of the pledge and that flag salute that I described to you earlier—this flag salute, palm in the air, hands raised, stiffed-armed. This statute, however, if possible, went even further than the statute in *Minersville* by providing that any child who failed to comport with this requirement would be suspended; then expelled; and once expelled, found to be a truant, whereupon his parents could be fined, or her parents might actually be sent to jail. This is compulsion, of course, of the highest order. I don't mean to denigrate that. It might be a kind of compulsion that is perfectly constitutional; or, at least, that is what the Court has suggested in *Minersville.*

This time, however, the Court changed its mind. And there are a number of opinions we need to consider here, or that we could consider, at least; but the two most important are the majority opinion by Justice Jackson and the inevitable dissent by Felix Frankfurter. One word about Justice Jackson, because I don't believe we have encountered him up to this point in the course. As you read his opinion, you may want to remember that it is 1943, and that later, Justice Jackson will become the chief prosecutor at the Nuremberg War Trials.

He begins in *Barnette* by saying, "One's right to life, liberty, and property, to free speech, a free press, freedom of worship and assembly, and other fundamental rights may not be submitted to vote. They depend on the outcome of no election." What an extraordinary claim, fundamentally at odds—you can probably see—with the kind of claim made by Felix Frankfurter, writing for a majority in *Minersville*.

Jackson continues:

> The freedoms asserted by these appellees does not bring them into collision with rights asserted by any other individual. Nor is there any question in this case that their behavior is peaceable and orderly. The sole conflict is between authority and the rights of the individual.

I think it's important to stop here for a moment, although we are hardly done with Jackson's opinion. That last sentence I quoted to you suggested, "The sole conflict," he wrote, "is between the authority and the rights of the individual." And surely it is possible to describe the conflict in *West Virginia v. Barnette,* or the conflict in *Minersville,* in precisely those terms.

But that is not the only way to describe what happened in this case. One might rewrite that sentence to make it read, "The sole conflict is between the community and the rights of the individual," because let us not forget that it is the community's interest in the promotion in the spirit of patriotism that is the genesis behind this statute, behind this requirement. Does the Constitution inevitably tell us, is there anything in the First Amendment that tells us, without ambiguity, how to resolve a conflict between the individual and the community? It will not do simply to describe it in those terms. One needs to resolve it in those terms.

Here is how Justice Jackson tried to get at that problem: "the very purpose of a Bill of Rights was to withdraw certain subjects from the vicissitudes of political controversy, to place them beyond the reach of majorities…."

Now, think about the importance of that claim. In trying to reconcile this problem between the community's interest and the individual liberty, in trying to resolve the problem that I called "the problem of decisional authority" just a little earlier in this lecture, Justice Jackson does not so much depend upon the language, or the meaning even, of the First Amendment; but instead counsels us to look at the entire purpose of the Bill of Rights *writ large*. And in doing so, he suggests that there is, inevitably, always a tension between our commitment to liberty and our commitment to democratic self-governance; but that tension must be resolved, he says, by understanding that the whole point of the Bill of Rights was to withdraw certain subjects from the political arena.

Now, he doesn't actually say this, but I think it is a fair interpretation of his decision to suggest that, in trying to reconcile liberty with community, we must understand that that is not necessarily an even-handed contest; it is a prejudiced contest. I mean prejudiced in the sense that we must start from an assumption that, at least with regard to those liberties contained in the Bill of Rights, we should err on the side of protecting liberty; because that is the whole idea, the very central purpose of the Bill of Rights itself.

Then, Justice Jackson concludes; "The case," he wrote, "is made difficult not because the principles of its decision are obscure, but because the flag involved is our own." Now, surely he must have a point here. Surely there is a kind of emotional baggage that handicaps our ability to take a look at this problem objectively. He adds to that (and I will paraphrase here) that one of the central purposes of the Bill of Rights is to protect a freedom of liberty, more generally, and that freedom to differ will not be worth much if the freedom to differ is limited to items, or to matters, or to ideas that do not much matter themselves. We must, if we are to take liberty seriously, protect the liberty to differ in areas that strike to the very core of our social being, of who we are as a people.

He claims that "the case is made difficult not because the principles of its decisions are obscure;" I might add that that is certainly true. The principles of the decision are not obscure at all. But I think the case is made difficult for more reasons than the one he advances alone, that the "flag involved is our own." I think the case is made difficult because it is not, perhaps, as obvious to some people as it was to Jackson, that in reconciling these two liberties, one is clearly of greater significance than the other. I think reasonable people might disagree about how to strike that balance. Certainly, Justice Frankfurter disagreed about how to strike the balance.

Now, at the point of being too repetitive, I can't stress enough that we are only three years past *Minersville,* and that it was Justice Frankfurter who had written the majority opinion in *Minersville*. His dissent in *Barnette* is impassioned. He begins, "One who belongs to the most vilified and persecuted minority in history is not likely to be insensitive to the freedoms guaranteed by our Constitution." I want to stop here.

Justice Frankfurter is referring of course to his Jewish heritage. One might wonder—I know that I always do—why he feels compelled to open with such a personal statement. ("One who belongs to the most vilified and persecuted minority in history is not likely to be insensitive to the freedoms guaranteed by our Constitution.") Surely, at some point, Frankfurter must have felt as though he had been criticized unfairly, perhaps as being insensitive to the needs of these poor children, or to the violence directed against Jehovah's Witnesses, more generally.

He continues, "Were my purely personal attitude relevant, I should wholeheartedly associate myself with the general libertarian views in the Court's opinion." Why tell us that? Why does it matter what his personal opinion would be? Justice Frankfurter has a lesson he wants us to learn, and that lesson, as we have seen before, is that there is a difference between a judge's appeal to his or her own personal identity or personal set of beliefs and their obligation to interpret the Constitution. And Frankfurter tells us, in hauntingly personal terms, that there are times where the Constitution has taken him—as indeed, it must take every interpreter—to places that he would rather not go; that there is a sharp divide; and in this case, obviously, an emotionally painful divide between what he thinks the Constitution commands him to do and what he would like to do.

He continues reinforcing this theme: "But as judges, we are neither Jew nor Gentile, neither Catholic nor agnostic." He does not, as it turns out, invoke the image of the blind statue of justice, with the scales being weighted on either side; but that might have been the image that he could have used. Justice is blind; or, we should say, justice is agnostic. He wants to point to an image of a Supreme Court justice that brings to the decision no personal prejudice, no personal opinion; a human being; a blank slate; a perfectly objective, a perfectly sterile interpreter of the Constitution. And, in some ways, that may be a noble ideal. Certainly it is an ideal that has motivated

©2006 The Teaching Company Limited Partnership

justices, at least since *Lochner,* if not since the beginning of the Western legal system.

And I suppose one might respond that that kind of dispassion, even if it is a constitutional ideal, might sometimes blind us—hence, the blindfold—and it might be an exceptionally high price to pay. And let's think about who might pay that price. Clearly, Frankfurter paid a price; you can see the emotional turmoil that he is engulfed in. But let's not forget too, that the Gobitis children had to pay that price, and lots of other children had to pay that price. Perhaps that is a price we all pay for living in a constitutional democracy.

I hope you can see why these two cases are controversial; but if not, let me add to them one final point: they underscore for us, yet again, how difficult it is to determine when it is that judges should step in and set aside a decision reached by the majoritarian process. Stripped of all the emotion, stripped of all the facts, that is the underlying issue in the two flag salute cases. When, if ever, should judges set aside a result or a decision reached by legislatures? And, unfortunately, the Constitution gives us no clear guidance as to that issue.

Now, let me finish with just one other quick case. It's a fun case, I think, but a significant one. In *Wooley v. Maynard,* decided in 1977, the Court ruled that the state of New Hampshire could not prosecute an individual who had masked over the phrase "Live Free or Die" on the license plate of his car. In this case, *Wooley* involved a Jehovah's Witness who objected to that phrase.

In writing for the Court, Chief Justice Burger did what you undoubtedly would have done; he compared the case to *Barnette,* noting:

> Here, as in *Barnette,* we are faced with a state measure which forces an individual as part of his daily life—indeed constantly, while his automobile is in public view—to be an instrument for fostering public adherence to an ideological point of view he finds unacceptable.

And that is why I have called these cases the "right to silence cases;" because there may be times when our right to silence is every bit as important in validating First Amendment values as our right to speak.

Lecture Twenty-Four
Why Is Freedom of Religion so Complex?

Scope:

The relationship between matters of the soul and matters of state is a subject of intense controversy in the United States. In this lecture, we begin an extended inquiry into freedom of religion. As we shall see, the Court's work in this area is complicated and often confusing. In part, this is because the First Amendment includes not one but two guarantees designed to protect religious freedom—the establishment clause and the free exercise clause. Although they overlap, the two clauses also point in different directions and seek to achieve different things. Moreover, the Founders either decided not to or neglected to give us a definition of *establishment* and *free exercise* and even of *religion* itself. Finally, in recent years a sharply divided Court has hinted at sweeping changes in the long-settled doctrines that make up freedom of religion jurisprudence.

Outline

I. Every polity must reconcile the demands of religious faith (and denial) with the beliefs of others, as well as with the collective welfare of the community.

   A. In the United States, the parameters of this conflict are sketched out by the religion clauses of the First Amendment. This amendment, as most folks know, has two critical components:

   1. The first is the establishment clause, which provides that "Congress shall make no law respecting an establishment of religion."

   2. The second provides that Congress shall not prohibit the "free exercise" of religion.

   3. We shall see that these two provisions have occasioned an astonishingly complex and often confusing jurisprudence.

   4. Sometimes, that confusion is directly traceable to the existence of the two clauses—they do not always work in tandem, and indeed, they sometimes seem to pull in different directions.

B. There are other provisions as well, most notably Article VI, which provides that there shall be no religious test as a qualification for public office.

C. We should note, however, that these prohibitions applied only to the federal government until well into the 20th century, when the religion clauses were incorporated through the Fourteenth Amendment. At the time of the Founding, for example, many states had established religions and required religious oaths for public office.

   1. As a consequence, almost all of the Court's work in this area is from the 20th century.

   2. It may be that some of the confusion and complexity we will encounter stems from just that fact—perhaps the Court needs more time, and perhaps there is something especially difficult about making 18th-century guarantees of religious freedom have meaning and coherence more than two centuries later.

   3. For example, how are we to reconcile the two clauses?

   4. One justice once pointed to the problem by asking us to imagine a lonely soldier stationed at a far outpost. He might plausibly claim that his right of free exercise is impinged if the military does not provide access to a chaplain or minister of his faith.

   5. But if the military obliges his demand, it runs the risk of favoring one religion over another or religion over nonreligion and, thus, might run afoul of the establishment clause.

   6. This conflict between the two clauses is not a necessary consequence—it follows from our specific interpretations of the clauses. Those interpretations might be the wrong ones, and the conflict may be artificial. But they point to difficulties in giving the clauses meaning.

II. The religion clauses, then, are among the most controversial and ambiguous of the Constitution's provisions, and the Court's efforts to give them meaning have produced a long and complex set of rulings and doctrines.

A. Consider two kinds of immediate problems:

B. First, under what conditions, if any, may a majority of the community express its belief in public spaces, such as the nation's elementary schools or at the opening of legislative sessions? For example, should students be allowed to pray at the beginning of a school day or at a school-sponsored event, such as a graduation?

    1. How are we to decide such cases? Neither the establishment clause nor the free exercise clause clearly settles the matter.

    2. In other words, we need some interpretive method to determine the answer.

C. Second, under what conditions, if any, should the community be permitted to regulate or prohibit the religious beliefs of individual citizens or religious groups? Should parents, for example, be permitted to withhold from their children certain types of medical treatments, such as blood transfusions, if such treatments violate their faith?

    1. These, too, are not mere abstractions. There are hundreds of such cases, and in most, if not all, of our choices they have profound consequences.

    2. Justice Felix Frankfurter once referred to such clashes as "great tragedies," as conflicts not between right and wrong but between competing conceptions of what is good and what is right.

III. Before we take up specific cases and issues, we should consider, at a higher level of abstraction, what the religion clauses were intended to accomplish.

A. I don't mean so much that we should engage in a search for the Framers' intent. Instead, I think we should consider what the clauses are meant to accomplish to determine what ends they mean to achieve.

B. One possible purpose is to remove religion as a source of civil conflict. The clauses do this, we might argue, insofar as they immunize religion from state control.

C. They may also do it by encouraging and promoting religious pluralism.

1. By one survey, there are more than 200 major religious denominations in the United States and scores of so-called "minor" faiths.

2. The existence of so many religions may help to keep any one of them from establishing a foothold in the government, but it also increases the opportunity for conflict among them.

IV. Some of the difficulties in the Court's jurisprudence are not specific to the clauses but, instead, result from a familiar tension—the conflict between our commitment to individual liberty and the interests of the community.

A. As we shall see, these conflicts are especially pronounced in the religion cases.

B. It might be, however, that if we characterize the religion cases as just another example of this larger tension, we might miss something unique about religion as a constitutional liberty.

C. Consider this question, for example: Given that speech and expression are already protected, what was the need to include two guarantees for freedom of religion in the First Amendment?

1. One might argue that most, if not all, expressions of religious faith would be protected under the speech clauses.

2. Indeed, some cases about religious freedom seem as though they were decided on other grounds, such as *Minersville* and *Barnette*.

D. Some scholars and judges have argued that our inability or unwillingness to articulate a clear distinction between speech and religion reflects a failure to understand how or why the Founders took special care to protect religion.

V. Of course, another difficulty we will encounter will also seem familiar and is suggested by the foregoing issue. What is the definition of *religion*?

A. As we shall see, the Court's definition has changed dramatically over the years, but at no time has the Court been able to come up with a comprehensive, universal definition.

    1. Some of the Court's earliest cases are directly relevant to the question of definition, and many, interestingly, involve religious minorities.

    2. For example, the Mormon migration west raised a number of freedom of religion questions—often occasioned by the practice of polygamy.

    3. In *Reynolds v. United States* (1878), the Court upheld a federal statute that prohibited polygamy in the territories. Later, in *Davis v. Beason* (1890), the Court upheld a federal statute that not only prohibited polygamy but also made it a crime to belong to a religion that practiced it. Upon conviction, one could lose the right to vote.

    4. Writing for the Court, and taking care to define *religion*, Justice Field said, "The term 'religion' has reference to one's view of his relations to his Creator and to the obligations they impose in reverence for his being and character, and of obedience to his will."

    5. How does Justice Field know that this is the correct constitutional definition of *religion*?

    6. In a case decided almost a century later, this time involving the Amish, the Court again struggled with questions about definition. In *Wisconsin v. Yoder* (1972), the Court wrote, "To have the protection of the religion clauses, the claims must be rooted in religious belief."

    7. What is a religious, as opposed to a nonreligious, belief? The Court is not as clear here but did note: "Thoreau's choice was philosophical and personal, rather than religious."

    8. Finally, there is the case of *Thomas v. Review Board* (1981). In this case, the Court wrote, "Courts are not arbiters of scriptural interpretation."

9. One consequence of the failure to define religion is that it is equally difficult to determine what is included as what is excluded. More generally, it points to the problem of judicial power in a democracy.

B. In addition, there is an underlying issue that harkens back to familiar problems of judicial power: Who should decide whether any particular set of beliefs is "really" a religion?

   1. One possibility is that the courts should decide, but there are profound dangers here.

   2. A second possibility is to let individuals decide for themselves, but this, too, has several dangers, including the obvious one of abuse.

VI. Finally, we shall see over the next few lectures that few areas in civil liberties are in as much turmoil as religion. In recent years, the Court has hinted at substantial and far-reaching changes in long-settled rules and doctrines.

A. Part of the reason for this volatility may reflect deep-seated divisions in American society about what role matters of faith ought to play in the public square.

B. Again, this is part of the reason why our approach in this course is less focused on doctrine than overarching principles.

Essential Reading:

Phillip Hamburger, *Separation of Church and State*.

James H. Hutson, *Religion and the New Republic: Faith in the Founding of America*.

Mark De Wolfe Howe, *The Garden and the Wilderness*.

Supplementary Reading:

Lief Carter, *Constitutional Interpretation: Cases in Law and Religion*.

Stephen L. Carter, *The Culture of Disbelief: How American Law and Politics Trivialize Religious Devotion*.

Louis Fisher, *Religious Liberty in America: Political Safeguards*.

John T. Noonan, Jr., *The Luster of Our Country: The American Experience of Religious Freedom.*

Questions to Consider:

1. Are the religion clauses really necessary? Wouldn't matters of faith and belief be protected under the speech and association protections of the First Amendment? Why would the Founders include special guarantees for religious freedom?

2. Do we need a definition of religion? Why? Suppose we could determine, with reasonable certainty, how the Founders defined religion. Should we be bound by an 18th-century understanding of what religion is or means?

3. Why are two clauses necessary? Do the establishment and free exercise clauses point to different religious freedoms? Where, if at all, do they overlap?

Lecture Twenty-Four—Transcript
Why Is Freedom of Religion so Complex?

The constitutional dimension of the relationship between matters of the soul and matters of state is—and probably always has been—a subject of intense controversy in the United States. In this lecture, we will begin an extended inquiry into freedom of religion. We shall see that the Court's work in this area is often complicated, always confusing. In part, this is because the First Amendment's freedom of religion guarantees, like its freedom of speech guarantees, are multiple and complex. We shall see, as we take up these materials, that part of the complexity is directly traceable to that multiplicity of provisions in the First Amendment, which was also true as we saw in our speech cases. There are several speech clauses; sometimes they conflict with each other; sometimes they pull in different directions; and the same is true of the Constitution's two religion clauses.

The first clause is, of course, the establishment clause. It is worth quoting at the start. The establishment clause provides that "Congress shall make no law respecting an establishment of religion." The second, the free exercise clause, states simply that "Congress shall not prohibit the free exercise of religion."

From these two small clauses, the Court has generated a tremendous jurisprudence, a complicated jurisprudence, and, indeed, a jurisprudence that might be described "charitable," as in "coherent." We shall see that problems of incoherence, or perhaps, to put it more gently, problems of consistency, have characterized the Court's work in this field from the very beginning. That might suggest that these problems of interpretation, that these jurisprudential difficulties, reach back as far as the Founding. That is misleading; that's simply not true. Astonishingly, the Court's work in the field of freedom of religion is almost entirely a product of the 20th century. There is a straightforward, simple reason for this. You will recall the incorporation doctrine, the doctrine through which different parts of the Bill of Rights were made applicable to the states. Because of the incorporation doctrine, the First Amendment's freedom of religion provisions were not really made applicable to the states until the 1940s and thereafter. As a consequence, almost all of the Court's work post-dates World War II.

The Court hasn't had that long a time, in other words, to construct a coherent jurisprudence; and I think the Court should be forgiven, partly for that reason, but also because the underlying issues raise matters of public controversy and academic difficulty that will, of course, take time to resolve. The religion clauses are among the most controversial and ambiguous of the Constitution's provisions. The Court's efforts to give these two clauses meaning have produced an amazingly complex set of rules, an amazingly complex set of doctrines; doctrines and rules so complex that I do not think any single justice can fully comprehend them all, and I am confident that no student of the Constitution can make sense of them all.

When I say no student can make sense of them all, I mean only this: we can understand what the Court has said, but we cannot always reconcile its various rulings. In part, there is another reason, and that is because the two clauses themselves—the establishment clause on the one hand, the free exercise clause on the other—may pull in different directions. Surely, when read together, they point to the need to protect a wide range of religious belief and activity. But the two clauses do, at times, seem to pull in different directions. And indeed, in a later lecture, I will spend time talking about the ways in which we might even want to define religion differently, depending upon which clause we are interpreting.

But for now, I'll consider one small example where the two clauses might pull in different directions. Imagine, as one Supreme Court justice once wrote, "a lonely soldier, stationed at a foreign outpost. He might well claim that his free exercise of religion is impeded if the state does not provide him access, say, to a chaplain, or to a minister of his religious faith."

On the other hand, if the state were to accommodate—I use the word "accommodate" deliberately because it would become an important part of the Supreme Court's jurisprudence—this soldier's religious belief, one might well argue that the state, through the expenditure of monetary resources, has tended to establish that religion or to aid that religion. And this one Supreme Court justice suggested that, "there lies at least one fundamental conflict between the two."

There may be times, in other words—as awful as it might seem— when we have to choose between the two religion clauses; or, as a scholar might say, we might have to rank order their values. And if we do, then we encounter the same fundamental problem we have encountered in nearly every lecture in this course: how do we assign value to these different constitutional provisions? How do we avoid the charge—if we are a judge—that we are simply making it up? Where does the Constitution give us any guidance about which of these two provisions ought to trump the other in the event that they conflict?

Now, I want to be clear about this. This potential conflict on the hypothetical that I have given you isn't a necessary conflict. It's not an inevitable conflict. It is a conflict caused by the way we interpret the two provisions. And other justices have suggested that the conflict that I have described is entirely artificial, one entirely of the Court's own making, and that if we properly understood how to interpret the establishment clause, as well as how to interpret the free exercise clause, we could alleviate any such conflicts.

At stake in how we interpret these two different provisions are important issues about how we make sense of the Constitution as a whole. And, if you'll permit me, it is worth remembering, again, that these are not abstract issues. These are not abstract constitutional issues. They are not abstract theological issues. Behind them are persons, real live persons of faith, persons who choose not to believe, and communities that constantly find themselves involved in disputes about the limits of individual belief and the extent of community power. There is rarely a holiday season that goes by where these kinds of conflicts don't transcend mere constitutional conflicts and become political, everyday conflicts that many of us struggle with in our own communities.

I'd like you to consider two other kinds of problems very briefly, problems that are implicit in nearly every freedom of religion case. So, consider this problem first: under what conditions, if any (and there may be none), may a majority of the community express its beliefs, its shared religious beliefs, in public spaces, such as the nation's elementary schools, or at the opening of legislative sessions? Consider this example: should students be allowed to pray at the beginning of a school day, or at school-sponsored events, such as graduations, for example? These are live problems. When I say they are live problems, I mean they are not theoretical abstractions. They are the kinds of problems that communities wrestle with on an ongoing basis. They are the kinds of problems, of course, that judges must wrestle with.

Think in the abstract now about how thin these provisions are about freedom of religion. How can you possibly find the meaning you need in order to resolve a question as complicated and as controversial as, should students be allowed to pray at the beginning of the school day? Where would you go for meaning? It isn't enough simply to point in the general direction of the "No" establishment clause. The truth is that the establishment clause, as written, doesn't tell you what the correct answer is in that case; nor does the free exercise clause. These two provisions—much like the provisions we considered when we took up the freedom of expression cases—are provisions that point to a class of problems; they don't point to a class of answers.

Or consider another set of questions: under what conditions (again, if any) should the community be permitted to regulate, or even to prohibit, the religious beliefs of individual citizens or particular religious groups? Maybe that's too abstract. Consider a more particular version of the problem: should parents, for example, be permitted to withhold from their children certain types of medical treatments, such as blood transfusions, if it violates their faith? And I hope you'll understand that that, of course, is not an abstraction. Those cases populate the federal courts and state courts—to a lesser extent—every year. And in all of them, we have individuals struggling with their dual commitments to their faith and to United States' Constitution, as citizens of the United States. These are what Felix Frankfurter once described as "great tragedies." And he meant "tragedy" in the Greek sense; not of a clear conflict between right and wrong, but a conflict between competing notions of the good, or competing notions of what is right. Many of the cases we shall see are driven by religious minorities.

I'd like to step back just for a second. I don't believe that at any point in this course I have ever asked you to consider, or even myself to consider, whether or not the Court's work in any particular area— or even whether the Constitution's commitments in any particular area—are good or bad, correctly decided or wrongly decided. I've never asked you, in other words, to consider whether or not the particular constitutional provision we're concerned with—or even the Constitution, more generally—should be considered a success or a failure, or whether the Court's work ought to be considered a success or a failure. But I'd like to do that now. Before we open up specific cases or even specific problems, I think we might ask ourselves, have the religion clauses accomplished what they were intended to accomplish? Of course, there are lots of ways to ask that question; lots of ways to answer that question. I'd like to suggest one just to start.

If we think that the purposes of both clauses were, among other things, first to promote faith or to promote communities of faith; and the second purpose was to keep the state out of the business of regulating faith, how would we measure success or failure? One way to think about that is to acknowledge a sociological fact: there are over 200 major religious denominations in the United States, and scores of what might be called "minor" religious denominations. If one purpose of the religion clauses was to let religion bloom in the United States, then we might well conclude that the great amount of religious diversity that exists in the United States is a testimony to the success of the Constitution's religion provisions. And they might also be a source of continuing difficulty; because that great diversity of religious belief, one might argue, simply increases the number of opportunities for persons of faith to bump up against the rights of other persons, or to bump up against community interests, more generally. Diversity is obviously a strength—it may well be a purpose of the First Amendment—but it is also a source of ongoing conflict.

Some of the difficulties that surround the Court's decisions are a consequence not only of the specific problems that we associate with freedom of religion, but of a larger tension that, by now, is a familiar part of this course: the relationship between individual liberty, more generally, and community interests, more generally, as well. One could argue, I think, that when we take up freedom of religion as a distinct area of constitutional inquiry, that, at the most basic level, we do nothing different than we have done before; that we are interested in seeing, in other words, how the Constitution—perhaps speaking through judges—regulates or mediates the relationship between individual and community.

I don't have any great difficulty with conceptualizing our work in that way; but I worry that doing so might lead us to ignore questions about whether there is something unique and special about our protections for religion. In other words, let me ask this question in a more blunt, direct way. Having protected speech in the opening provisions of the First Amendment, why were the Founders interested in protecting religion?

One might well argue that the speech provisions cover almost all religious questions. You'll recall, when we did the *Minersville* case and *Barnette,* that the judges themselves seemed to switch back and forth between describing that case as a "speech case" and a "religion case," and we'll see that continue through our examination of these cases. The Court will not often spend time thinking carefully about whether this is a religion case or a speech case. It won't be precise in trying to identify the nature of the underlying liberty interest.

Some scholars, and perhaps some judges, have concluded that our unwillingness to really clearly articulate the distinctions between speech and religion is a function of an ongoing problem in our constitutional community; and that is some underlying discomfort with problems of religion, more generally. In other words, some scholars—and to a lesser extent, a few judges—think that our inability to get a clear grasp on the problem of, what is the difference between speech and religion, is indicative of a larger problem in our constitutional society; and that is that we are uncomfortable with notions of faith, more generally; in part because many of us think faith is the ultimate issue of privacy, and that there is something deeply disturbing about having matters of private belief enter the public square. That is a problem that I would like you to think about as we work our way through the Court's opinions.

Now, of course, there's another difficulty (this one I'm sure you saw coming), and that is simply this: if we're going to protect freedom of religion, we are going to need a definition of religion; and more particularly, we'll need a definition of establishment and we'll need a definition of free exercise. I guess you can tell what I am going to say next. The Court has worked on this problem for a long time, and it has come up with a clear and unequivocal answer: We don't know what the definition of religion is.

Now, you'll recall that I said earlier that the Court really has only entered the field of religion past World War II, after the incorporation doctrine made it clear. But, interestingly, there are a couple of 19th century cases. They're very interesting on their own terms, and they're interesting, too, for what they have to say about the definition of religion. They also inaugurate a recurrent fact of jurisprudence. Let me start with that.

I say these early cases inaugurate a fact of the Court's religious jurisprudence simply to point out this: the vast majority of cases that the Court has decided have been driven, as I said before, by religious minorities. And it is really quite remarkable how many of the cases we will take up involve, for example, the Jehovah's Witnesses. The early cases were driven by adherence of the Mormon faith. So consider a quick review of American history.

In the middle-to-late 19th century, Mormons were driven consistently to the West. I tried to say this as delicately as I can. Any student of American history knows that we might describe the Mormon migration as a migration based on persecution, and there is certainly an element of truth in that. But other scholars will argue that the Mormons willingly went west, and were never especially welcome in any community they entered, not simply because of hostility to their faith, but because of hostility to their politics.

Mormons were astute political organizers, and they tended to overrun local communities—not illegally, but through the ballot box. There was great controversy surrounding the Mormon religion and the Mormon expansion westward. Ultimately, the Mormons expanded into the western territories. This becomes important for understanding the First Amendment issue, because when they moved into the territories, they no longer were in states. The territories were administered by the federal government; hence, the First Amendment would apply; and hence, we get our early freedom of religion cases by virtue of federal authority over the western territories.

Now, if you know anything about the history of the Mormon migration west, you know that it was deeply political, often times violent; and opposition to the Mormons often centered upon the practice of polygamy, which, at one point in the Church's history, was an acceptable part of their religious creed. This tended to offend the sensibilities of a great many citizens. And throughout the late-1800s, the federal government passed laws designed to inhibit, to criminalize, the practice of polygamy by members of the Mormon Church.

The Court first took up these issues in a case called *Reynolds v. United States*, especially in the context of the Mormon religion; and in that case, the Court upheld the federal statute that criminalized polygamy. The same issue came to the Court just a little bit later in the well-known case of *Davis v. Beason*, decided in 1890.

Now, there are very interesting factual issues associated with *Davis*. In *Davis,* we have a federal statute that not only prohibited polygamy, but which also made it a crime to belong to a religion that practiced or even said it believed in polygamy. One of the consequences of conviction for violating this statute would be the deprivation of your right to vote. That's an extraordinary statute.

I'm interested in *Davis* in this context, however, because of what it has to say about the definition of religion itself. And I want to quote at some length from Justice Field's majority opinion for the Court. He wrote, "The term 'religion' has reference to one's view of his relations to his Creator and to the obligations they impose in reverence for his being in character and of obedience to his will."

Before we take up the particulars of that definition, it is worth asking, I think, a more fundamental question: how does he know that that is the definition of religion? And of course, it will not do to say, well he found it, for example, in some King James Version of the Bible, or any other religious text you might find. That won't do. We are not interested in whether this is a sensible or defensible definition of religion. That is not our inquiry. Our inquiry is, is that the constitutional definition of religion?

Field starts with the same problem we start with. There is nothing in the constitutional text that actually defines the term. So he must be looking for some other source of constitutional meaning. Is it a precedent? Is it something Madison wrote in *The Federalist Papers*? Is it something Thomas Jefferson wrote to the Baptists? Is it something that reaches back further? You'll recall that, in almost all of our Founding documents, there are references to a creator, even in the Mayflower Compact. Where does this definition come from? And, interestingly, Field feels no compulsion to answer that question. He simply assumes that this definition is, of course the definition of religion, as if there could be no other. And, of course, if you read it carefully, "Our relationship to our Creator," it assumes a creator. It assumes obligations.

And, of course, later scholars and later judges have found—or at least they think they have found—in Field's definition a fundamentally Christian definition of religion, a fundamentally theistic definition of religion; one that might exclude non-theistic traditions as well as non-Christian traditions. And, of course, as it turns out, later courts, as you might expect, have tried to move away from this Christian theistic notion of what religion is. They have tried to accommodate, for example, non-theistic traditions such as Buddhism. But we still have the same difficulty. If we can't be sure that the Constitution privileges a theistic definition, how can we be sure that it doesn't? We have the same underlying problem of ambiguity.

The Court has also taken up the definitional question in lots of different places. Here is another one. This one, decided by the Court in 1972, *Wisconsin v. Yoder*, was a case involving the Amish community in Wisconsin, where the Court said, "A way of life, however virtuous and admirable, may not be interposed as a barrier to state action." You see the kind of problem I'm having here—the problem I love dealing with—is a way of life, especially a virtuous one, by definition a religion? And the Court's suggestion here is, no. In another part of the opinion, the Court suggests that, in order for something to qualify as religion, it must have a religious component. I am enamored of that definition. In order for it to be a religion, it must be religious. Of course, we can't decide if it's religious without knowing what religion is; and, of course, the whole process becomes entirely circular.

In the same decision, *Wisconsin v. Yoder*, the Court wrote, "To have the protection of the religion clauses, the claims must be rooted in religious belief." And there's the problem; of course, they must be rooted in religious belief. But we don't know what constitutes a religious belief. The Court, however, to its credit, tries to give us some guidance.

The Court continues in *Wisconsin v. Yoder*: "Thoreau's choice was philosophical and personal, rather than religious." How do we know? How can we possibly know? So there's something different between a religious way of life—which is immune, at least sometimes, to state regulation—and a way of life that is grounded merely in the philosophical or the personal. A fascinating distinction. I'm not sure how tenable it is; but on some level, I don't care if it's tenable. I'm interested in whether or not it's a distinction that could plausibly be traced back to the Constitution. That is our fundamental obligation. And, of course, as you might imagine, there was nothing in

Wisconsin v. Yoder that could trace that definition back to the Constitution, because it is probably an impossible task.

Here's another case, also directly relevant to the question of definition. It's called *Thomas v. Review Board*. In it, the Court said, "Courts are not arbiters of scriptural interpretation." Now, why would the Court have been compelled to make such a statement? This points to another set of problems, an independent set of problems, but also a set of problems that's grounded in the difficulty of defining religion. What if, speaking just colloquially, we think that the person in front of us is using religion as a dodge or a cover for something else?

This is not an abstract problem either. Remember, there are real human beings who sometimes pay the price of what might be called "religious fraud." I urge you, when you are done with this lecture, to consult your outline; and in it, you will find an address where you should send me money. And in return for your money, I will perform for you a personal miracle. You name it; I will do it for you. I expect to get some money. And I expect not to be prosecuted, because if you try to prosecute me, how are you going to prove that I don't really believe what I am saying? How are you going to prove that my set of fundamental beliefs isn't a religious belief? That I am the architect of the known universe; that I am the Aristotelian first cause; that I am the cause of your being; and the object, or at least should be, of your reverence. How are you going to prove that that isn't a religious belief?

This points to the problem of definition. If you don't have a definition, not only can't you tell what is included, you will not be able to tell what is excluded. And it points to the problem that we have dealt with repeatedly, the problem of power. What I mean by this is the following: in our search for a definition of religion, we have only a number of options that are open to us, and none of them looks especially attractive.

Option number one: we allow the Court, or the nation's courts more generally, to determine what is really a religion and what is not. Hence, the *Thomas v. Review Board*: "Courts are not arbiters of scriptural interpretation." Courts don't want to be in the business of deciding what's really a religion. Who would want to be in that business, other than an egomaniac? And Courts especially don't want to be in the business if they can't find anything in the

Constitution that gives them guidance. One option for the definition of religion is to allow the Court to do it.

Now let me paint this picture a little more darkly. One option is that the Court should decide. What are the courts? They're instrumentalities of the state. Do you really want the state, acting even through seemingly innocuous and benign judges, to be in the business of saying, "This one is really a religion; that one, however, we think is fraud"? I hope you can see the potential dangers here.

Here's another possibility: let everybody decide for themselves. So, when I say, "I am a religion," that's it. There's no state inquiry into the authenticity of my belief. If I think I'm a religion, then I'm a religion. And this, at least, gets us out of the danger of the state involving itself on a daily basis about what's really a religion and what isn't. Surely, the First Amendment couldn't permit that. But the alternative now is something that we've dismissed too easily before: a genuine problem of fraud; a genuine problem that real harm will be done to real individuals if we don't exercise some control over the definition. The question of power, then, refers to the question of who has the constitutional authority to determine what counts as a religion for purposes of the freedom of religion clauses.

Now, permit me just to sort of foreshadow the kinds of issue we will take up. In the next two or three lectures, we will consider the following issues. We will begin with the school prayer cases, and then we will move to a review of establishment clause cases and issues, more generally. And after those two lectures, we will then take up the free exercise clause, which we will see is in even more doctrinal turmoil in the Court's establishment clause jurisprudence. And then, finally, in our last lecture on freedom of religion, I will consider, again, the interaction between the establishment clause and the free exercise clause, and try to figure out ways in which they complement each other and where they might conflict.

Timeline of Cases Discussed in the Course

All cases were before the U.S. Supreme Court unless otherwise noted.

- Chief Justices of the U.S. Supreme Court are listed before cases during which they held office. Chief Justices who died in office are marked †.
- Winning parties are indicated in ***boldface italics***.
- A case marked with an asterisk (*) offered rulings so mixed or so complicated that the designation of an overall winner may be misleading.
- Informal names for some cases are noted in parentheses.

Chief Justice Oliver Ellsworth, March 8, 1796–December 15, 1800

1798 *Calder v. Bull*, 3 U.S. 386*

Chief Justice John Marshall, February 4, 1801–July 6, 1835†

1803 *Marbury v. Madison*, 5 U.S. 137*

1810 *Fletcher v. **Peck***, 10 U.S. 87 (Yazoo Land Fraud Case)

1825 *Eakin v. Raub*, 12 Sergeant & Rawle 330* (Pennsylvania State Supreme Court)

1833 *Barron v. **Baltimore***, 32 U.S. 243

Chief Justice Brooke Taney, March 28, 1836–October 12, 1864†

1837 *Charles River Bridge v. **Warren Bridge***, 36 U.S. 420

1857 *Dred Scott v. **Sandford***, 60 U.S. 393*

Chief Justice Salmon Portland Chase, December 15, 1864–May 7, 1873†

1873 *Butchers' Benevolent Association of New Orleans v. **Crescent City Live-Stock Landing & Slaughter-House Company***, 83 U.S. 36 (Slaughter-House Cases)

1873 *Bradwell v. **State of Illinois***, 83 U.S. 130

Chief Justice Morrison Remick Waite, March 4, 1874–March 23, 1888†

1874 *Minor v. **Happersett***, 88 U.S. 162

1877*Munn v. **Illinois***, 94 U.S. 113 (Granger Cases)

1878*Reynolds v. **United States***, 98 U.S. 145

Chief Justice Melville Weston Fuller, October 8, 1888–July 4, 1910†

1890*Davis v. **Beason, Sheriff***, 133 U.S. 333

1896*Plessy v. **Ferguson***, 163 U.S. 537

1905***Lochner*** v. New York, 198 U.S. 45

Chief Justice Edward Douglass White, December 19, 1910–May 19, 1921†

1919*Schenck v. **United States***, 249 U.S. 47

Chief Justice William Howard Taft, July 11, 1921–February 3, 1930

1923***Meyer*** v. Nebraska, 262 U.S. 390

1925*Pierce v. **Society of Sisters***, 268 U.S. 510

1925***Gitlow*** v. New York, 268 U.S. 652

1927*Buck v. **Bell***, 274 U.S. 200

1927*Whitney v. **California***, 274 U.S. 357

1928*Olmstead v. **United States***, 277 U.S. 438

Chief Justice Charles Evans Hughes, February 24, 1930–June 30, 1941

1937*West Coast Hotel v. **Parrish***, 300 U.S. 379

1937*Palko v. **Connecticut***, 302 U.S. 319

1938***Missouri ex rel. Gaines*** v. Canada 305 U.S. 337

1940***Minersville*** v. Gobitis, 310 U.S. 586 (Flag Salute Case I)

Chief Justice Harlan Fiske Stone, July 3, 1941–April 22, 1946†

1942*Chaplinsky v. **New Hampshire***, 315 U.S. 568

1942*Jones v. **Opelika***, 316 U.S. 584

1943*West Virginia v. **Barnette***, 319 U.S. 624 (Flag Salute Case II)

1944*Korematsu v. **United States***, 323 U.S. 214

Chief Justice Frederick Moore Vinson, June 24, 1946–September 8, 1953†

1947*Everson v. **Board of Education***, 330 U.S. 1

1948*McCollum* v. *Illinois*, 333 U.S. 203

1950*Sweatt* v. *Painter*, 339 U.S. 629

1951*Dennis* v. *United States*, 341 U.S. 494

1952*Beauharnais* v. *Illinois*, 343 U.S. 250

Chief Justice Earl Warren, October 5, 1953–June 23, 1969

1954*Brown* v. *Board of Education I*, 347 U.S. 483 (School Desegregation Case I, Brown I)

1955*Brown* v. *Board of Education II*, 349 U.S. 294

1957*Yates* v. *United States*, 354 U.S. 298

1957*Roth* v. *United States*, 354 U.S. 476

1958*Cooper* v. *Aaron*, 358 U.S. 1

1960*Talley* v. *California*, 362 U.S. 60

1961*Noto* v. *United States*, 367 U.S. 290

1961*Hoyt* v. *Florida*, 368 U.S. 57

1962*Engel* v. *Vitale*, 370 U.S. 421* (School Prayer Case)

1963*Abington Township School District* v. *Schempp*, 374 U.S. 203 (School Prayer Case)

1963*Sherbert* v. *Verner*, 374 U.S. 398

1965*Griswold* v. *Connecticut*, 381 U.S. 479

1966*Harper* v. *Virginia Board of Elections*, 383 U.S. 663

1967*Loving* v. *Virginia*, 388 U.S. 1

1968*United States* v. *O'Brien*, 391 U.S. 367 (Draft Card Case)

1969*Tinker* v. *Des Moines School District*, 393 U.S. 503

1969*Brandenburg* v. *Ohio*, 395 U.S. 444

Chief Justice Warren Earl Burger, June 23, 1969–September 26, 1986

1971*Cohen* v. *California*, 403 U.S. 15

1971*Lemon* v. *Kurtzman*, 403 U.S. 602*

1971*Reed* v. *Reed*, 404 U.S. 71

1972*Eisenstadt* v. *Baird*, 405 U.S. 438

1972*Wisconsin* v. *Yoder*, 406 U.S. 205 (Amish School Case)

1972*Furman* v. *Georgia*, 408 U.S. 238

1973*Roe* v. *Wade*, 410 U.S. 116 (Abortion Case)

1973*Doe* v. *Bolton*, 410 U.S. 179

1973*San Antonio School District* v. *Rodriguez*, 411 U.S. 1

1973 *Frontiero* v. *Richardson*, 411 U.S. 677

1973 *Miller* v. *California*, 413 U.S. 15*

1973 *Paris Adult Theatre I* v. *Slaton*, 413 U.S. 49

1976 *Massachusetts Board of Retirement* v. *Murgia*, 427 U.S. 307

1976 *Planned Parenthood of Missouri* v. *Danforth*, 428 U.S. 52

1976 *Gregg* v. *Georgia*, 428 U.S. 153*

1976 *Craig* v. *Boren*, 429 U.S. 190

1977 *Moore* v. *City of East Cleveland*, 431 U.S. 494

1977 *Trimble* v. *Gordon*, 430 U.S. 762

1977 *Wooley* v. *Maynard*, 430 U.S. 705

1978 *Regents of the University of California* v. *Bakke*, 438 U.S. 265*

1981 *Michael M.* v. *Superior Court of Sonoma County*, 450 U.S. 464

1981 *Thomas* v. *Review Board*, 450 U.S. 707

1982 *Mississippi University for Women* v. *Hogan*, 458 U.S. 718

1983 *Akron* v. *Akron Center for Reproductive Health*, 462 U.S. 416

1983 *Planned Parenthood* v. *Ashcroft*, 462 U.S. 476

1984 *Lynch* v. *Donnelly*, 465 U.S. 668

1984 *Clark* v. *Community for Creative Nonviolence*, 468 U.S. 288

1985 *Wallace* v. *Jaffree*, 472 U.S. 38

1985 *Cleburne* v. *Cleburne Living Center*, 473 U.S. 432

1985 *American Booksellers Association, Inc.* v. *Hudnut*, 771 F.2d 323 (U.S. Court of Appeals, 7th Circuit)

1986 *Bowers* v. *Hardwick*, 478 U.S. 186 (Homosexual Sodomy Case I)

Chief Justice William Hubbs Rehnquist, Sept. 26, 1986–Sept. 3, 2005†

1987 *McCleskey* v. *Kemp*, 481 U.S. 279

1987 *Nollan* v. *California Coastal Commission*, 483 U.S. 825

1989 *DeShaney* v. *Winnebago County*, 489 U.S. 189

1989 *Michael H.* v. *Gerald D.*, 491 U.S. 110

1989 *Texas* v. *Johnson*, 491 U.S. 397

1990 *Employment Division, Ore. Dept. of Human Resources* v. *Smith*, 494 U.S. 872 (Peyote Case)

1990 *Cruzan* v. *Director, Missouri Dept. of Health*, 497 U.S. 261

1991*Barnes* v. *Glen Theatre*, 501 U.S. 560

1992*RAV* v. *City of St. Paul*, 505 U.S. 377

1992*Lee* v. *Weisman*, 505 U.S. 577

1992*Planned Parenthood* v. *Casey*, 505 U.S. 833*

1992*Lucas* v. *South Carolina Coastal Council*, 505 U.S. 1003

1993*Herrera* v. *Collins*, 506 U.S. 390

1993*Baehr* v. *Lewin*, 74 Haw. 645 (Hawaii State Supreme Court)

1993*Church of the Lukumi Babalu Aye, Inc.* v. *Hialeah*, 508 U.S. 520

1993*Wisconsin* v. *Mitchell*, 508 U.S. 476

1993*Heller* v. *Doe*, 509 U.S. 312

1994*Callins* v. *Collins*, 510 U.S. 1141

1996*Romer* v. *Evans*, 517 U.S. 620

1996*United States* v. *Virginia*, 518 U.S. 515

1997*Boerne* v. *Flores*, 521 U.S. 507

1997*Vacco, Attorney General of New York* v. *Quill*, 521 U.S. 793

1997*Reno* v. *American Civil Liberties Union*, 521 U.S. 844

1997*Washington* v. *Glucksberg*, 521 U.S. 702

1999*Baker* v. *Vermont*, 170 Vt 194, 744 A. 2d 864 (Vermont State Supreme Court)

2000*Erie* v. *Pap's A.M.*, 529 U.S. 277

2000*Troxel* v. *Granville*, 530 U.S. 57

2000*Stenberg* v. *Carhart*, 530 U.S. 914 (Partial Birth Abortion Case)

2002*Ashcroft* v. *Free Speech Coalition*, 535 U.S. 234

2002*Tahoe-Sierra Preservation Council* v. *Tahoe Regional Planning Agency*, 535 U.S. 302

2002*Atkins* v. *Virginia*, 536 U.S. 304

2002*Zelman* v. *Simmons-Harris*, 536 U.S. 639

2003*Virginia* v. *Black*, 538 U.S. 343*

2003*Gratz* v. *Bollinger*, 539 U.S. 244

2003*Grutter* v. *Bollinger*, 539 U.S. 306

2003*Lawrence* v. *Texas*, 539 U.S. 558 (Sodomy Case II)

2003*Goodridge* v. *Mass. Dept. of Public Health*, 798 N.E.2d 241 (Massachusetts State Supreme Court)

2005*Roper* v. *Simmons*, 543 U.S. 551

2005*Kelo* v. *New London*, 545 U.S. _ _ _

2005 *McCreary County v. **ACLU*** 545 U.S. _ _ _
2005 *Van Orden v. **Perry***, 545 U.S. _ _ _

Chief Justice John Roberts, Sept. 29, 2005–

Annotated List of Cases—Alphabetical Order

types of opinions

Opinion of the Court: an opinion supported by a majority of the voting justices.

Judgment of the Court: a decision supported by a plurality of the justices voting; does not become a binding precedent for future courts.

Concurring opinion: an opinion by one or more justices that agrees with the result reached by the majority but disagrees with part of the reasoning.

Opinion concurring in judgment: an opinion by one or more justices that agrees with the result reached by a majority or plurality of the Court but offers a different opinion in support of that conclusion.

Dissenting opinion: an opinion by one or more justices that disagrees with the result reached by the majority.

Seriatim opinion: a judicial decision with separate opinions from each judge instead of a majority or plurality opinion announced by the Court.

Note: winning parties are indicated in ***boldface italics***, except for cases with rulings so mixed or so complicated— marked with an asterisk (*)—that the designation of an overall winner may be misleading.

*Abington Township School District v. **Schempp***, 374 U.S. 203 (1963) (School Prayer Case): Vote 7 (White, Brennan, Goldberg, Black, Warren, Douglas, Harlan II)–1 (Stewart)
> Opinion of the Court: Clark; Concurring opinions: Goldberg (Harlan II), Douglas; Dissenting opinion: Stewart

The Court upheld the school prayer decision in *Engel v. Vitale* (370 U.S. 412, 1962) by confirming that a state may not impose any sort of religious requirement in schools.

*Akron v. **Akron Center for Reproductive Health***, 462 U.S. 416 (1983): Vote 5 (Stevens, Powell, T. Marshall, Brennan, Burger)–4 (O'Connor, Rehnquist, White, Blackmun)
> Opinion of the Court: Powell; Dissenting opinion: O'Connor (Rehnquist)

The Court found that parts of the city of Akron's 1978 ordinance imposing several regulations on abortion violated a woman's reproductive rights under *Roe v. Wade*.

American Booksellers Association, Inc. v. *Hudnut*, 771 F.2d 323 (U.S. Court of Appeals, 7th Circuit, 1985):
> Opinion of the Court: Easterbrook (Cudahy); Concurring opinion: Swygert

The 7th Circuit Court of Appeals ruled that an Indianapolis ordinance that criminalized some forms of pornography as a civil rights violation itself violated the First Amendment.

Ashcroft v. ***Free Speech Coalition***, 535 U.S. 234 (2002): Vote 6 (Stevens, Kennedy, Souter, Thomas, Ginsburg, Breyer)–3 (Rehnquist, O'Connor, Scalia)
> Opinion of the Court: Kennedy; Opinion concurring in judgment: Thomas; Dissenting opinions: Rehnquist (Scalia), O'Connor (Rehnquist, Scalia)

The Court agreed with the 9th Circuit that the provisions of the Child Pornography Prevention Act of 1996 were insufficiently related to the state's legitimate interest in prohibiting pornography that actually involved minors.

Atkins v. *Virginia*, 536 U.S. 304 (2002): Vote 6 (Stevens, O'Connor, Kennedy, Souter, Ginsburg, Breyer)–3 (Rehnquist, Scalia, Thomas)
> Opinion of the Court: Stevens; Dissenting opinions: Rehnquist (Scalia, Thomas), Scalia (Rehnquist, Thomas)

The Court decided that the execution of a mentally retarded person would violate the Eighth Amendment's ban on cruel and unusual punishment.

Baehr v. *Lewin*, 74 Haw. 645 (Hawaii State Supreme Court) (5 May 1993):
> Opinion of the Court: Levinson; Concurring opinion: J. Burns; Dissenting opinion: Heen

The Hawaii Supreme Court ruled that the state must show compelling reason for denying same-sex couples equal access to legal marriage.

Baker v. *Vermont*, 170 Vt 194, 744 A. 2d 864 (Vermont State Supreme Court, 1999):
> Opinion of the Court: Amestoy; Concurring opinion: Dooley; Opinion concurring in part and dissenting in part: Johnson

In this case, the Vermont Supreme Court ruled that the exclusion of same-sex couples from the benefits and protections of marriage under state law violated the common benefits clause of the Vermont Constitution.

Barnes v. *Glen Theatre*, 501 U.S. 560 (1991): Vote 5 (Rehnquist, O'Connor, Scalia, Kennedy, Souter)–4 (B. White, T. Marshall, Blackmun, Stevens)
>   Judgment of the Court: Rehnquist; Opinions concurring in judgment: Scalia, Souter; Dissenting opinion: B. White (T. Marshall, Blackmun, Stevens)

In this case, a majority ruled that an Indiana law prohibiting nude dancing performed as entertainment did not violate the First Amendment.

Barron v. ***Baltimore***, 32 U.S. 243 (7 Pet. 243) (1833): Unanimous vote (J. Marshall, W. Johnson, Duvall, Story, Thompson, McLean, Baldwin)
>   Opinion of the Court: J. Marshall

In this case, the Court ruled that the Fifth Amendment, in particular, and the Bill of Rights, more generally, did not apply to the actions of state governments.

Beauharnais v. ***Illinois***, 343 U.S. 250 (1952): Vote 5 (Vinson, Frankfurter, Burton, Clark, Minton)–4 (Black, Reed, Douglas, R. Jackson)
>   Opinion of the Court: Frankfurter; Dissenting opinions: Black (Douglas), Reed (Douglas), Douglas, R. Jackson

The Court upheld a state law that prohibited libelous statements about certain groups against a claim that the statute violated the First Amendment.

Boerne v. *Flores*, 521 U.S. 507 (1997): Vote: 6 (Ginsberg, Thomas, Scalia, Stevens, Rehnquist, Kennedy)– 3 (Souter, Breyer, O'Connor)
>   Opinion of the Court: Kennedy; Concurring opinions: Stevens, Scalia; Dissenting opinions: Souter, Breyer, O'Connor

The Court ruled that Congress exceeded its Fourteenth Amendment enforcement powers by enacting the Religious Freedom Restoration Act (RFRA).

Bowers v. *Hardwick*, 478 U.S. 186 (1986) (Homosexual Sodomy Case I): Vote 5 (Burger, B. White, Powell, Rehnquist, O'Connor)–4 (Brennan, T. Marshall, Blackmun, Stevens)

Opinion of the Court: B. White; Concurring opinions: Burger, Powell; Dissenting opinions: Blackmun (Brennan, T. Marshall, Stevens), Stevens (Brennan, T. Marshall)

The Court upheld a Georgia statute that criminalized consensual sodomy. Later overruled in *Lawrence v. Texas*.

Bradwell v. State of Illinois, 83 U.S. 130 (1873): Vote 8 (Clifford, Swayne, Miller, Davis, Field, Strong, Bradley, Hunt)–1 (S. P. Chase)

Opinion of the Court: Miller; Concurring opinion: Bradley (Swayne, Field); Dissenting without opinion: S. P. Chase

The Court maintained that the right to admission to practice in the courts of a state is not a privilege or immunity of a citizen of the United States.

Brandenburg v. Ohio, 395 U.S. 444 (9 June 1969): Unanimous vote (Warren, Black, Douglas, Harlan II, Brennan, Stewart, White, T. Marshall); Did not participate: Fortas

Opinion of the Court: *Per curiam*; Concurring opinions: Black, Douglas (Black)

The Court ruled that if speech incites imminent unlawful action, it may be restricted, but the burden of proof in all speech cases rests on the state to show that action will result, rather than on the defendant to show that it will not.

Brown v. Board of Education I, 347 U.S. 483 (1954) (School Desegregation Case/Brown I): Unanimous vote (Warren, Black, Reed, Frankfurter, Douglas, R. Jackson, Burton, Clark, Minton)

Opinion of the Court: Warren

The Court decided that segregation in public education is inherently unequal and, thus, a violation of the equal protection clause of the Fourteenth Amendment.

Brown v. Board of Education II, 349 U.S. 294 (1955): Unanimous vote (Warren, Black, Reed, Frankfurter, Douglas, Burton, Clark, Minton, Harlan II)

Opinion of the Court: Warren

The Court ordered the states to end segregation in public elementary schools with "all deliberate speed."

Buck v. Bell, 274 U.S. 200 (1927): Vote: 8 (Taft, Holmes, Van Devanter, McReynolds, Brandeis, Sutherland, Sanford, Stone)–1 (Butler)

Opinion of the Court: Holmes; Dissenting without opinion:

Butler

The Court upheld a Virginia law that permitted involuntary sterilization in some cases.

Butchers' Benevolent Association of New Orleans v. **Crescent City Live-Stock Landing & Slaughter-House Company**, 83 U.S. 36 (1873) (Slaughter-House Cases): Vote 5 (Miller, Clifford, Strong, Hunt, Davis)–4 (Field, Chase, Swayne, Bradley)

> Opinion of the Court: Miller; Dissenting opinions: Field, Bradley, Swayne

The Court ruled that the privileges and immunities clause of the Fourteenth Amendment did not make the Bill of Rights applicable to the states.

Calder v. Bull, 3 U.S. 386 (1798)*: Vote 4 (Cushing, Iredell, Paterson, S. Chase)–0

> Seriatim opinions: Cushing, Iredell, Paterson, S. Chase; Did not participate: Ellsworth, Wilson

The Court held that the *ex post facto* clause in Article I applies only to *laws* that address the criminal law, not to civil matters or cases involving the right to property.

Callins v. **Collins**, 510 U.S. 1141 (1994): No vote recorded because no overall opinion issued—just a denial of a cert petition for the case to be heard.

> Concurring opinion (concurring with the denial): Scalia; Dissenting opinion: Blackmun

In this denial of a *certiorari* petition, the Supreme Court refused to accept an appeal from a defendant who had been sentenced to death by a Texas jury.

Chaplinsky v. **New Hampshire**, 315 U.S. 568 (1942): Unanimous vote (Stone, Roberts, Black, Reed, Frankfurter, Douglas, Murphy, Byrnes, R. Jackson)

> Opinion of the Court: Murphy

The Court ruled that the First Amendment does not protect fighting words. The Court also held that lewd, obscene, profane, and libelous words are not protected under the First Amendment.

Charles River Bridge v. **Warren Bridge**, 36 U.S. 420 (1837): Vote 4 (Taney, Baldwin, Wayne, Barbour)–3 (McLean, Story, Thompson)

> Opinion of the Court: Taney; Concurring opinion: Baldwin; Dissenting opinions: McLean, Story, Thompson

In this case involving the right to property, the Taney Court stressed the authority of the state to regulate private property in the public interest by noting the states' need to respond to changing technologies and economic realities in the early 19th century.

Church of the Lukumi Babulu Aye, Inc. v. *Hialeah*, 508 U.S. 520 (1993): Unanimous vote (Rehnquist, B. White, Blackmun, Stevens, O'Connor, Scalia, Kennedy, Souter, Thomas)
> Opinion of the Court: Kennedy; Concurring opinion: Scalia (Rehnquist); Opinions concurring in judgment: Blackmun (O'Connor), Souter

The Court ruled that a city ordinance designed to prohibit certain kinds of animal sacrifice by members of the Santeria religion violated the free exercise clause.

Clark v. *Community for Creative Nonviolence*, 468 U.S. 288 (1984): Vote 7 (White, Burger, Blackmun, Powell, Rehnquist, Stevens, O'Connor)–2 (Brennan, J. Marshall)
> Opinion of the Court: White; Concurring opinion: Burger; Dissenting opinion: J. Marshall (Brennan)

The Court decided that National Park Service regulations prohibiting overnight camping did not violate the First Amendment, although it conceded that, in some circumstances, sleeping might be considered expressive conduct.

Cleburne v. *Cleburne Living Center*, 473 U.S. 432 (1985): Unanimous vote (Stevens, Powell, Rehnquist, O'Connor, T. Marshall, Brennan, Burger, White, Blackmun)
> Opinion of the Court: White; Concurring opinions: Marshall (Blackmun), Stevens (Burger)

The Court ruled that the denial of a special use permit to Cleburne Living Center, Inc., discriminated against the mentally retarded and violated the equal protection clause of the Fourteenth Amendment.

Cohen v. *California*, 403 U.S. 15 (1971): Vote 5 (Douglas, Harlan II, Brennan, Stewart, T. Marshall)–4 (Burger, Black, B. White, Blackmun)
> Opinion of the Court: Harlan II; Dissenting opinion: Blackmun (Burger, Black, B. White)

In deciding whether a state can outlaw an "offensive" word altogether, the Court decided that "the state has no right to cleanse public debate to the point where it is grammatically palatable to the most squeamish."

*Cooper v. **Aaron***, 358 U.S. 1 (1958): *Per curiam* vote (signed by all nine justices)
> Concurring opinion: Frankfurter

This case reaffirmed the Court's position in *Brown v. Board of Education*, 347 U.S. 483 (1954), and reinstated the Court's authority as the ultimate interpreter of the Constitution.

***Craig** v. Boren*, 429 U.S. 190 (1976): Vote 7 (Brennan, Stewart, B. White, T. Marshall, Blackmun, Powell, Stevens)–2 (Burger, Rehnquist)
> Opinion of the Court: Brennan; Concurring opinions: Powell, Stevens, Blackmun; Opinion concurring in judgment: Stewart; Dissenting opinions: Burger, Rehnquist

The Court struck down an Oklahoma law prohibiting the sale of 3.2 percent beer to males under 21 and women under 18 as a violation of the equal protection clause.

*Cruzan v. **Director, Missouri Dept. of Health***, 497 U.S. 261 (1990): Vote 5 (Rehnquist, B. White, O'Connor, Scalia, Kennedy)–4 (Brennan, T. Marshall, Blackmun, Stevens)
> Opinion of the Court: Rehnquist; Concurring opinions: O'Connor, Scalia; Dissenting opinions: Brennan (Marshall, Blackmun), Stevens

In this case, the Court ruled that under the Fourteenth Amendment's due process clause, every person has a right to refuse medical treatment, even if that decision would lead to death. However, the Court found that this right may be limited by the state's interest in preserving life.

*Davis v. **Beason, Sheriff***, 133 U.S. 333 (1890): Unanimous vote (Fuller, Miller, Field, Bradley, Harlan I, Gray, Blatchford, L. Larmar, Brewer)
> Opinion of the Court: Field

The Court upheld an Idaho territorial law that denied the right to vote to any person who advocated or practiced polygamy or who belonged to an organization that did so.

*Dennis v. **United States***, 341 U.S. 494 (1951): Vote 7 (Vinson, Reed, Frankfurter, R. Jackson, Burton, Clark, Minton)–2 (Black, Douglas)

Opinion of the Court: Vinson; Opinion concurring in judgment: Frankfurter; Concurring opinion: R. Jackson; Dissenting opinions: Black, Douglas; Did not participate: Clark

In this case, the Court examined the constitutionality of the Smith Act as applied to 11 leaders of the Communist party. The Court concluded that the government could not only limit speech directly inciting unlawful action, or conspiring to promote such action, or teaching that such action should occur but may also penalize the act of conspiring to organize a group that would teach that such action ought to occur.

DeShaney v. **Winnebago County**, 489 U.S. 189 (1989): Vote 6 (Scalia, Stevens, O'Connor, Kennedy, Rehnquist, White)–3 (T. Marshall, Brennan, Blackmun)

> Opinion of the Court: Rehnquist; Dissenting opinions: Brennan (T. Marshall), Blackmun

In this case, the Court ruled that a state's failure to protect an individual against private violence does not violate the Fourteenth Amendment.

Dred Scott v. **Sandford**, 60 U.S. 393 (1856–1857): Vote 7 (Taney, Wayne, Catron, Daniel, Nelson, Crier, Campbell)–2 (McLean, Curtis)

> Opinion of the Court: Taney; Concurring opinions: Wayne, Nelson (Grier), Grier, Daniel, Campbell, Catron; Dissenting opinions: McLean, Curtis

In this case from its December 1856 term, the Court ruled in March 1857 that no person of African descent can be a citizen of the United States or any state.

Eakin v. Raub, 12 Sergeant & Rawle 330 (Pennsylvania State Supreme Court) (1825)*:

> Opinion of the Court: Chief Justice Tilghman; Dissenting opinion: Gibson

In this case, the Supreme Court of Pennsylvania considered a case of adverse possession. It is important because in his well-known dissent, Justice Gibson criticized John Marshall's opinion in *Marbury v. Madison* (1803).

Eisenstadt v. **Baird**, 405 U.S. 438 (1972): Vote 6 (Douglas, Brennan, Stewart, B. White, T. Marshall, Blackmun)–1 (Burger)

Opinion of the Court: Brennan; Concurring opinions: Douglas, B. White (Blackmun); Dissenting opinion: Burger; Did not participate: Powell, Rehnquist

The Court decided that the Massachusetts statute that allowed only licensed physicians or pharmacists to distribute contraceptives for the purpose of preventing pregnancy to married persons violated the equal protection clause.

Employment Division, Ore. Dept. of Human Resources v. *Smith*, 494 U.S. 872 (1990): Vote 6 (Rehnquist, White, Stevens, O'Connor, Scalia, Kennedy)–3 (Brennan, Marshall, Blackmun)

Opinion of the Court: Scalia; Opinion concurring in judgment: O'Connor (Brennan, Marshall, Blackmun); Dissenting opinion: Blackmun (Brennan, Marshall)

The Court upheld a drug conviction against a claim that the use of the drug was protected by the free exercise clause. In so ruling, the Court also held that neutral state laws with an adverse impact on the free exercise clause need not be measured against the compelling state interest test.

Engel v. Vitale, 370 U.S. 421 (1962) (School Prayer Case)*: Vote 6 (Warren, Black, Douglas, Clark, Harlan II, Brennan)–1 (Stewart)

Opinion of the Court: Black; Concurring opinion: Douglas; Dissenting opinion: Stewart; Did not participate: Frankfurter, B. White

In this case, the Court ruled that a state law requiring prayers in public schools was a violation of the establishment clause of the First Amendment.

Erie v. *PAP's A.M.*, 529 U.S. 277 (2000): Vote 7 (O'Connor, Rehnquist, Kennedy, Souter, Breyer, Scalia, Thomas)–2 (Ginsberg, Stevens)

Opinion of the Court: O'Connor; Concurring opinion: Scalia (Thomas); Opinion concurring in part and dissenting in part: Souter; Dissenting opinion: Stevens (Ginsburg)

The Court held that a public indecency ordinance applied to prohibit nude dancing did not violate the First Amendment.

*Everson v. **Board of Education***, 330 U.S. 1 (1947): Vote 5 (Vinson, Black, Reed, Douglas, Murphy)–4 (Frankfurter, R. Jackson, W. Rutledge, Burton)

Opinion of the Court: Black; Dissenting opinions: R. Jackson (Frankfurter), W. Rutledge (Frankfurter, R. Jackson, Burton)

The Court affirmed that the establishment clause of the First Amendment applied to the states by incorporation through the Fourteenth Amendment and that the framers had intended the clause to create a wall of separation between church and state.

Fletcher v. Peck, 10 U.S. 87 (1810) (Yazoo Land Fraud Case): Vote 5 (J. Marshall, Washington, W. Johnson, Livingston, Todd)–0
> Opinion of the Court: J. Marshall; Concurring opinion: W. Johnson; Did not participate: Cushing, S. Chase

In this case, the Court ruled that a Georgia statute designed to set aside the Yazoo land frauds was unconstitutional because it infringed on the property rights of innocent third-party purchasers.

Frontiero v. Richardson, 411 U.S. 677 (1973): Vote 8 (Burger, Douglas, Brennan, Stewart, B. White, T. Marshall, Blackmun, Powell)–1 (Rehnquist)
> Judgment of the Court: Brennan; Opinions concurring in judgment: Stewart, Powell (Burger, Blackmun); Dissenting opinion: Rehnquist

In this case, the Court ruled that discrimination on the basis of sex ought to be considered semi-suspect, not a suspect classification, like race.

Furman v. Georgia, 408 U.S. 238 (1972): Vote 5 (Douglas, Brennan, Stewart, B. White, T. Marshall)–4 (Burger, Blackmun, Powell, Rehnquist)
> Opinion of the Court: *Per curiam*; Opinions concurring in judgment: Douglas, Brennan, Stewart, B. White, T. Marshall; Dissenting opinions: Burger (Blackmun, Powell, Rehnquist), Blackmun, Powell (Burger, Blackmun, Rehnquist), Rehnquist (Burger, Blackmun, Powell)

The Court held that the death penalty schemes in Georgia and Texas were cruel and unusual in violation of the Eighth Amendment, but that the death penalty itself was not, by definition, such a violation.

Gitlow v. New York, 268 U.S. 652 (1925): Vote 7 (Taft, Van Devanter, McReynolds, Sutherland, Butler, Sanford, Stone)–2 (Holmes, Brandeis)
> Opinion of the Court: Sanford; Dissenting opinion: Holmes (Brandeis)

In this case, the Court for the first time put forward the doctrine of incorporation, by which the Fourteenth Amendment "incorporated" some of the liberties protected in the Bill of Rights and applied them to the states.

Goodridge v. *Mass. Dept. of Public Health*, 798 N.E. 2d 941 (Mass. State Supreme Court, 2003):
> Opinion of the Court: Marshall; Concurring opinion: Greaney; Dissenting opinions: Spina, Sosman, Cordy

The Massachusetts Supreme Court found that the state may not deny the benefits of civil marriage to two individuals of the same sex.

Gratz v. *Bollinger*, 539 U.S. 244 (2003): Vote 6 (Rehnquist, O'Connor, Scalia, Kennedy Thomas; Breyer)–3 (Stevens, Souter, Ginsburg)
> Opinion of the Court: Rehnquist; Concurring opinions: Thomas, O'Connor; Opinion concurring in judgment: Breyer; Dissenting opinions: Stevens, Ginsberg, Souter

The Court ruled that the use of racial preferences in the University of Michigan's undergraduate admissions violated the equal protection clause of the 14th Amendment.

Gregg v. Georgia, 428 U.S. 153 (1976)*: Vote 7 (Stewart, Powell, Stevens; B. White, Burger, Rehnquist, Blackmun)–2 (Brennan, T. Marshall)
> Judgment of the Court: Stewart; Concurring opinion: B. White (Burger, Rehnquist); Opinions concurring in judgment: White (Burger, Rehnquist), Blackmun; Dissenting opinions: Brennan, T. Marshall

The Court ruled that the death penalty does not violate the cruel and unusual punishment clause when states take steps to ensure that its application is not arbitrary and capricious.

Griswold v. *Connecticut*, 381 U.S. 479 (1965): Vote 7 (Warren, Douglas, Clark, Harlan II, Brennan, B. White, Goldberg)–2 (Black, Stewart)
> Opinion of the Court: Douglas; Concurring opinion: Goldberg (Warren, Brennan); Opinions concurring in judgment: Harlan II, B. White; Dissenting opinions: Black (Stewart), Stewart (Black)

The Court found that a Connecticut statute regulating access to information about contraceptives violated the right of marital privacy as protected by the First, Third, Fourth, Fifth, Ninth, and Fourteenth Amendments.

*Grutter v. **Bollinger***, 539 U.S. 306 (2003): Vote 5 (Ginsberg, Souter, Breyer, Stevens, O'Connor)–4 (Scalia, Thomas, Rehnquist, Kennedy)

> Opinion of the Court: O'Connor; Concurring opinion: Ginsberg; Dissenting opinions: Kennedy, Thomas, Scalia

The Court found that the University of Michigan's law school did not violate the equal protection clause by considering race as a factor in the admissions process.

Harper v. Virginia Board of Elections, 383 U.S. 663 (1966): Vote 6 (Warren, Douglas, Clark, Brennan, B. White, Fortas)–3 (Black, Harlan II, Stewart)

> Opinion of the Court: Douglas; Dissenting opinions: Black, Harlan II (Stewart)

The Court declared the use of a poll tax in Virginia elections unconstitutional under the equal protection clause.

Heller v. Doe, 509 U.S. 312 (1993): Vote 6 (Kennedy, O'Connor, Rehnquist, White, Scalia, Thomas)–3 (Blackmun, Souter, Stevens)

> Opinion of the Court: Kennedy; Concurring in opinion in part: O'Connor; Dissenting opinions: Blackmun, Souter (Blackmun, Stevens)

The Court ruled that Kentucky's involuntary commitment of mentally retarded persons did not violate the equal protection clause under the Fourteenth Amendment.

*Herrera v. **Collins***, 506 U.S. 390 (1993): Vote 6 (Rehnquist, B. White, O'Connor, Scalia, Kennedy, Thomas)—3 (Blackmun, Stevens, Souter)

> Opinion of the Court: Rehnquist; Concurring opinions: O'Connor (Kennedy), Scalia (Thomas); Opinion concurring in judgment: B. White; Dissenting opinion: Blackmun (Stevens, Souter)

The Court considered whether the Constitution permits the government to execute a person who claimed that new evidence had emerged that would prove him not guilty of the crime. The plaintiff filed a petition for *habeas corpus* relief, but the Court struck down his request, claming that federal *habeas corpus* relief was limited to constitutional issues only.

*Hoyt v. **Florida***, 368 U.S. 57 (1961): Unanimous vote (Warren, Black, Frankfurter, Douglas, Clark, Harlan II, Brennan, Whittaker, Stewart)

> Opinion of the Court: Harlan II; Concurring opinion: Warren, Black, Douglas

The Court upheld a Florida law that did not require women to serve on juries because Florida had no deliberate intent to exclude women from jury participation.

*Jones v. **Opelika***, 316 U.S. 584 (1942): Vote: 5 (Roberts, Reed, Frankfurter, Byrnes, R. Jackson)–4 (Stone, Black, Douglas, Murphy)

> Opinion of the Court: Reed; Dissenting opinions: Stone (Black, Douglas, Murphy), Murphy (Stone, Black, Douglas), Black, Douglas, Murphy

The Court ruled that Alabama's ordinance prohibiting the selling of books without a license did not violate the plaintiff's First Amendment rights to freedom of press and religion because by selling some of the books, the plaintiff was engaging in commercial activity.

*Kelo v. **New London***, 545 U.S. _ _ _ (2005): Vote 5 (Stevens, Kennedy, Souter, Ginsburg, Breyer)–4 (O'Connor, Rehnquist, Scalia, Thomas)

> Opinion of the Court: Stevens; Concurring opinion: Kennedy; Dissenting opinions: O'Connor (Rehnquist, Scalia, Thomas), Thomas

The Court ruled that municipal governments may take private property and transfer it to other private parties without violating the takings clause, provided that the transfer is part of an overall plan for economic development.

*Korematsu v. **United States***, 323 U.S. 214 (1944): Vote: 6 (Stone, Black, Reed, Frankfurter, Douglas, W. Rutledge)–3 (Roberts, Murphy, R. Jackson)

> Opinion of the Court: Black; Concurring opinion: Frankfurter; Dissenting opinions: Roberts, Murphy, R. Jackson

The Court held that the Executive Order for relocation that only applied to Japanese Americans did not deprive the plaintiff of his due process rights.

***Lawrence** v. Texas*, 539 U.S. 558 (2003) (Sodomy Case II): Vote 6 (Kennedy, Stevens, Souter, Ginsburg, Breyer, O'Connor)–3 (Scalia, Rehnquist, Thomas)

Opinion of the Court: Kennedy; Concurring opinion: O'Connor; Dissenting opinions: Scalia (Rehnquist, Thomas), Thomas

The Court overruled its decision in *Bowers v. Hardwick* and declared prohibition of homosexual sodomy unconstitutional in *Lawrence v. Texas.*

*Lee v. **Weisman**,* 505 U.S. 577 (1992): Vote 5 (Blackmun, Stevens, O'Connor, Kennedy, Souter)–4 (Rehnquist, B. White, Scalia, Thomas)

Opinion of the Court: Kennedy; Concurring opinions: Blackmun (Stevens, O'Connor), Souter (Stevens, O'Connor); Dissenting opinion: Scalia (Rehnquist, B. White, Thomas)

The Court upheld its decision in *Engel* by ruling that a school policy of including a prayer as part of an official school ceremony violated the establishment clause.

Lemon v. Kurtzman, 403 U.S. 602 (1971)*: Multiple votes

Opinion of the Court: Burger; Concurring opinions: Douglas (Black, T. Marshall), Brennan; Opinion concurring in judgment (Pennsylvania case): B. White; Dissenting opinion (Rhode Island cases): B. White; Did not participate (Pennsylvania case): T. Marshall

In this case, the Court developed a test for determining whether a state statue violates the establishment clause of the Constitution by aiding religion. The Court defined the three prongs of the test as follows: a state must have a secular legislative purpose; the principal or primary effect must be one that neither advances nor inhibits religion; and the statue must not foster an excessive government entanglement with religion.

Lochner v. New York, 198 U.S. 45 (1905): Vote 5 (Fuller, Brewer, Brown, Peckham, McKenna)–4 (Harlan I, E. White, Holmes, Day)

Opinion of the Court: Peckham; Dissenting opinions: Harlan I (E. White, Day), Holmes

In this case, the Court ruled that a New York law that regulated the working conditions of bakery employees violated the right of contract.

Loving v. Virginia, 388 U.S. 1 (1967): Unanimous vote (Warren, Black, Douglas, Clark, Harlan II, Brennan, Stewart, B. White, Fortas)

Opinion of the Court: Warren; Opinion concurring in judgment: Stewart

The court ruled that a Virginia law that prohibited interracial marriage was a violation of the Fourteenth Amendment's equal protection clause.

Lucas v. South Carolina Coastal Council, 505 U.S. 1003 (1992): Vote 6 (Rehnquist, B. White, O'Connor, Scalia, Thomas, Kennedy)–3 (Blackmun, Stevens, Souter)

    Opinion of the Court: Scalia; Concurring opinion: Kennedy; Dissenting opinions: Blackmun, Stevens, Souter

In this case, the Court ruled that a South Carolina law limiting the development of private property as a part of a coastal land preservation program was a violation of the takings clause of the Fifth Amendment.

Lynch v. Donnelly, 465 U.S. 668 (1984): Vote: 5 (Burger, B. White, Powell, Rehnquist, O'Connor)–4 (Brennan, T. Marshall, Blackmun, Stevens)

    Opinion of the Court: Burger; Concurring opinion: O'Connor; Dissenting opinions: Brennan (T. Marshall, Blackmun, Stevens), Blackmun (Stevens)

The Court decided that a municipal display of holiday decorations that included a crèche and some non-religious objects did not violate the First Amendment.

Marbury v. Madison, 5 U.S. 137 (1803)*: Vote 5 (J. Marshall, Paterson, S. Chase, Washington, Moore)–0

    Opinion of the Court: J. Marshall; Did not participate: Cushing

In this case, John Marshall concluded that the Court possesses the power of judicial review.

***Massachusetts Board of Retirement** v. Murgia*, 427 U.S. 307 (1976): Vote 7 (Burger, Brennan, Stewart, B. White, Blackmun, Powell, Rehnquist)–1 (T. Marshall)

    Opinion of the Court: *Per curiam*; Dissenting opinion: T. Marshall; Did not participate: Stevens

The Court decided that the equal protection clause does not require strict scrutiny for a claim of discrimination based on age.

*McCleskey v. **Kemp***, 481 U.S. 279 (1987): Vote 5 (Rehnquist, B. White, Powell, O'Connor, Scalia)–4 (Brennan, T. Marshall, Blackmun, Stevens)

Opinion of the Court: Powell; Dissenting opinions: Brennan (T. Marshall, Blackmun, Stevens), Blackmun (Brennan, T. Marshall, Stevens), Stevens (Blackmun)

The Court rejected a claim that Georgia's system of capital punishment was unconstitutional because it discriminated on the basis of race.

McCollum v. *Illinois*, 333 U.S. 203 (1948): Vote 5 (Black, Frankfurter, R. Jackson, Rutledge, Burton)–1 (Reed)

Opinion of the Court: Black; Concurring opinions: Frankfurter, Jackson; Dissenting opinion: Reed

The Court ruled that religious instruction in public schools violates the establishment clause.

McCreary County v. *ACLU*, 545 U.S. _ _ _ (2005): Vote 5 (Souter, Stevens, O'Connor, Ginsberg, Breyer)–4 (Scalia, Rehnquist, Thomas, Kennedy)

Opinion of the Court: Souter; Concurring opinion: O'Connor; Dissenting opinion: Scalia (Rehnquist, Thomas)

The Court ruled that the public display of the Ten Commandments in a Kentucky courtroom was unconstitutional.

Meyer v. *Nebraska*, 262 U.S. 390 (1923): Vote 7 (Taft, McKenna, Van Devanter, McReynolds, Brandeis, Butler, Sanford)–2 (Holmes, Sutherland)

Opinion of the Court: McReynolds; Dissenting opinion: Holmes, Sutherland

The Court ruled that a Nebraska statute that prohibited the teaching of languages other than English to children violated the Fourteenth Amendment.

Michael H. v. *Gerald D.*, 491 U.S. 110 (1989): Vote 5 (Scalia, O'Connor, Kennedy, Rehnquist, Stevens)–4 (Brennan, White, Blackmun, J. Marshall)

Opinion of the Court: Scalia; Concurring opinions: O'Connor, Stevens; Dissenting opinions: Brennan (Blackmun, J. Marshall), White

The Court upheld a California law under which a child born to a married woman living with her husband was presumed to be a child of the marriage.

Michael M. v. **Superior Court of Sonoma County**, 450 U.S. 464 (1981): Vote 5 (Burger, Stewart, Blackmun, Powell, Rehnquist)–4 (Brennan, B. White, T. Marshall, Stevens)

> Judgment of the Court: Rehnquist; Concurring opinion: Stewart; Opinion concurring in judgment: Blackmun; Dissenting opinions: Brennan (B. White, T. Marshall), Stevens

The Court sustained a California statutory rape law that punished males for sexual relations with a female under the age of 18 years but not females engaged in the same behavior with underage males.

Miller v. California, 413 U.S. 15 (1973)*: Vote 5 (Burger, B. White, Blackmun, Powell, Rehnquist)–4 (Douglas, Brennan, Stewart, T. Marshall)

> Opinion of the Court: Burger; Dissenting opinions: Douglas, Brennan (Stewart, T. Marshall)

In this case, the Court developed a three-part test for defining obscenity, which is not protected under the First Amendment. Justice Burger concluded, "At a minimum, prurient, patently offensive depiction or description of sexual conduct must have serious literary, artistic, political, or scientific value to merit First Amendment protection."

Minersville v. *Gobitis*, 310 U.S. 586 (1940) (Flag Salute Case I): Vote 8 (Hughes, McReynolds, Roberts, Black, Reed, Frankfurter, Douglas, Murphy)–1 (Stone)

> Opinion of the Court: Frankfurter; Concurring without opinion: McReynolds; Dissenting opinion: Stone

The Court upheld a Pennsylvania law that required all public school children to begin each day with a salute to the American flag. The Court decided that the law was not a violation of freedom of speech or religion.

Minor v. **Happersett**, 88 U.S. 162 (21 Wall. 162) (1874): Unanimous vote (Waite, Clifford, Swayne, Miller, Davis, Field, Strong, Bradley, Hunt)

> Opinion of the Court: Waite

The Court ruled unanimously that a woman's right of suffrage was not protected by the Constitution.

Mississippi University for Women v. **Hogan**, 458 U.S. 718 (1982): Vote 5 (Brennan, B. White, T. Marshall, Stevens, O'Connor)–4 (Burger, Blackmun, Powell, Rehnquist)

Opinion of the Court: O'Connor; Dissenting opinions: Burger, Blackmun, Powell (Rehnquist)

The Court ruled that the Mississippi University's nursing school for women violated the equal protection clause of the Fourteenth Amendment by not allowing men to attend.

Missouri ex rel. Gaines v. *Canada*, 305 U.S. 337 (1938): Vote 6 (Hughes, Brandeis, Stone, Roberts, Black, Reed)–2 (McReynolds, Butler)

Opinion of the Court: Hughes; Dissenting opinion: McReynolds (Butler)

The Court ruled that the racially discriminatory admissions policy of the all-white University of Missouri law school violated the equal protection clause.

Moore v. *City of East Cleveland*, 431 U.S. 494 (1977): Vote 5 (Brennan, T. Marshall, Blackmun, Powell, Stevens)–4 (Burger, Stewart, B. White, Rehnquist)

Judgment of the Court: Powell; Concurring opinion: Brennan (T. Marshall); Opinion concurring in judgment: Stevens; Dissenting opinions: Burger, Stewart (Rehnquist), B. White

The Court decided an East Cleveland housing ordinance that allowed only immediate family members to live together violated the due process clause of the Fourteenth Amendment.

Munn v. *Illinois*, 94 U.S. 113 (1877) (Granger Cases): Vote 7 (Waite, Clifford, Swayne, Miller, Davis, Bradley, Hunt)–2 (Field, Strong)

Opinion of the Court: Waite; Dissenting opinion: Field (Strong)

In this case, the Court decided that state laws regulating how much railroads could charge to move goods and people was not a violation of the right to property.

Nollan v. *California Coastal Commission*, 483 U.S. 825 (1987): Vote 5 (Rehnquist, B. White, Powell, O'Connor, Scalia)–4 (Brennan, T. Marshall, Blackmun, Stevens)

Opinion of the Court: Scalia; Dissenting opinions: Brennan (T. Marshall), Blackmun, Stevens (Blackmun)

The Court ruled that a coastal development permit issued by the California Costal Commission violated the takings clause of the Fifth Amendment because it deprived the plaintiffs of the reasonable use of their property.

Noto v. United States, 367 U.S. 290 (1961): Vote 7 (Harlan II, Frankfurter, Whittaker, Clark, Stewart, Black, Douglas)–2 (Brennan, Warren)

> Opinion of the Court: Harlan; Concurring opinions: Black, Douglas; Remand to lower court with request to dismiss: Brennan (Warren)

In this case, the Court distinguished sharply between the advocacy of illegal action, which may be prohibited under the First Amendment, and the advocacy of ideas, which may not be prohibited.

*Olmstead v. **United States***, 277 U.S. 438 (1928): Vote 5 (Taft, Van Devanter, McReynolds, Sutherland, Sanford)–4 (Holmes, Brandeis, Butler, Stone)

> Opinion of the Court: Taft; Dissenting opinions: Holmes (Stone), Brandeis (Stone), Butler (Stone), Stone

The Court ruled that the Fourth Amendment did not prohibit the use of wiretaps to monitor private telephone conversations without an actual trespass onto private property.

*Palko v. **Connecticut***, 302 U.S. 319 (1937): Vote 8 (Hughes, McReynolds, Brandeis, Sutherland, Stone, Roberts, Cardozo, Black)–1 (Butler)

> Opinion of the Court: Cardozo; Dissenting without opinion: Butler

The Court ruled that the Fourteenth Amendment did not incorporate the guarantee against double jeopardy in the Fifth Amendment. Palko was executed.

*Paris Adult Theatre I v. **Slaton***, 413 U.S. 49 (1973): Vote 5 (Burger, B. White, Blackmun, Powell, Rehnquist)–4 (Douglas, Brennan, Stewart, T. Marshall)

> Opinion of the Court: Burger; Dissenting opinions: Douglas, Brennan (Stewart, T. Marshall)

The Court upheld a Georgia statute that outlawed "hard-core" pornography.

*Pierce v. **Society of Sisters***, 268 U.S. 510 (1925): Unanimous vote (Taft, Holmes, Van Devanter, McReynolds, Brandeis, Sutherland, Butler, Sanford, Stone)

> Opinion of the Court: McReynolds

The Court concluded that an Oregon law requiring a public school education for children ages 8 to 16 was a violation of parents' right to direct the upbringing and education of their children.

Planned Parenthood of Missouri v. *Danforth*, 428 U.S. 52 (1976): Multiple votes
>Opinion of the Court: Blackmun; Concurring opinion: Stewart (Powell); Dissenting opinions: B. White (Burger, Rehnquist), Stevens

In this case, the Court responded to several provisions of a 1974 Missouri act passed in response to *Roe v. Wade*, including a provision that required a married woman to obtain the consent of her husband for an abortion.

Planned Parenthood v. Ashcroft, 462 U.S. 476 (1983): Multiple votes
>Judgment of the Court: Powell; Opinion concurring in judgment: O'Connor (B. White, Rehnquist); Dissenting opinion: Blackmun (Brennan, T, Marshall, Stevens)

The Court upheld a Missouri regulation requiring parental consent for "unemancipated minors" to obtain an abortion, coupled with a provision that provided, in some cases, for an alternative process for judicial approval.

Planned Parenthood v. Casey, 505 U.S. 833 (1992)*: Vote 5 (Blackmun, Stevens, O'Connor, Kennedy, Souter)–4 (Rehnquist, B. White, Scalia, Thomas)
>Judgment of the Court: O'Connor, Kennedy, Souter; Concurring opinion: Stevens; Opinion concurring in judgment: Blackmun; Dissenting opinions: Rehnquist (B. White, Scalia, Thomas), Scalia (Rehnquist, B. White, Thomas)

A plurality of the Court refused to overrule *Roe* but in the process worked several substantial changes in the Court's abortion jurisprudence, including eliminating the trimester and viability framework and replacing the compelling state interest test with the undue burden test.

Plessy v. Ferguson, 163 U.S. 537 (1896): Vote 7 (Fuller, Field, Gray, Brown, Shiras, E. White, Peckham)–1 (Harlan I)
>Opinion of the Court: Brown; Dissenting opinion: Harlan I; Did not participate: Brewer

In announcing the separate but equal doctrine, the Court ruled that Louisiana's separate car law did not violate the equal protection clause of the Fourteenth Amendment.

RAV v. City of St. Paul, 505 U.S. 377 (1992): Unanimous vote (Rehnquist, B. White, Blackmun, Stevens, O'Connor, Scalia, Kennedy, Souter, Thomas)

>   Opinion of the Court: Scalia; Opinions concurring in judgment: B. White (Blackmun, Stevens, O'Connor), Blackmun, Stevens (B. White, Blackmun)

In this case, the Court struck down a St. Paul ordinance that forbade placing "on public or private property a symbol or object," such as a burning cross or a Nazi swastika, "which one knows or has reasonable grounds to know arouses anger, alarm, or resentment in others on the basis of race, color, creed, religion or gender."

Reed v. Reed, 404 U.S. 71 (1971): Unanimous vote (Burger, Douglas, Brennan, Stewart, B. White, T. Marshall, Blackmun, Powell, Rehnquist)

>   Opinion of the Court: Burger

The Court found that an Idaho statue giving preference to males in the administration of a decedent's estate violated the equal protection clause of the Fourteenth Amendment.

Regents of the University of California v. Bakke, 438 U.S. 265 (1978)*: Multiple votes

>   Judgment of the Court: Powell; Opinions concurring in part and dissenting in part: Brennan, B. White, T. Marshall, Blackmun, Stevens (Burger, Stewart, Rehnquist), B. White, T. Marshall, Blackmun

A plurality of the Court held that public universities may not constitutionally use numerical quotas in their admissions programs but may use race as a criterion in admissions.

*Reno v. **American Civil Liberties Union***, 521 U.S. 844 (1997): Vote 7 (Stevens, Scalia, Kennedy, Souter, Thomas, Ginsburg, Breyer)–2 (Rehnquist, O'Connor)

>   Opinion of the Court: Stevens; Opinion concurring in part and dissenting in part: O'Connor (Rehnquist)

The Court ruled that a federal law prohibiting the transmission of obscene or indecent messages on the Internet to recipients younger than 18 years of age was unconstitutional because it was overbroad.

*Reynolds v. **United States***, 98 U.S. 145 (1878): Unanimous vote (Waite, Clifford, Swayne, Miller, Strong, Bradley, Hunt, Harlan I; Field)

Opinion of the Court: Day; Opinion concurring in part and dissenting in part: Field

In this case, the Court sustained the constitutionality of a congressional statute that forbade polygamy as applied to the territory of Utah.

***Roe** v. Wade*, 410 U.S. 116 (1973) (Abortion Case): Vote 7 (Burger, Douglas, Brennan, Stewart, T. Marshall, Blackmun, Powell)–2 (B. White, Rehnquist)

Opinion of the Court: Blackmun; Concurring opinions: Burger, Douglas, Stewart; Dissenting opinions: B. White (Rehnquist), Rehnquist

The Court ruled that a right to an abortion was part of the Fourteenth Amendment's concept of personal liberty and privacy. The Court also devised an elaborate scheme, based on the state's interests in protecting the fetus at the point of viability and the mother's health, that permits the state to regulate the abortion decision at certain points in the pregnancy, provided that the state's interest is "compelling."

Romer** v. **Evans, 517 U.S. 620 (1996): Vote 6 (Stevens, O'Connor, Kennedy, Souter, Ginsburg, Breyer)–3 (Rehnquist, Scalia, Thomas)

Opinion of the Court: Kennedy; Dissenting opinion: Scalia (Rehnquist, Thomas)

The Court invalidated a Colorado constitutional amendment that barred local governments from enforcing any regulation or conferring any entitlement that granted homosexuals protected minority status.

Roper** v. **Simmons, 543 U.S. 551 (2005): Vote 5 (Kennedy, Stevens, Breyer, Ginsburg, Souter)–4 (Rehnquist, Scalia, O'Connor, Thomas)

Opinion of the Court: Kennedy; Concurring opinion: Stevens (Ginsburg); Dissenting opinions: O'Connor, Scalia (Rehnquist, Thomas)

The Court ruled that the Eighth Amendment forbids the execution of offenders who were under the age of 18 when their crimes were committed.

Roth** v. **United States, 354 U.S. 476 (1957): Vote 6 (Warren, Frankfurter, Burton, Clark, Brennan, Whittaker)–3 (Black, Douglas, Harlan II)

Opinion of the Court: Brennan; Opinion concurring in judgment: Warren; Opinion concurring in part and dissenting in part: Harlan II; Dissenting opinion: Douglas (Black)

In this case, the Court established that the test for obscenity is "whether to an average person, applying contemporary community standards, the dominant theme of the material taken as a whole appeals to prurient interest."

San Antonio School District v. *Rodriguez*, 411 U.S. 1 (1973): Vote 5 (Burger, Stewart, Blackmun, Powell, Rehnquist)–4 (Douglas, Brennan, B. White, T. Marshall)

Opinion of the Court: Powell; Concurring opinion: Stewart; Dissenting opinions: Brennan, B. White (Douglas, Brennan), T. Marshall (Douglas)

The Court found that a public school education is not a fundamental right under the due process clause and that economic classifications are not entitled to strict scrutiny under the equal protection clause.

Schenck v. *United States*, 249 U.S. 47 (1919): Unanimous vote (E. White, McKenna, Holmes, Day, Van Devanter, Pitney, McReynolds, Brandeis, Clarke)

Opinion of the Court: Holmes

In upholding the Espionage Act of 1917, the Court, speaking through Justice Holmes, established the clear and present danger test.

Sherbert v. *Verner*, 374 U.S. 398 (1963): Vote 7 (Warren, Black, Douglas, Clark, Brennan, Stewart, Goldberg)–2 (Harlan II, B. White)

Opinion of the Court: Brennan; Concurring opinion: Douglas; Opinion concurring in judgment: Stewart; Dissenting opinion: Harlan II (B. White)

In this case, the Court ruled that a secular regulation that "substantially burdens" a religious practice must be justified by a compelling state interest. Parts of this case were later overruled by *Employment Division v. Smith* (1989).

Stenberg v. *Carhart*, 530 U.S. 914 (2000): Vote 5 (Stevens, O'Connor, Souter, Ginsburg, Breyer)–4 (Rehnquist, Scalia, Kennedy, Thomas)

Opinion of the Court: Breyer; Concurring opinions: Stevens (Ginsberg), O'Connor, Ginsberg (Stevens); Dissenting opinions: Rehnquist, Scalia, Kennedy (Rehnquist), Thomas (Rehnquist, Scalia)

The Court concluded that a Nebraska law that banned dilation and evacuation procedures during abortion procedures (or so-called partial-birth abortions) was unconstitutional because it was too broad and did not include a health exception.

Sweatt v. Painter, 339 U.S. 629 (1950): Unanimous vote (Vinson, Black, Reed, Frankfurter, Douglas, R. Jackson, Burton, Clark, Minton)
    Opinion of the Court: Vinson
The Court ordered the state of Texas to admit an African-American student to its all-white law school, even though the state did have a separate law school for African-Americans.

*Tahoe-Sierra Preservation Council v. **Tahoe Regional Planning Agency***, 535 U.S. 302 (2002): Vote 6 (Stevens, O'Connor, Kennedy, Souter, Ginsberg, Breyer)–3 (Rehnquist, Scalia, Thomas)
    Opinion of the Court: Stevens; Dissenting opinions: Rehnquist (Scalia, Thomas), Thomas (Scalia)
The Court refused to rule that a series of local statutes that placed moratoria on land development in advance of a comprehensive land-use plan necessarily constituted a "temporary taking" under the Fifth Amendment.

Talley v. California, 362 U.S. 60 (1960): Vote 6 (Black, Warren, Douglas, Brennan, Stewart; Harlan II)–3 (Clark, Frankfurter, Whittaker)
    Opinion of the Court: Black; Concurring opinion: Harlan; Dissenting opinion: Clark
The Court found that a California ordinance restricting the distribution of anonymous handbills violates the First Amendment.

*Texas v. **Johnson***, 491 U.S. 397 (1989): Vote 5 (Brennan, T. Marshall, Blackmun, Scalia, Kennedy)–4 (Rehnquist, B. White, Stevens, O'Connor)
    Opinion of the Court: Brennan; Concurring opinion: Kennedy; Dissenting opinions: Rehnquist (B. White, O'Connor), Stevens
In overturning a criminal conviction for burning a U.S. flag, the Court ruled that the defendant's actions were constitutionally protected under the First Amendment because he was expressing a political viewpoint and because his actions qualified as symbolic speech.

***Thomas** v. Review Board*, 450 U.S. 707 (1981): Vote: 8 (Burger,

Brennan, Stewart, B. White, T. Marshall, Blackmun, Powell, Stevens)–1 (Rehnquist)

>Opinion of the Court: Burger; Opinion concurring in judgment: Blackmun; Dissenting opinion: Rehnquist

The Court decided that a state decision denying unemployment benefits to the plaintiff impermissibly interfered with his free exercise of religion.

Tinker v. *Des Moines School District*, 393 U.S. 503 (24 Feb. 1969): Vote 7 (Warren, Douglas, Brennan, Stewart, B. White, Fortas, T. Marshall)–2 (Black, Harlan II)

>Opinion of the Court: Fortas; Concurring opinions: Stewart, B. White; Dissenting opinions: Black, Harlan II

In this case, the Court held that the decision of school administrators to prohibit students from wearing armbands to protest the war in Vietnam was an unconstitutional infringement of symbolic speech.

Trimble v. *Gordon*, 430 U.S. 762 (1977): Vote 5 (Stevens, T. Marshall, Powell, Brennan, White)–4 (Rehnquist, Blackmun, Stewart, Burger)

>Opinion of the Court: Powell; Dissenting opinions: Rehnquist, Blackmun, Stewart, Burger

The Court struck down an Illinois inheritance statute that disadvantaged nonmarital children as a violation of the equal protection clause.

Troxel v. *Granville*, 530 U.S. 57 (2000): Vote 6 (Rehnquist, O'Connor, Souter, Thomas, Ginsburg, Breyer)–3 (Stevens, Scalia, Kennedy)

>Judgment of the Court: O'Connor; Opinions concurring in judgment: Souter, Thomas; Dissenting opinions: Stevens, Scalia, Kennedy

In this case, the Court struck down Washington's third-party visitation statute, noting that it interfered with parents' due process right "to make decisions concerning the care, custody, and control" of their children.

United States v. *O'Brien*, 391 U.S. 367 (1968) (Draft Card Case): Vote 7 (Fortas, Stewart, White, Harlan II, Black, Warren, Brennan)–1 (Douglas)

>Opinion of the Court: Warren; Concurring opinion: Harlan II; Dissenting opinion: Douglas; Did not participate: T. Marshall

In upholding a conviction based on the burning of a draft card, the Court developed a three-part test to determine when the First Amendment protects symbolic speech or expressive conduct.

United States v. Virginia, 518 U.S. 515 (1996): Vote 7 (Rehnquist, Stevens, O'Connor, Kennedy, Souter, Ginsburg, Breyer)–1 (Scalia)
> Opinion of the Court: Ginsburg; Opinion concurring in judgment: Rehnquist; Dissenting opinion: Scalia; Did not participate: Thomas

In this case, the Court struck down the males-only admissions policy of the Virginia Military Institute as a violation of the equal protection clause. The Court ruled that for sex discrimination to be constitutional, the government must present an "exceedingly persuasive justification" to treat men and women differently.

Vacco, Attorney General of New York v. Quill, 521 U.S. 793 (1997): Unanimous vote (Ginsberg, Souter, Thomas, Breyer, Scalia, Stevens, Rehnquist, O'Connor, Kennedy)
> Opinion of the Court: Rehnquist; Concurring opinions: O'Connor, Ginsburg, Souter, Stevens, Breyer

The Court found that New York's ban on physician-assisted suicide did not violate the equal protection clause because the ban was rationally related to the state's interest in protecting medial ethics.

Van Orden v. Perry, 545 U.S. _ _ _ (2005): Vote 5 (Rehnquist, Scalia, Kennedy, Thomas, Breyer)–4 (Ginsberg, O'Connor, Souter, Stevens)
> Opinion of the Court: Rehnquist; Concurring opinion: Breyer (Scalia, Thomas); Dissenting opinion: Stevens (Ginsberg)

The Court ruled that a monument of the Ten Commandments on the Texas state capitol building grounds did not violate the First Amendment's establishment clause.

Virginia v. Black, 538 U.S. 343 (2003)*: Vote 7 (Ginsberg, Breyer, Scalia, Rehnquist, Kennedy, O'Connor, Stevens)–2 (Thomas, Scalia)
> Opinion of the Court: O'Connor; Concurring opinions: Scalia (Rehnquist), Souter (Kennedy, Ginsburg); Dissenting opinion: Thomas

The Court ruled that Virginia's cross-burning statue prohibiting the burning of a cross to intimidate any person or group did not violate the First Amendment.

*Wallace v. **Jaffree**,* 472 U.S. 38 (1985): Vote 6 (Brennan, T. Marshall, Blackmun, Powell, Stevens, O'Connor)–3 (Burger, B. White, Rehnquist)

Opinion of the Court: Stevens; Concurring opinion: Powell; Opinion concurring in judgment: O'Connor; Dissenting opinions: Burger, B. White, Rehnquist

The Court struck down an Alabama statute that requited a one-minute "moment of silence" at the beginning of the school day as a violation of the establishment clause.

***Washington** v. Glucksberg,* 521 U.S. 702 (1997): Unanimous vote (Rehnquist, Stevens, O'Connor, Scalia, Kennedy, Souter, Thomas, Ginsburg, Breyer)

Opinion of the Court: Rehnquist; Concurring opinions: Ginsburg, Breyer, Stevens, Souter, O'Connor (Ginsburg, Breyer)

The Court decided that Washington's prohibition against physician-assisted suicide does not violate the due process clause of the Fourteenth Amendment.

*West Coast Hotel v. **Parrish**,* 300 U.S. 379 (1937): Vote 5 (Hughes, Brandeis, Stone, Roberts, Cardozo)–4 (Van Devanter, McReynolds, Sutherland, Butler)

Opinion of the Court: Hughes; Dissenting opinion: Sutherland (Van Devanter, McReynolds, Butler)

The Court upheld a wages and hours statute and, thus, overruled *Lochner v. New York.*

*West Virginia v. **Barnette**,* 319 U.S. 624 (1943): Vote 6 (Stone, Black, Douglas, Murphy, R. Jackson, W. Rutledge)–3 (Roberts, Reed, Frankfurter)

Opinion of the Court: R. Jackson; Concurring opinions: Black (Douglas), Murphy; Dissenting opinion: Frankfurter; Dissenting without opinion: Roberts, Reed

The Court ruled that a state law requiring students in public elementary schools to salute the flag violated the First Amendment. This case overruled *Minersville v. Gobitis* (1940).

*Whitney v. **California**,* 274 U.S. 357 (1927): Unanimous vote (Taft, Holmes, Van Devanter, McReynolds, Brandeis, Sutherland, Butler, Sanford, Stone)

Opinion of the Court: Sanford; Concurring opinion: Brandeis (Holmes)

The Court upheld the California Criminal Syndicalism Act of 1919, which made it a crime to organize or knowingly become a member of an organization that aims to bring about revolutionary change through the use of violence.

Wisconsin v. *Mitchell*, 508 U.S. 476 (1993): Unanimous vote (Rehnquist, B. White, Blackmun, Stevens, O'Connor, Scalia, Kennedy, Souter, Thomas)
>   Opinion of the Court: Rehnquist

The Court unanimously upheld a state hate crime law that provided for up to five years' additional imprisonment for an offender who intentionally selected his or her victim because of the person's race, religion, color, disability, sexual orientation, national origin, or ancestry.

*Wisconsin v. **Yoder***, 406 U.S. 205 (1972) (Amish School Case): Vote 6 (Burger, Brennan, Stewart, B. White, T. Marshall, Blackmun)–1 (Douglas)
>   Opinion of the Court: Burger; Concurring opinions: Stewart (Brennan), B. White (Brennan, Stewart); Dissenting opinion: Douglas; Did not participate: Powell, Rehnquist

The Court held that the First Amendment protected the religious rights of the Amish to withdraw their children from public schools at the age of 14.

*Wooley v. **Maynard***, 430 U.S. 705 (1977): Vote 6 (Burger, Brennan, Stewart, T. Marshall, Powell, Stevens)–3 (B. White, Blackmun, Rehnquist)
>   Opinion of the Court: Burger; Dissenting opinions: B. White (Rehnquist, Blackmun), Rehnquist (Blackmun)

The Court ruled that under the First Amendment, New Hampshire could not force a citizen to display the words "Live Free or Die" on a license plate.

Yates v. *United States*, 354 U.S. 298 (1957): Vote 6 (Warren, Black, Frankfurter, Douglas, Burton, Harlan II)–1 (Clark)
>   Opinion of the Court: Harlan II; Opinion concurring in judgment: Burton; Opinion concurring in part and dissenting in part: Black (Douglas); Dissenting opinion: Clark; Did not participate: Brennan, Whittaker

The Court overturned the convictions of 14 communist leaders on the grounds that the Smith Act undermined free speech.

Zelman v. *Simmons-Harris*, 536 U.S. 639 (2002): Vote: 5 (Rehnquist, O'Connor, Scalia, Kennedy, Thomas)–4 (Stevens, Souter, Ginsburg, Breyer)

> Opinion of the Court: Rehnquist; Concurring opinions: O'Connor, Thomas; Dissenting opinions: Stevens, Souter (Stevens, Ginsburg, Breyer), Breyer (Stevens, Souter)

The Court upheld an Ohio school voucher plan against a claim that the plan violated the establishment clause of the First Amendment.

Glossary

advisory opinion: A formal opinion issued by a court about a hypothetical or nonadversarial state of affairs or when no concrete case or controversy is to be decided.

affidavit: A written and signed declaration of facts made before a notary public or a similar officer.

affirm: A decision by a higher or superior court to uphold or confirm a decision by a lower or inferior court.

amicus curiae: "Friend of the court"; a person or group, not a litigant in the case, that submits a brief on an issue before the court.

appeal: A request asking a higher court to review a trial or lower-court decision to decide whether it was correct.

appellant: A person or group who appeals a judicial decision from a lower court. This is the party listed first in the title of a decision.

appellate jurisdiction: When a higher or superior court has the authority to review the judgment and proceedings of an inferior or lower court.

appellee: The person or group who won the suit in a lower court and against whom an appeal is taken. This is the party listed second in the title of a decision.

balancing: A method of constitutional interpretation in which judges weigh one set of interests or rights against another set of interests or rights. This method is often found in First Amendment cases or in cases where two or more rights are in apparent tension.

bench trial: A trial, in a lower court, by a judge and without a jury.

Brandeis brief: A lawyer's brief that utilizes not only case law and other legal materials but also a wide variety of non-legal materials, such as legislative findings, public policy documents, and data from social science. Named after Justice Louis Brandeis, who as a lawyer was among the first to use such materials.

brief: A written argument of law submitted by lawyers explaining why a case should be decided in favor of their client.

case and controversy (also "case or controversy"): A matter before a court in which the parties suffer real and direct harm and seek judicial resolution. The phrase often refers to Article III, Section 2 of the Constitution. Contrast with **advisory opinion**.

certification, writ of: Similar to an appeal, this is a process in which a lower court forwards a case to, and requests guidance from, an appellate court regarding unresolved legal questions.

certiorari, **writ of**: This is a method of appeal to the Supreme Court and the primary means by which the Court sets its docket. Technically, it is an order issued by the Supreme Court directing the lower court to transmit records for a case the Court has accepted on appeal.

circuit court: An appellate court; in the federal judicial system, each circuit covers several states; in most states, the court's jurisdiction is by county.

comity: Courtesy, or the respect a court owes to other branches and levels of government.

common law: A type of legal system that is based primarily on judicial decisions rather than legislative action and statutory law.

complaint: A written statement by the plaintiff indicating legally and factually how he or she has been harmed by the defendant.

concurring opinion: An opinion by a judge who agrees with the result reached by the majority or plurality but disagrees with all or part of the reasoning.

constitutional court: A court with the authority to review whether governmental action conforms with the national constitution; in the United States, such courts are created under Article III.

counsel: The lawyers of record in a case.

de facto: In fact or practice.

defendant: The person named as the offender in a civil complaint or, in a criminal case, the person accused of the crime.

de jure: In law or official policy.

deposition: An oral statement, whether by a defendant or a witness, usually taken by an attorney, that may later be used at trial. See also **discovery.**

dicta (*obiter dicta*): Statements by a court that are not strictly necessary to reach the result in the case or that are not necessarily relevant to the result of the case. *Dicta* do not have the binding force of precedent.

discovery: The process before trial in which attorneys investigate what happened, often by using written interrogatories and taking oral depositions.

dissenting opinion: An opinion filed by a judge or judges who do not agree with the result reached by the majority of the court.

distinguish: To show why a case differs from another case and, thus, does not legally control the result.

diversity jurisdiction: The authority of federal courts to hear cases in which the litigants are citizens of different (or diverse) states.

docket: A full record of a court's proceedings.

doctrinalism: A method of constitutional interpretation that decides cases by appealing to specific doctrines, such as the "clear and present danger" test, and a way of organizing constitutional law more generally. This method is often found in First Amendment and equal protection cases.

doctrinal test: A set of guidelines, usually established through precedent, that the Court uses to adjudicate specific cases in specific areas of constitutional law. For example, the Court uses a three-part doctrinal test called the Miller test, first formulated in *Miller v. California* (1973), to determine whether materials are obscene. Other examples include the *Lemon v. Kurtzman* (1971) test for cases determining when a law has the effect of establishing religion, and the clear and present danger test in cases of subversive speech. Closer to terms of art than definitions, doctrinal tests typically have meanings that are much more fluid and dynamic than those of many other legal concepts: They change may from judge to judge and case to case.

due process: A requirement of fair and regular procedures; in the United States, there are two due process clauses, one in the Fifth

Amendment, which applies to the federal government, and one in the Fourteenth Amendment, which applies to the states.

en banc: "In the bench" or "full bench." Refers to cases in which all the judges of the court participate. For example, in federal circuit courts, cases are usually decided, not *en banc*, but by a smaller panel of three judges. See also **panel**.

error, writ of: A writ—or an order—sent by a higher court to a lower court instructing it to send the case to the higher court for review for possible error.

ex parte: "From one side; on one side." A hearing at which only one of the sides to a case is present.

ex post facto: "After the fact"; a law that makes something illegal that was not illegal when it was done or that increases the penalty for the act after it has occurred. In the United States, *ex post facto* applies only to the criminal law.

ex rel.: "On behalf of" (Latin: *ex relatione*); typically, when the government brings a case on behalf of a private party that has an underlying interest in the case, as in *Missouri ex rel. Gaines v. Canada* (1938).

federal question jurisdiction: A case based on, or that involves, the application of the U.S. Constitution, acts of Congress, and treaties of the United States.

habeas corpus, writ of: "You have the body"; a writ from a judge or a court sent to an officer or official asking him or her to explain why he has authority to detain or imprison a certain individual.

impeachment: The constitutional process in which the House of Representatives may accuse high officers of the federal government of misconduct. The trial of an impeached officer takes place in the Senate.

incorporation: In constitutional doctrine, the process by which the Supreme Court made the Bill of Rights applicable to the states through the due process clause of the Fourteenth Amendment.

injunction: A judicial order, usually temporary in duration, that prohibits or compels the performance of a specific act to prevent irreparable damage or injury.

interrogatories: Written questions, prepared by an attorney, that must be completed under oath by the other party, usually with the assistance of counsel, during the process of discovery. See also **deposition**.

issue presented: The legal issue or constitutional controversy raised by the facts of the case.

judgment: A final decision by a court. It usually determines the respective rights and claims of the parties but is subject to **appeal**.

judicial review: The authority of a court to review legislation, executive orders, and other forms of state action for their conformity with constitutional provisions.

jurisdiction: The authority of a court to entertain, or hear, a case.

jurisprudence: The study of law and legal philosophy.

justiciability: Whether a case may be heard by a court or is suitable for a judicial resolution. See also **jurisdiction**.

legislative court: A court created by Congress under its Article I powers; in contrast to Article III courts, judges on such courts generally do not receive lifetime tenure.

litigant: A party to a lawsuit, whether plaintiff, defendant, petitioner, or respondent.

majority opinion: An opinion by a majority of sitting judges or justices. Majority opinions typically have the force of law. See also **precedent.**

mandamus, **writ of**: "We command"; an order by a court to a governmental official directing that official to take a particular course of action or to comply with a judicial order.

martial law: A condition under which rule by military authorities replaces that of civilian authorities and courts martial replace civilian courts. See also **habeas corpus.**

moot: "Unsettled; undecided." A situation in which the underlying legal or constitutional controversy has been resolved or changed so that a judicial resolution is not possible or must be hypothetical.

natural law, natural rights: A system of law or rights based on "nature" or a higher law that transcends human authority.

opinion: A written explanation by a judge that sets forth the legal basis and rationale for his or her decision.

opinion of the court: An opinion by a majority of the judges or justices hearing a case. Compare with **plurality opinion**.

oral argument: Proceeding where attorneys explain their positions to a court and answer questions from the judges.

original jurisdiction: The authority of a court to hear a case in the first instance or as a trial court. Contrast with **appellate jurisdiction**.

originalism: A method of constitutional interpretation that seeks the "original" meaning of a constitutional provision or the intent of its drafters.

overrule: Where a decision by a court specifically repudiates or supersedes a statement of law made in an earlier case. Contrast with **distinguish.**

panel: A group of appellate judges, usually three, that decides cases. Also, a group of potential jurors for a trial court.

parties: The litigants in a case, including the plaintiff and the defendant, or on appeal, the appellants and appellees. The parties are typically named in the title of a case.

per curiam: "By the bench"; a collective decision issued by a court for which no individual judge or justice claims authorship or is identified by name.

per se: "In or by itself"; intrinsic, in the nature of the thing.

petitioner: The party who seeks a writ from a judge or the assistance of the court.

plaintiff: A person in a civil lawsuit who files the complaint against one or more defendants.

plurality opinion: The opinion in a case by a group of judges or justices that commands the most votes, but not an absolute majority of the court.

police powers: The powers reserved to state or local government to protect the "health, safety, welfare, and morals of the community."

political question doctrine: A rule of judicial power which holds that cases primarily involving political instead of legal issues should not be decided by courts but, instead, should be left to the other branches of government.

precedent: A court decision in an earlier case that is similar to the case at hand. Precedents are typically binding, in the sense that other courts must follow the rule established in the precedent, or explain why the rule does not apply (see **distinguish**) or why the precedent should be **overruled**.

prima facie: "At first sight"; the evidence needed to establish a case until it is contested by opposing evidence.

procedure: The code or rules that govern how a lawsuit proceeds. Different areas of law and different courts have different rules of procedure.

prudentialism: A method of constitutional interpretation that advises judges to avoid setting broad rules for future cases, as well as a particular understanding of the limited role courts should play in a constitutional democracy.

record: A full and written account of the proceedings in a lawsuit.

recuse: The process by which a judge decides not to participate in a case, usually because he or she has or appears to have a conflict of interest. A judge normally will not set forth the reasons for his or her recusal.

remand: The process by which an appellate court sends a case back to a lower court for further proceedings, often with specific instructions of law.

reserved powers: Powers, or areas of governance, that remain with the states, as confirmed by the Tenth Amendment.

respondent: The party against whom legal action is sought or taken.

reverse: When a higher court sets aside, or overrules, an erroneous decision by a lower court.

ripeness: A requirement that a case must be sufficiently developed factually before it may be heard by a court. Contrast with **moot.**

seriatim opinion: "In series"; usually a reference to a judicial decision where each judge issues a separate opinion instead of a majority opinion announced by the court.

sovereign immunity: A doctrine that holds that the government may not be sued without its consent.

standing: A doctrine requiring a plaintiff to demonstrate that he or she has a real, direct, and personal concern in a case before the court will hear the case.

stare decisis: "Let the decision stand." The practice of adhering to settled law and prior decisions. See **precedent.**

state action: Actions for which the state bears responsibility, either directly or indirectly; a requirement for a judicial remedy under the Constitution. In other words, the Constitution does not apply to private action.

statute: A law passed by a legislature. Compare with **common law**.

stay: A suspension of court proceedings.

structuralism: This method of constitutional interpretation suggests that the meaning of any particular or specific constitutional provision should be found by understanding how it relates to the constitutional text as a whole. This method is often found in separation of powers and federalism cases.

subpoena: A command to a witness to appear in a court or before a judge and give testimony.

textualism: A method of constitutional interpretation that stresses the actual wording of the constitutional provision in question, and which argues that we should read the words first for their ordinary meaning.

tort: A private civil wrong or breach of a legal duty owed to another person.

vacate: To set aside.

venue: The location or jurisdiction where a case in a lower court is tried.

verdict: A decision by a jury or a judge.

vested rights: A doctrine which holds that longstanding property rights must be respected by the government absent an urgent claim of public need.

writ: A written order by a court ordering an individual or a party to comply with its terms.

Biographical Notes

Note: Names of current justices are printed in capital letters.

ALITO, SAMUEL ANTHONY, JR. (b. 1950). Associate Justice; after an undergraduate degree from Princeton University and a J.D. from Yale Law School, he served as a law clerk for Leonard I. Garth of the United States Court of Appeals for the Third Circuit from 1976 to 1977. Thereafter he worked in several different capacities for the Department of Justice and was U.S. Attorney, District of New Jersey, from 1987 to 1990. He was appointed to the United States Court of Appeals for the Third Circuit in 1990. Nominated by President George W. Bush, he joined the Supreme Court on January 31, 2006.

Black, Hugo (1886–1971). Associate Justice; nominated by President Roosevelt. He served from 1937 until his retirement in 1971. Black had been an Alabama state judge and U.S. senator (1926–1937). He was a firm supporter of Roosevelt's New Deal programs in the Senate; his youthful membership in the Ku Klux Klan did not block his confirmation. Black was a First Amendment absolutist on the Court, strongly supporting free speech, separation of church and state, and strict textual analysis of the Constitution. His most important opinions include *Everson v. Ewing Township* (1947), *McCollum v. Board of Education* (1948), *Engel v. Vitale* (1962), and dissents in *Chambers v. Florida* (1940), *Betts v. Brady* (1942), *Adamson v. California* (1947), *Griswold v. Connecticut* (1965), and *Tinker v. Des Moines* (1969).

Blackmun, Harry (1908–1999). Associate Justice; nominated by President Nixon in 1970, he served until 1994. Blackmun attended Harvard University, where he earned his bachelor's degree in mathematics and studied law under the guidance of Felix Frankfurter. In 1959, President Eisenhower appointed Blackmun to the United States Court of Appeals for the Eighth Circuit, where his opinion in *Jackson v. Bishop* (1968) determined that physical abuse of prisoners was in violation of the Eighth Amendment. He voted to strike down laws interfering with reproductive rights and filed emotional separate opinions in *Webster v. Reproductive Health Services* (1989) and *Planned Parenthood v. Casey* (1992). His opinion in Roe was joined by six other justices, while in *Casey,* no other justice joined his opinion. Blackmun also wrote strong dissents in *Bowers v. Hardwick* (1986) and *DeShaney v. Winnebago County* (1989).

Brandeis, Louis D. (1856–1941). Associate Justice; nominated by President Wilson. He served from 1916 until his retirement in 1939 as the first Jewish justice. He argued the case of *Muller v. Oregon* in 1908, introducing the famous "Brandeis brief" and the use of social science in law. Brandeis also advocated the right to privacy in an influential law review article in 1890 and was opposed to the "bigness" in business and government. He wrote important opinions in *Whitney v. California* (1927), *Erie v. Tompkins* (1938), *Olmstead v. United States* (1928), and *New State Ice Co. v. Liebmann* (1932).

Brennan, William J., Jr. (1906–1997). Associate Justice; nominated by President Eisenhower in 1956, he served until 1990. He completed his law degree at Harvard and entered private practice in New Jersey. He authored important opinions in the areas of free expression, criminal procedure, and reapportionment. Brennan wrote the Court decision in *Cooper v. Aaron* (1958) that forced school officials to accelerate classroom integration and in *Baker v. Carr* (1962). In *United Steelworkers of America v. Weber* (1979), he wrote for the Court that federal anti-discrimination law does not bar employers from adopting race-based affirmative action programs to boost the number of blacks in the work force and management. Also, Brennan's opinion in *New York Times v. Sullivan* (1964) required public figures who sue for libel to prove "actual malice." He delivered the majority opinion in *Edwards v. Aguillard* (1987) that invalidated the required teaching of "creation science."

BREYER, STEPHEN G. (b. 1938). Associate Justice; nominated by President Clinton in 1994. Breyer graduated from Stanford University, and also received a B.A. from Magdalen College, Oxford, and a law degree from Harvard Law School, where he then taught, as well as at the Kennedy School of Government. He served as a law clerk to Justice Goldberg during the 1964 term. During 1980–1990, he served as a judge of the United States Court of Appeals for the First Circuit, and as Chief Judge during 1990–1994. Breyer wrote the plurality opinion declaring that the government may not require cable TV operators to segregate and block leased access channels that feature offensive or indecent programming in *Denver Area Consortium v. Federal Communications Commission* (1996). He dissented in the *Bush v. Gore* (2003) decision.

Burger, Warren Earl (1907–1995). Fifteenth Chief Justice; nominated by President Nixon. He served from 1969 until his retirement in 1986. Burger attended St. Paul's College of Law, now known as The William Mitchell College of Law. He went on to become a federal appeals judge. His most important opinions include *Swann v. Charlotte-Mecklenburg School District* (1971), *Milliken v. Bradley* (1974), and *Nixon v. United States* (1974), which upheld a subpoena for the Watergate tapes and resulted in Nixon's resignation. Burger's other benchmark decisions include *Miller v. California* (1973), defining obscenity, and *Lemon v. Kurtzman* (1971), concerning state establishment of religion.

Douglas, William O. (1898–1980). Associate Justice; nominated by President Cleveland in 1939, he left office in 1975, having served the Court for thirty-six years—the longest of any justice. Douglas graduated from Columbia Law School in 1925, began teaching at Yale Law School in 1927, and became a member of the Securities and Exchange Commission in 1936 (and chair in 1937). He expressed strong opinions in First Amendment rights cases, including *Terminiello v. City of Chicago* (1949) and *Dennis v. United States* (1952), and wrote the lead opinion in *Griswold v. Connecticut* (1965). Some of his other important opinions include *Skinner v. Oklahoma* (1942) and a dissent in *Roth v. United States* (1957).

Frankfurter, Felix (1882–1965). Associate Justice; nominated by President Roosevelt in 1939, he served until 1962. Frankfurter was born in Vienna; emigrated with his parents to New York, where he attended City College; and then went on to Harvard Law School, where he earned a reputation as an expert in Constitutional and federal law. He advised Woodrow Wilson during the Paris Peace Conference of 1919, maintained an active interest in Zionist causes, and helped to found the American Civil Liberties Union in 1920. In *Minersville School District. v. Gobitis* (1940) flag salute case, Frankfurter's opinion for the Court concluded that a public school was permitted to expel a student who refused, for religious reasons, to salute the American flag. His last opinion before retiring was a long dissent to *Baker v. Carr* (1962), in which he argued that legislative apportionment was a political rather than judicial matter.

GINSBURG, RUTH BADER (b. 1933). Associate Justice; nominated by President Clinton in 1993 as the first Jewish woman

Justice. Ginsburg received her undergraduate degree from Cornell University, attended Harvard Law School, and received her LL.B. from Columbia Law School. She served as a law clerk to Edmund L. Palmieri, Judge of the United States District Court for the Southern District of New York, from 1959–1961. She was a professor of law at Rutgers University School of Law (1963–1972) and Columbia Law School (1972–1980). Ginsburg also served as the ACLU's General Counsel and was on the National Board of Directors during 1974–1980. She was appointed a judge of the United States Court of Appeals for the District of Columbia Circuit in 1980. Majority opinions authored by Ginsberg include *United States v. Virginia* (1996). In *Bush v. Gore* (2000), Ginsberg dissented. She also voted against the execution of minors in *Roper v. Simmons* (2005).

Harlan, John M., II (1899–1971). Associate Justice; nominated by President Eisenhower, he served from 1955 until his death in 1971. Harlan was educated at Princeton and was a Rhodes Scholar at Oxford where he read law. He took an American law degree at New York Law School in 1925. President Eisenhower appointed Harlan to the United States Court of Appeals for the Second Circuit, where he served for ten months. Eisenhower promoted him to the High Court. He argued for a broad interpretation of the Fourteenth Amendment's due process clause, evidenced in his dissenting opinion to *Poe v. Ullman* (1961). Harlan dissented in *Mapp v. Ohio* (1961) and *Miranda v. Arizona* (1966), which expanded the protections of defendants in criminal cases, and again in *Reynolds v. Sims* (1964).

Holmes, Oliver Wendell, Jr. (1841–1933). Associate Justice; nominated by President Taft in 1902, he served until his retirement in 1932 at age 90. He was a Harvard law professor, edited the *American Law Review*, and was Chief Justice of the Massachusetts Supreme Court. Holmes played an important role in shaping Legal Realism. His benchmark opinions include *Schenck v. United States* (1919) and the opinion for the Court in *Buck v. Bell* (1927). His dissents in *Northern Securities Co. v. U. S.* (1904), *Lochner v. New York* (1905), *Dr. Miles Medical v. J. D. Park & Sons* (1911), *American Column & Lumber v. U. S.* (1921), and *Abrams v. United States* (1919) earned him the reputation "The Great Dissenter."

Hughes, Charles Evan (1962–1948). Eleventh Chief Justice; nominated by President Hoover in 1930, Hughes served until his retirement in 1941. Hughes was governor of New York (1907–1910), appointed to the Supreme Court as an associate justice in 1910 by President Taft, resigned in 1916 to run a losing race against Democratic candidate Woodrow Wilson in 1918, and later became Secretary of State (1921–1925). Hughes's *West Coast Hotel* (1937) decision abandoned a line of cases that had read the due process clauses of the Fifth and Fourteenth amendments as providing expansive protection for freedom of contract and the right of property.

Jackson, Robert (1892–1954). Associate Justice; nominated by Franklin Roosevelt, he served from 1941 until 1954, taking a leave of absence during 1945–46 to serve as the chief prosecutor of the Nuremburg Trials. Jackson formulated a three-tier test for evaluating claims of presidential power in *Youngstown Sheet & Tube Co. v. Sawyer* (1952), which remains one of the most widely-cited opinions in Supreme Court history. He also wrote the majority opinion in *West Virginia State Board of Education v. Barnette* (1943), which overturned mandatory saluting of the American flag. He dissented in *Korematsu v. United States* (1944).

KENNEDY, ANTHONY (b. 1936). Associate Justice; nominated by President Reagan in 1988. Kennedy received his B.A. in Political Science from Stanford University, and an LL.B. from Harvard Law School. He was Professor of Constitutional Law at McGeorge School of Law, University of the Pacific. In 1975, he was appointed to the United States Court of Appeals for the Ninth Circuit by President Ford. Kennedy joined the opinion of *Atkins v. Virginia* (2002), declaring execution of the mentally ill unconstitutional. He also wrote the opinion of the court in *Roper v. Simmons* (2005), invalidating the execution of felons. Kennedy joined the opinion of O'Connor and Souter in *Planned Parenthood v. Casey* (1993) but dissented in *Stenberg v. Carhart* (2002), which supported partial-birth abortions. He authored the Court's opinion in *Lawrence v. Texas* (2003).

Marshall, John (1755–1835). Fourth Chief Justice; nominated by President Adams. He served from 1801 until his death in 1835. Marshall had been a Virginia state legislator, U.S. envoy to France, a U.S. representative from Virginia, and U.S. Secretary of State under Adams. Marshall established that the courts were entitled to exercise judicial review, or the power to strike down laws that violated the Constitution. Thus, Marshall has been credited with cementing the position of the judiciary as an independent and influential branch of government. His most important opinions include *Marbury v. Madison* (1803), *McCulloch v. Maryland* (1819), *Dartmouth College v. Woodward* (1819), and *Gibbons v. Ogden* (1824).

Marshall, Thurgood (1908–1993). Associate Justice; nominated by President Johnson. He served from 1967 until his retirement in 1991 and was the first black justice on the Court. He headed the NAACP legal staff from 1938 until 1961 and argued many benchmark civil rights cases before the Court. Of the thirty-two cases he argued before the Supreme Court, Marshall won twenty-nine. These cases include *Dong v. Florida* (1940), *Smith v. Allwright* (1944), *Shelley v. Kraemer* (1948), *Sweatt v. Painter* (1950), and *McLaurin v. Oklahoma State Regents* (1950). His most famous case as a lawyer was *Brown v. Board of Education of Topeka* (1954). His most important opinions include *Stanley v. Georgia* (1969), *Furman v. Georgia* (concurrence, 1972), and *San Antonio School District v. Rodriguez* (1973).

Murphy, Frank (1890–1949). Associate Justice; nominated by President Roosevelt in 1939, he served from 1940 through 1949. Murphy was elected Governor of Michigan in 1936; his settlement of the automobile strike (1937) in Flint, Michigan, made him a national figure. While serving the Court, his decisions protected citizens against discrimination in *Falbo v. United States* (1944), *West Virginia State Board of Education v. Barnette* (1943), and *Korematsu v. United States* (1944). He sought to protect labor workers picketing in *Thornhill v. Alabama,* (1940). He worked to uphold the Fourth Amendment, dissenting in *Wolf v. Colorado* (1949).

O'Connor, Sandra Day (b. 1930). The Supreme Court's 102nd Justice and first female Justice; nominated by President Reagan in 1985, she retired in 2006. O'Connor received her B.A. and LL.B. from Stanford University. She was appointed to the Arizona State Senate in 1969 and was subsequently reelected to two two-year terms. In 1975, she was elected Judge of the Maricopa County Superior Court and served until 1979, when she was appointed to the Arizona Court of Appeals. In *Grutter v. Bollinger* (2003), she maintained that the state's legitimate interest in using race as a factor for admission had gradually declined over the past 25 years as minority test scores improved, and that the Court should continue to monitor the strength of that interest until it decided that it was no longer sufficient to merit racial distinctions. O'Connor was instrumental in the Court's refashioning of its position on the right to abortion in 1992. In *Planned Parenthood v. Casey* (1992), O'Connor wrote the decision with Justices Kennedy and Souter that reaffirmed the constitutionally protected right to abortion established in *Roe v. Wade* (1973) but also lowered the standard that legal restrictions on abortion must meet in order to pass constitutional muster.

Powell, Lewis (1907–1998). Associate Justice; nominated by President Nixon in 1971, after turning down a nomination two years before. Often the swing vote, Powell's opinion in *Regents of the University of California v. Bakke* (1978) and *Bowers v. Hardwick* (1986); concerning the latter, he stated he had never met a homosexual person. After his retirement from the Court in 1987, he expressed remorse for his majority opinion in *McCleskey v. Kemp* (1987), where he voted to uphold the death penalty despite a study purporting to confirm that the penalty was applied disproportionately to African-Americans. Powell dissented in *Furman v. Georgia* (1972) but also helped rewrite the opinion in the compromise four years later in *Gregg v. Georgia* (1976).

Rehnquist, William H. (1924–2005). Sixteenth Chief Justice; nominated by President Nixon in 1972, he served for fourteen years until President Reagan appointed him Chief Justice in 1986, replacing Chief Justice Burger. Rehnquist served on the Supreme Court until his death in 2005. He received a B.A., M.A., and LL.B. from Stanford University and an M.A. from Harvard University. He served as a law clerk for Justice Robert H. Jackson during the 1951 and 1952 terms, practiced law in Phoenix, Arizona (1953–1969), and served as Assistant Attorney General, Office of Legal Counsel (1969–1971). Rehnquist wrote many important opinions, including dissents in *Roe v. Wade* (1972) and *Wallace v. Jaffree* (1985). He joined the majority in *Bowers v. Hardwick* (1986). Rehnquist presided over the Clinton impeachment hearings.

ROBERTS, JOHN G., JR. (b. 1955). Seventeenth Chief Justice; nominated by President George W. Bush in 2005. Roberts graduated from Harvard where he earned his undergraduate and law degrees. He then clerked for Henry Friendly of the United States Court of Appeals for the Second Circuit (1979–1980), and then-Associate Justice Rehnquist. He served as Associate Counsel to President

Reagan, White House Counsel's Office (1982–1986), and Principal Deputy Solicitor General, U.S. Department of Justice (1989–1993). He was appointed to the United States Court of Appeals for the District of Columbia Circuit in 2003. Roberts joined Justice Scalia's dissent in *Gonzales v. Oregon* (2006), where the Court decided that an Oregon state law permitting physician-assisted suicide did not conflict with the Controlled Substances Act. Roberts also wrote the unanimous decision in *Rumsfeld v. Forum for Academic and Institutional Rights* (2006).

SCALIA, ANTONIN (b. 1936). Associate Justice; nominated by President Reagan in 1986. He received his B.A from Georgetown University and the University of Fribourg, Switzerland, and his law degree from Harvard Law School. He was in private practice in Cleveland, Ohio (1961–1967), and then served as a professor of law at the University of Virginia and the University of Chicago. In 1982, President Reagan appointed him to the United States Court of Appeals for the District of Columbia Circuit. His most notable decisions include preventing personal property form being searched without a warrant in *Kyllo v. United States* (2001). Scalia also wrote strongly worded dissents in *Lawrence v. Texas* (2003), *Webster v. Reproductive Health Services* (1999), and *Planned Parenthood v. Casey* (1992).

SOUTER, DAVID H. (b. 1939). Associate Justice; nominated by President George W. Bush in 1990. Souter graduated from Harvard College, earned a B.A. in jurisprudence from Oxford University, and received his law degree from Harvard in 1966. In 1983, he was appointed an Associate Justice to the Supreme Court of New Hampshire. He became a judge of the United States Court of Appeals for the First Circuit in 1990. Souter joined the plurality opinion of *Planned Parenthood v. Casey* (1992), along with Kennedy and O'Connor. He dissented in *Bush v. Gore* (2000). Souter voted to affirm a state ban on nude dancing in *Barnes v. Glen Theatre* (1991) and concurred in *Lee v. Weisman* (1992).

STEVENS, JOHN PAUL (b. 1920). Associate Justice; nominated by President Ford in 1975. Previously, Stevens served as a judge of the United States Court of Appeals for the Seventh Circuit, nominated by President Nixon. He voted to reinstate capital punishment in the United States, opposed the affirmative action program at issue in *Regents of the University of California v. Bakke*

(1978), and refused to recognize a right to burn the flag as a speech act in *Texas v. Johnson* (1994). Later, Stevens supported a different affirmative program at the University of Michigan Law School, challenged in *Grutter v. Bollinger* (2003). In *Cleburne v. Cleburne Living Center* (1985), Stevens argued against the Supreme Court's famous "strict scrutiny" doctrine for laws involving "suspect classifications."

Stewart, Potter (1915–1985). Associate Justice; nominated by President Eisenhower in 1958, he served until his retirement in 1981. In 1954, Stewart was appointed to the United States Court of Appeals for the Sixth Circuit. Stewart dissented from the Court's decision in *Griswold v. Connecticut* (1965), but he changed his views and joined the Court's decision in *Roe v. Wade* (1973). Stewart is known for his views in the obscenity case of *Jacobellis v. Ohio* (1964), where he wrote in his short concurrence that "hard-core pornography" was hard to define, but that "I know it when I see it."

Story, Joseph (1779–1845). Associate Justice; nominated in 1811 by President Madison, he served until his death. In 1829, Story also accepted a newly-created position as Dane Professor of Law at Harvard University. Story devoted his efforts to equity jurisprudence and contributed significantly to patent law. In 1819, he attracted attention by his vigorous denunciation of the slave trade, and in 1820, he called on his fellow members of the Massachusetts Convention to revise the state constitution. He is also remembered for his ruling in *Amistad* (1841) in favor of kidnapped Africans.

Taney, Roger (1777–1864). Fifth Chief Justice; nominated by President Jackson in 1836, he served until 1864 as the first Roman Catholic to hold this position. Educated at Dickinson College before a law degree was required, Taney practiced law in Maryland was elected to the Maryland State Senate, and served as Attorney General of the United States. The Taney Court overturned the Marshall Court's decision in the *Dartmouth College v. Woodward* (1819) that had limited the power of the states to regulate corporations and reversed the Marshall Court's previous holding that states could not charter banks. In the *Charles River Bridge v. Warren Bridge* (1837) Taney declared that a state charter of a private business conferred only privileges expressly granted and that any ambiguity must be decided in favor of the state. He is also known for the benchmark decision of *Dred Scott v. Stanford* (1857).

THOMAS, CLARENCE (b. 1948). Associate Justice; nominated by President George W. Bush in 1991. Thomas attended Conception Seminary, graduated from Holy Cross College, and received his law degree from Yale University. He served as Assistant Secretary for Civil Rights in the U.S. Department of Education (1981–1982) and as Chairman of the U.S. Equal Employment Opportunity Commission (1982–1990). He became a judge of the United States Court of Appeals for the District of Columbia Circuit in 1990. In *McIntyre v. Ohio Elections Commission* (1995), Thomas wrote a concurring opinion agreeing with a majority of the Court that a law banning anonymous campaign literature violated the First Amendment. He concurred with the Court's decision in *United States v. Lopez* (1995) invalidating a federal law prohibiting possession of a firearm in a school zone, and he voted to expand personal gun rights under the Second Amendment in *Printz v. United States* (1997). Thomas also voted to uphold the school voucher program in *Zelman v. Simmons-Harris* (2002). He was the only Justice to side with the government in *United States v. Hubbell* (2000) and dissented with a divided court in *Lawrence v. Texas* (2003).

Vinson, Frederick (1890–1953). Thirteenth Chief Justice; nominated by President Truman. He served from 1946 until his death in 1953. Vinson served in the U.S. House of Representatives, became an associate justice of the U.S. Court of Appeals for the District of Columbia, and later became chief justice of the U.S. Emergency Court of Appeals. He made several significant decisions concerning internal security legislation. In *American Communications v. Douds* (1950), he found the requirement that members of labor unions swear to their non-membership in the Communist party unconstitutional; in *Dennis v. United States* (1951), he upheld the conviction of eleven leaders of the Communist party for violations of the Smith Act. His important opinions include *Sweatt v. Painter* (1948) and *Shelley v. Kraemer* (1948).

Warren, Earl (1891–1974). Fourteenth Chief Justice; nominated by President Eisenhower in 1953, and served until his retirement in 1969. Warren attended the University of California at Berkeley, where he earned his undergraduate and law degrees. In 1942, Warren was elected Governor of California, and he was twice re-elected. In 1948, he was the Republican nominee for Vice President of the

United States, and in 1952, he sought the Republican Party's nomination for President. Among his most important opinions is his unanimous decision for the Court in *Brown v. Board of Education* (1954).

Bibliography

The cases we read throughout this course are available in many places and formats. Full copies of the cases are available at most public libraries and there are several sites on the Internet, including the official site of the U.S. Supreme Court, which has most of the cases. However, the cases are often extremely long and include information not directly relevant to our inquiry. For this reason, I advise students to purchase a casebook, or a collection of edited cases. Many such collections are available. The readings and cases I have recommended are from Donald P. Kommers, John E. Finn, and Gary J. Jacobsohn, *American Constitutional Law: Essays, Cases, and Comparative Notes,* Volume 2, 2nd edition (Lantham, MD: Rowman & Littlefield Publishers: 2004), but any casebook will have most of the cases.

Essential Reading:

Amar, Akhil Reed. "Did the Fourteenth Amendment Incorporate the Bill of Rights Against States?" 19 *Harvard Journal of Law and Public Policy* 443 (1999). This important article discusses whether the Fourteenth Amendment should make the Bill of Rights applicable to state governments.

Banner, Stuart. *The Death Penalty: An American History.* Cambridge: Harvard University Press, 2003. A comprehensive history of the death penalty in the United States.

Berlin, Isiah. *Four Essays on Liberty.* 2nd ed. New York: Oxford University Press, 2002. The classic treatise on the differences between positive and negative liberties.

Burt, Robert A. "The Constitution of the Family." 1979 *Supreme Court Review* 329. Provides a comprehensive account of the role of the family in constitutional law.

Chafee, Zechariah, Jr. *Free Speech in the United States.* Cambridge: Harvard University Press, 1948. A classic history of freedom of speech in America.

Cooper, Phillip J., and Howard Ball. *The United States Supreme Court: From the Inside Out.* Englewood Cliffs, NJ: Prentice Hall College Division, 1995. Provides an excellent window into the structure and operation of the U.S. Supreme Court.

Ely, John Hart. "The Wages of Crying Wolf: A Comment on *Roe v. Wade*." 82 *Yale Law Journal* 920 (1973). This classic article marshals a series of criticisms about the Court's decision in *Roe v. Wade*.

———. *Democracy and Distrust*. Cambridge: Harvard University Press, 1981. Outlines an important theory about the proper role of the Court and the limits of judicial review in a constitutional democracy.

Greenawalt, Kent. *Fighting Words*. Princeton: Princeton University Press, 1995. Makes a set of arguments about the fighting words doctrine and the meaning of the First Amendment.

Hamburger, Phillip. *Separation of Church and State*. Cambridge: Harvard University Press, 2002. Examines the history and meaning of the establishment clause, tracing it from the 1840s.

Howe, Mark De Wolfe. *The Garden and the Wilderness*. Chicago: University of Chicago Press, 1965. This important book argues that religious freedoms are as much to protect religion from the state as the state from religion.

Hutson, James H. *Religion and the New Republic: Faith in the Founding of America*. Littleton, CO: Rowman & Littlefield Publishers, 2000. A collection of essays that explores the importance of religious faith at the Founding.

Kalven, Harry, Jr. *A Worthy Tradition: Freedom of Speech in America*. New York: Harper & Row, 1988. A comprehensive history of freedom of speech in the United States.

Ketcham, Ralph, ed. *The Federalist Papers*. New York: Signet Classics, 2003. This collection of essays on the Constitution is mandatory reading.

Kluger, Richard. *Simple Justice*: *The History of "Brown v. Board of Education" and Black America's Struggle for Equality*. New York: Vintage, 2004. The leading account of the facts and issues in *Brown. v. Board of Education*.

Kommers, Donald P., John E. Finn, and Gary Jacobsohn. *American Constitutional Law: Essays, Cases and Comparative Notes*. Vol. 2. Littleton, CO: Rowman & Littlefield, 2004. This casebook covers the major topics and issues in civil liberties and includes edited versions of the Court's most important cases.

Levinson, Sanford. *Constitutional Faith*. Princeton: Princeton University Press, 1989. Explores issues basic to the constitutional order, including questions about why and when the Constitution ought to be reaffirmed by individual citizens.

Phillips, Michael J. *The Lochner Court, Myth and Reality: Substantive Due Process from the 1890s to the 1930s.* Westport, CT: Praeger Publishers, 2000. This important book situates the Lochner decision against the Court's general treatment of substantive due process, arguing that the decision in Lochner is not representative of the Court's general approach.

Rubenfeld, Jed. "The Right of Privacy." 102 *Harvard Law Review* 737 (1989). Offers a comprehensive set of arguments about the origins, meanings, and limits of privacy as a constitutional concept.

Sunstein, Cass R. *Democracy and the Problem of Free Speech.* New York: Free Press, 1995. Examines the relationship between democratic theory and the First Amendment, calling for a New Deal vision of the First Amendment, in which political speech is more fully protected than commercial speech.

Weschler, Herbert. "Toward Neutral Principles of Constitutional Law." 73 *Harvard Law Review* 1 (1959). An important article on the necessity of neutral principles in constitutional interpretation.

Whittington, Keith. *Constitutional Interpretation: Textual Meaning, Original Intent, and Judicial Review.* Lawrence, KS: University Press of Kansas, 2001. Examines and evaluates various methods of constitutional interpretation and how they influence our understanding of judicial review.

Supplementary Reading:

Abel, Richard. *Speech and Respect.* London: Sweet & Maxwell, 1994. Discusses the relationship among speech, respect, and human dignity.

Ackerman, Bruce. *Private Property and the Constitution.* New Haven: Yale University Press, 1978. A comprehensive account of the importance of property to the constitutional order.

Baer, Judith A. *Equality under the Constitution: Reclaiming the Fourteenth Amendment.* Ithaca, NY: Cornell University Press, 1983. Argues for a reinvigorated and more expansive conception of equal protection of the laws.

Barber, Sotirios A. *Welfare and the Constitution.* Princeton: Princeton University Press, 2003. This important book argues for a broader understanding of welfare rights as basic constitutional rights.

Beard, Charles. *An Economic Interpretation of the Constitution.* Reissue ed. New York: Free Press, 1986. A classic treatise that argues that the Founders meant for the Constitution to protect the propertied classes.

Becker, Theodore. *The Declaration of Independence: A Study in the History of Political Ideas.* New York: Vintage, 1958. A classic examination of the political philosophy behind the Declaration of Independence.

Bedau, Hugo Adam. *The Death Penalty in America: Current Controversies.* Reprint ed. Oxford: Oxford University Press, 1998. A wide-ranging overview of various aspects of the death penalty.

Berns, Walter. *For Capital Punishment: Crime and the Morality of the Death Penalty.* Reprint ed. Lanham, MD: University Press of America, 1991. This book is still one of the best defenses of the constitutionality and sensibility of the death penalty.

———. *The First Amendment and the Future of American Democracy.* Reprint ed. Washington, DC: Regnery Publishing, 1976. Examines the argument that speech is a critical component of democracy.

Bernstein, Anita. "For and Against Marriage: A Revision," 102 *Michigan Law Review* 129 (2003). In this article, Bernstein provides an important and comprehensive overview of the arguments for and against marriage as an institution.

Bickel, Alexander M. *The Least Dangerous Branch: The Supreme Court at the Bar of Politics.* 2nd ed. New Haven: Yale University Press, 1986. Provides an excellent account of when and why the Supreme Court should defer to the democratic process.

Black, Charles L. *Capital Punishment: The Inevitability of Caprice and Mistake.* 2nd ed. New York: W.W. Norton & Co., 1981. Provides a set of arguments about why the death penalty is flawed and should be unconstitutional.

Bollinger, Lee C. *The Tolerant Society.* Reprint ed. New York: Oxford University Press, 1995. Argues that the First Amendment is critical to the development of a tolerant and informed society.

Bork, Robert H. "Neutral Principles and Some First Amendment Problems." 47 *Indiana Law Journal* 1 (1971). In this classic article, Judge Bork examines a number of critical problems raised by the Court's First Amendment jurisprudence.

————. *The Tempting of America*. New York: Free Press, 1997. In this influential book, Judge Bork argues in favor of a method of constitutional interpretation called "originalism" or "original understanding."

Brill, Alida. *Nobody's Businesses: Paradoxes of Privacy*. Reprint ed. Redwood City, CA: Addison-Wesley, 1991. Provides a comprehensive overview of privacy as a legal concept and the difficulties that inhere in it, arguing that privacy issues are related to prenatal rights, the right to die, and the AIDS crisis.

Carter, Lief. *Constitutional Interpretation: Cases in Law and Religion*. New York: Longman Publishing Group, 1991. This primer introduces readers to the religion clauses and addresses a set of cases and interpretive problems generated by the religion clauses.

Carter, Stephen L. *The Culture of Disbelief: How American Law and Politics Trivialize Religious Devotion*. Garden City, NY: Anchor, 1994. Argues that American law and culture tend to devalue the importance of religious faith.

————. *Reflections of an Affirmative Action Baby*. Reprint ed. New York: Basic Books, 1992. Examines the arguments surrounding affirmative action.

Cogan, Neal. *The Complete Bill of Rights: The Drafts, Debates, Sources, and Origins*. New York: Oxford University Press, 1997. Contains a complete history and a collection of documents relating to the Bill of Rights.

Cord, Robert. *Separation of Church and State: Historical Fact and Current Fiction*. Brooklyn, NY: Carlson Publishing, 1982. Examines the history of the establishment clause.

Cortner, Richard C. *The Supreme Court and the Second Bill of Rights: The Fourteenth Amendment and the Nationalization of the Bill of Rights*. Madison, WI: University of Wisconsin Press, 1980. Traces the rise of the incorporation doctrine through the Fourteenth Amendment.

Curtis, Michael Kent. *No State Shall Abridge: The Fourteenth Amendment and the Bill of Rights*. Durham, NC: Duke University Press, 1986. An excellent history of the relationship between the Fourteenth Amendment and the Bill of Rights.

Downs, Donald A. *The New Politics of Pornography*. Chicago: University of Chicago Press, 1989. Provides an overview of pornography as a political and constitutional issue.

———. *Nazis in Skokie: Freedom, Community, and the First Amendment*. Notre Dame: University of Notre Dame Press, 1986. A compelling account of the Nazi march in Skokie, Illinois.

Davidson, Kenneth M., Ruth Bader Ginsburg, and Herma Hill Kay. *Text, Cases, and Materials on Constitutional Aspects of Sex-Based Discrimination*. St. Paul, West Publishing Company, 1974. This is an edited collection of materials, including Supreme Court and lower court cases, that address the constitutional issues surrounding sex discrimination.

Dworkin, Ronald. *Life's Dominion*. Reprint ed. New York: Vintage, 1994. Addresses human life values and the role they play in the constitutional order.

———. *Sovereign Virtue: The Theory and Practice of Equality*. Cambridge: Harvard University Press, 2002. Presents a series of arguments about the meaning and importance of equality in the legal system.

Ely, Richard. *The Guardian of Every Other Right: The Constitutional History of Property Rights*. New York: Oxford University Press, 1992. Provides a complete history of the right to private property in the American constitutional system.

Emerson, Thomas. *The System of Freedom of Expression*. New York: Vintage Books, 1971. Covers an important theory of freedom of speech.

Epstein, Richard. *Takings: Private Property and the Power of Eminent Domain*. Reprint ed. Cambridge: Harvard University Press, 1989. Provides a comprehensive account of the takings clause and argues for its reinvigoration.

Farber, Daniel. *Lincoln's Constitution*. Chicago: University of Chicago Press, 2003. This important new book examines the constitutional philosophy of President Lincoln as forged by the Civil War.

Fehrenbacher, Donald E. *The Dred Scott Case*. New York: Oxford University Press, 2001. The complete account of the facts and issues in *Dred Scott*.

Finkelman, Paul. *An Imperfect Union: Slavery, Federalism, and Comity*. Chapel Hill, NC: University of North Carolina Press, 1981. Examines the role of slavery and Federalism in the formation of the Union.

Fisher, Louis. *Religious Liberty in America: Political Safeguards*. Lawrence, KS: University Press of Kansas, 2002. Examines the role of religious liberty in the political system and how it is protected by political as much as judicial institutions.

Fishkin, James S. *Justice, Equal Opportunity, and the Family*. New Haven: Yale University Press, 1983. Explores the relationship between the family and the constitutional values of merit and equality.

Formicola, Jo Renee, and Hubert Morken. *Everson Revisited: Religion, Education, and Law at the Crossroads*. Littleton, CO: Rowman & Littlefield Publishers, 1997. A complete history of the facts and issues in the case of *Everson v. School Board* (1947).

Garrow, David J. *Liberty and Sexuality: The Right to Privacy and the Making of Roe v. Wade*. Updated ed. Berkeley: University of California Press, 1998. A complete history of the facts and issues in *Roe v. Wade* (1973).

Gerstmann, Evan. *The Constitutional Underclass: Gays, Lesbians and the Failure of Class-Based Equal Protection*. Chicago: University of Chicago Press, 1999. Argues that current equal protection doctrines fail to protect gays and lesbians.

———. *Same-Sex Marriage and the Constitution*. Cambridge University Press, 2003. In this provocative book, Gerstmann argues that the right to marry must be fundamental, and should extend to same sex couples.

Gillman, Howard. *The Constitution Besieged*. Durham, NC: Duke University Press, 1995. Argues that *Lochner* was not motivated by laissez-faire market views but, instead, was an effort to preserve a conception of the police power that held that it could be used only in a neutral manner to benefit the general welfare.

Ginsburg, Ruth B. "Speaking in a Judicial Voice." 67 *New York University Law Review* 1185 (1993). Justice Ginsburg defends intermediate scrutiny.

Glendon, Mary Ann. *Abortion and Divorce in Western Law*. Reprint ed. Cambridge: Harvard University Press, 1989. A comprehensive and comparative account of abortion and divorce policies in Western democracies.

Gordon, Sarah Barringer. *The Mormon Question: Polygamy and Constitutional Conflict in Nineteenth-Century America*. Chapel Hill: University of North Carolina Press, 2002. A history of polygamy and the Mormon conflict in the United States.

Harvie, J. Wilkinson, III. *From Brown to Bakke*. New York: Oxford University Press, 1993. Examines the Court's work on race and affirmative action up to the *Bakke* case.

Horwitz, Morton. *The Transformation of American Law, 1780–1860*. Cambridge: Harvard University Press, 1979. This classic book traces the transformation of property as a constitutional right from the Founding to the Civil War.

Hull, Elizabeth. *Without Justice for All: The Constitutional Rights of Aliens*. Westport, CT: Greenwood Press, 1985. Examines the constitutional rights of aliens.

Irons, Peter. *The Courage of Their Convictions: Sixteen Americans Who Fought Their Way to the Supreme Court*. Reprint ed. New York: Penguin, 1990. Each of the 16 chapters in this book explores the personalities and issues involved in a famous Supreme Court case.

Kauper, Thomas. "Penumbras, Peripheries, Things Fundamental and Things Forgotten." 64 *Michigan Law Review* 235 (1965). Explores the doctrine of fundamental rights advanced in *Griswold v. Connecticut*.

Kirp, David L., Mark G. Yudof, and Marlene Strong Franks. *Gender Justice*. Reprint ed. Chicago: University of Chicago Press, 1986. Examines the relationship among gender, justice, and equality.

Lahav, Pnina. "Holmes and Brandeis: Libertarian and Republican Justifications of Free Speech." 4 *Journal of Law and Politics* 451 (1987). Explores the philosophical arguments behind the Holmes-Brandeis understanding of freedom of speech.

Law, Sylvia. "Rethinking Sex and the Constitution." 132 *University of Pennsylvania Law Review* 955 (1984). Explores the relationship between gender and basic constitutional rules and principles.

Lawrence, Charles, and Mari J. Matsuda. *We Won't Go Back: Making the Case for Affirmative Action*. Boston: Houghton Mifflin, 1997. Advances a series of arguments in favor of affirmative action.

Lessig, Lawrence. "Reading the Constitution in Cyberspace." 45 *Emory Law Journal* 869 (1996). A pioneering article about the Constitution and its role in cyberspace.

Leuchtenberg, William. *The Supreme Court Reborn: The Constitutional Revolution in the Age of Roosevelt*. Oxford University Press, 1995. This is an important collection of essays that explores the Roosevelt Court, with particular emphasis upon how the various social and political movements of the 1930s influenced the Court and its relationship with the Roosevelt administration.

Levy, Leonard. *Origins of the Bill of Rights*. New Haven: Yale University Press, 2001. An important history of the origins of the Bill of Rights.

———. *The Emergence of a Free Press*. Chicago: Ivan R. Dee, Publisher, 2004. A history of freedom of the press and its meaning at the Founding.

———. *The Establishment Clause: Religion and the First Amendment*. 2nd/rev. ed. Chapel Hill, NC: University of North Carolina Press, 1994. This important book provides a complete history of the origins and original purposes of the establishment clause.

Low, Susan Bloch, and Thomas Krattenmaker, eds. *Supreme Court Politics: The Institution and Its Procedures*. Minneapolis, MN: West Publishing Company, 1994. Offers detailed information about the Court, its internal operation, and its procedures.

MacKinnon, Catherine A. *Only Words*. Reprint ed. Cambridge: Harvard University Press, 1996. Makes an important argument that certain kinds of speech, including pornography, should be limited because they can harm.

Malbin, Michael. *Religion and Politics*. Washington, DC: American Enterprise Institute Press, 1978. Examines the religion clauses and what they meant at the Founding.

Marilley, Suzanne M. *Woman Suffrage and the Origins of Liberal Feminism in the United States*. Cambridge: Harvard University Press, 1996. A history of the right to vote for women and the rise of liberal feminism as a political movement.

McConnell, Michael. "Free Exercise and the *Smith* Decision." 57 *University of Chicago Law Review* 1109 (1990). This important article examines and criticizes the Court's decision in the celebrated Peyote case (*Employment Division v. Smith*), decided in 1990.

———. "The Right to Die and the Jurisprudence of Tradition," *Utah Law Review* 665 (1997). In this important law review article, McConnell rejects the claim that there should be a constitutionally recognized right to privacy.

McGrath, C. Peter. *Yazoo:Law and Politics in the New Republic: The Case of Fletcher v. Peck*. New York: W.W. Norton, 1966. A complete account of the Yazoo land fraud and the case of *Fletcher v. Peck*.

Meisel, Alan. *The Right to Die,* 2nd ed. New York: John Wiley, 1995. Although it is somewhat dated, this book provides a comprehensive overview of the legal and constitutional issues that surround the right to die, including an overview of various right to die statutes and cases.

Mill, John Stuart. *On Liberty*. New York: Penguin Books, 1975. Presents a classic argument about the meaning of liberty and the conditions under which it can be limited.

Miller , John C. *Crisis in Freedom*: *The Alien and Sedition Acts*. Mattituck, NY: Amereon Ltd., 2002. A complete history of the Alien and Sedition Acts.

Myrdal, Gunnar. *An American Dilemma: The Negro Problem and American Democracy*. Reprint ed. New Brunswick, NJ: Transaction Publishers, 1996. The classic account of race in the United States.

Nieman, Donald G. *Promises to Keep: African-Americans and the Constitutional Order, 1776 to the Present*. New York: Oxford University Press, 1991. An overview of the role that race has played in American constitutional history.

Noonan, John T., Jr. *The Luster of Our Country: The American Experience of Religious Freedom*. Berkeley: University of California Press, 2000. Examines the history and role of religious freedom in American constitutional history.

Okin, Susan Moller. *Justice, Gender, and the Family*. Reprint ed. New York: Basic Books, 1991. Explores the relationship between the family and gender in the legal order and how current conceptions fail to promote the ideal of justice.

Paul, Ellen Frankel, and Howard Dickman, eds. *Liberty, Property, and the Foundations of the American Constitution*. Albany, NY:

State University of New York Press, 1989. Examines the centrality of liberty and property to the constitutional order and provides a history of property as a constitutional right.

Posner, Richard. *Sex and Reason.* Cambridge: Harvard University Press, 1992. Explores the relationship among sex, public policy, and the Constitution, often through the use of economic analysis.

Rabban, David. *Free Speech in Its Forgotten Years.* New York and Cambridge: Cambridge University Press, 1999. Explores the meaning of free speech before the First World War.

Ravitch, Frank S. *School Prayer and Discrimination: The Civil Rights of Minorities and Dissenters.* Boston: Northeastern University Press, 1999. Boston: Northeastern University Press, 2001. Ravitch argues that treating the prayer in schools controversy as a First Amendment problem only is insufficient to protect the rights of religious minorities.

Rehnquist, William H. *The Supreme Court: How It Was, How It Is.* Revised and updated ed. New York: Vintage, 2002. Examines the history and functions of the Supreme Court.

Sarat, Austin. *When the State Kills: Capital Punishment and the American Condition.* Princeton: Princeton University Press, 2001. Argues that the death penalty plays a "major and dangerous role in the modern economy of power."

Scalia, Antonin. *A Matter of Interpretation: Federal Courts and the Law.* Princeton: Princeton University Press, 1998. Justice Scalia sketches a theory about the role of courts in a democratic society.

Siegan, Bernard. *Economic Liberties and the Constitution.* Chicago: University of Chicago Press, 1981. A classic account of property rights and economic liberties.

Siegel, Reva B. "Text in Contest: Gender and the Constitution from a Social Movement Perspective." 150 *University of Pennsylvania Law Review* 297 (2001). Examines the politics of gender and constitutional law.

Smith, James Morton. *Freedom's Fetters: The Alien and Sedition Laws and American Civil Liberties.* Ithaca, NY: Cornell University Press, 1966. A comprehensive history of the Alien and Sedition Acts.

Smith, Rogers. "The Constitution and Autonomy." 60 *Texas Law Review* 175 (1982). This important article examines autonomy as a constitutional interest.

Smith, Steven D. *Foreordained Failure: The Quest for a Constitutional Principle of Religious Freedom*. New York: Oxford University Press, 1999. Argues that no single principle can adequately account for the complexity of the religion clauses.

Sorauf, Frank. *The Wall of Separation: The Constitutional Politics of Church and State*. Princeton: Princeton University Press, 1976. An outstanding though dated account of the establishment clause and the constitutional politics surrounding it.

Strasser, Mark. *On Same-Sex Marriage, Civil Unions, and the Rule of Law: Constitutional Interpretation at the Crossroads*. Praeger, 2002. Strasser argues that the right of same sex couples to marry is indistinguishabele from other constitutional protections afforded to the family more generally.

Strossen, Nadine. *Defending Pornography: Free Speech, Sex, and the Fight for Women's Rights*. New York: New York University Press, 2000. Argues that a commitment to free speech, as well as to women's rights, must mean that pornography will sometimes be protected under the First Amendment.

Sunstein, Cass R. "*Lochner*'s Legacy." 87 *Columbia Law Review* 873 (1987). Undertakes a critical review of *Lochner v. New York*.

———. *One Case at a Time: Judicial Minimalism on the Supreme Court*. Cambridge: Harvard University Press, 2001. This important book argues that a correct understanding of the role of judicial review in a democracy calls for a restrained Court.

———. "The Right to Marry," 26 *Cardozo Law Review* 2081 (2005). Sunstein provides an excellent overview of the right to marry as a constitutional liberty.

———. *The Second Bill of Rights: FDR'S Unfinished Revolution and Why We Need It More Than Ever*. New York: Basic Books, 2004. Builds on a speech by Roosevelt to argue for a "second" bill of rights.

Thayer, James Bradley. "The Origin and Scope of the American Doctrine of Judicial Review." 7 *Harvard Law Review* (1883). The classic statement on behalf of judicial restraint in constitutional law.

Tribe, Laurence H. *Abortion: The Clash of Absolutes*. Updated/revised ed. New York: W.W. Norton & Company, 1992. Examines the constitutional issues surrounding abortion.

Tushnet, Mark. *Taking the Constitution away from the Courts.* Princeton: Princeton University Press, 1999. This book rejects judicial supremacy in constitutional interpretation and argues for the importance of extrajudicial constitutional interpretation.

Van Alstyne, William. "A Critical Guide to *Marbury v. Madison.*" *Duke Law Journal* 1 (1969). One of the leading studies of *Marbury v. Madison* (1803).

Van Burkleo, Sandra F. *Belonging to the World: Women's Rights and American Constitutional Culture.* New York: Oxford University Press, 2000. This comprehensive book examines the role of women's rights in the American constitutional order.

Warren, Samuel D., and Louis D. Brandeis. "The Right to Privacy." 4 *Harvard Law Review* 193 (1890). This article is the classic argument in favor of a right to privacy in the American legal order.

West, Robin. *Progressive Constitutionalism: Reconstructing the Fourteenth Amendment.* Durham, NC: Duke University Press, 1994. Argues for a more progressive account of the Fourteenth Amendment and the equal protection clause.

Whittington, Keith. "Extrajudicial Constitutional Interpretation: Three Objections and Responses." 80 *North Carolina Law Review* 773 (2002). Examines constitutional interpretation by nonjudicial actors.

Wildenthal, Bryan H. "The Lost Compromise: Reassessing the Early Understanding in Court and Congress on Incorporation of the Bill of Rights in the Fourteenth Amendment." 61 *Ohio Law Journal* 1051 (2000). Reexamines the history of the Fourteenth Amendment and the process of incorporation.

Wolters, Raymond. *The Burden of Brown.* Nashville: University of Tennessee Press, 1984. An examination of *Brown v. Board of Education* and its aftermath, both politically and constitutionally.

Woodward, C. Vann. *The Strange Career of Jim Crow.* Commemorative ed. New York: Oxford University Press, 2001. An important history and analysis of Jim Crow laws in the United States.

Zipursky, Benjamin C. "*DeShaney* and the Jurisprudence of Compassion." 65 *New York University Law Review* 1101 (1990). Examines the Court's decision in *DeShaney* and the role of compassion in the various opinions.

Internet References:

Cases

http://www.law.cornell.edu/supct/index.html. Cornell Law School's Legal Information Institute archive contains all opinions of the court issued since May of 1990. In addition, a collection of 610 of the most important historical decisions of the Court is available on CD-ROM and (with reduced functionality) over the Internet.

http://www.findlaw.com/casecode/. This is an excellent source for finding cases, both at the federal level and the state level. Searches Supreme Court cases by name or year from 1893 to the present; however, retrieves even earlier cases if searched by case number.

http://www.landmarkcases.org/. This useful site includes a wide range of materials about landmark cases, including secondary sources and a helpful glossary.

The Supreme Court and the Justices

http://www.supremecourtus.gov/. This is the official site of the Supreme Court. It has information about the history and operation of the Court and links to cases, as well as biographical information about the justices.

http://www.supremecourthistory.org/. The official site for the Historical Society of the Supreme Court, it is an excellent resource for information about the Court. It includes a timeline, biographies of the justices, and information about landmark cases.

http://www.oyez.org/oyez/frontpage. This is a superb multimedia site. It includes audio transcripts of oral arguments in major cases and a virtual tour of the Court, as well as biographical information for sitting justices, information about pending cases, and news items about the Court.

News and Press Coverage

http://news.findlaw.com/legalnews/us/sc/. This site carries news about the Supreme Court and other federal courts.

http://www.law.com/jsp/scm/index.jsp. Provides news and commentary about the Supreme Court.

http://jurist.law.pitt.edu/currentawareness/ussupremes.php. This comprehensive site includes news about the Supreme Court, as well as links to blogs and others sources of information and commentary about the Court.

Academic Centers/Journals

http://stu.findlaw.com/journals/. A comprehensive database of academic journals and law reviews.

http://www.lawreview.org/. This site allows students to do full text searches of online law reviews.

http://www.loc.gov/law/guide/lawreviews.html. A list of online law reviews.

Blogs

http://www.scotusblog.com/movabletype/. This well-established blog is dedicated to discussions about the Court and its cases.

http://scotus.blogspot.com/. This blog includes information about pending cases.

http://supremecourtwatch.tpmcafe.com/. This blog has commentary about current cases and Supreme Court news.

U.S. Constitution and Other Founding Documents

http://memory.loc.gov/ammem/help/constRedir.html. Hyperlinks to the Declaration of Independence, the Constitution, the Bill of Rights, later amendments, *The Federalist Papers*, and other materials.

http://www.law.indiana.edu/uslawdocs/declaration.html. The Declaration of Independence.

http://www.usconstitution.net/. A comprehensive, annotated online guide to the Constitution.

http://www.constitution.org/. Includes secondary information about the Constitution.

http://www.law.ou.edu/hist/federalist/. *The Federalist Papers*.

http://www.yale.edu/lawweb/avalon/federal/fed.htm. *The Federalist Papers*, annotated.

http://confinder.richmond.edu/. Links to other constitutions.

The Bill of Rights (Amendments I-X)

Transmitted October 2, 1789.
Ratified by three-fourths of the states, December 15, 1791.

The Conventions of a number of the States having, at the time of adopting the Constitution, expressed a desire, in order to prevent misconstruction or abuse of its powers, that further declaratory and restrictive clauses should be added, and as extending the ground of public confidence in the Government will best insure the beneficent ends of its institution;

Resolved, by the Senate and House of Representatives of the United States of America, in Congress assembled, two-thirds of both Houses concurring, that the following articles be proposed to the Legislatures of the several States, as amendments to the Constitution of the United States; all or any of which articles, when ratified by three-fourths of the said Legislatures, to be valid to all intents and purposes as part of the said Constitution, namely:

Amendment I

Congress shall make no law respecting an establishment of religion, or prohibiting the free exercise thereof; or abridging the freedom of speech, or of the press; or the right of the people peaceably to assemble, and to petition the government for a redress of grievances.

Amendment II

A well regulated militia, being necessary to the security of a free state, the right of the people to keep and bear arms, shall not be infringed.

Amendment III

No soldier shall, in time of peace be quartered in any house, without the consent of the owner, nor in time of war, but in a manner to be prescribed by law.

Amendment IV

The right of the people to be secure in their persons, houses, papers, and effects, against unreasonable searches and seizures, shall not be violated, and no warrants shall issue, but upon probable cause, supported by oath or affirmation, and particularly describing the place to be searched, and the persons or things to be seized.

Amendment V

No person shall be held to answer for a capital, or otherwise infamous crime, unless on a presentment or indictment of a grand jury, except in cases arising in the land or naval forces, or in the militia, when in actual service in time of war or public danger; nor shall any person be subject for the same offense to be twice put in jeopardy of life or limb; nor shall be compelled in any criminal case to be a witness against himself, nor be deprived of life, liberty, or property, without due process of law; nor shall private property be taken for public use, without just compensation.

Amendment VI

In all criminal prosecutions, the accused shall enjoy the right to a speedy and public trial, by an impartial jury of the state and district wherein the crime shall have been committed, which district shall have been previously ascertained by law, and to be informed of the nature and cause of the accusation; to be confronted with the witnesses against him; to have compulsory process for obtaining witnesses in his favor, and to have the assistance of counsel for his defense.

Amendment VII

In suits at common law, where the value in controversy shall exceed twenty dollars, the right of trial by jury shall be preserved, and no fact tried by a jury, shall be otherwise reexamined in any court of the United States, than according to the rules of the common law.

Amendment VIII

Excessive bail shall not be required, nor excessive fines imposed, nor cruel and unusual punishments inflicted.

Amendment IX

The enumeration in the Constitution, of certain rights, shall not be construed to deny or disparage others retained by the people.

Amendment X

The powers not delegated to the United States by the Constitution, nor prohibited by it to the states, are reserved to the states respectively, or to the people.